P9-CED-621

PLANNING PROGRAMS
FOR ADULT LEARNERS

PLANNING PROGRAMS FOR ADULT LEARNERS

A Practical Guide for Educators, Trainers, and Staff Developers

Rosemary S. Caffarella

Foreword by Malcolm S. Knowles

 JOSSEY-BASS PUBLISHERS
SAN FRANCISCO

Copyright © 1994 by Jossey-Bass Inc., Publishers, 350 Sansome Street, San Francisco, California 94104.

Jossey-Bass is a registered trademark of Jossey-Bass Inc., A Wiley Company.

No part of this publication may be reproduced, stored in a retrieval system, or transmitted in any form or by any means, electronic, mechanical, photocopying, recording, scanning, or otherwise, except as permitted under Sections 107 or 108 of the 1976 United States Copyright Act, without either the prior written permission of the Publisher or authorization through payment of the appropriate per-copy fee to the Copyright Clearance Center, 222 Rosewood Drive, Danvers, MA 01923, (978) 750-8400, fax (978) 750-4744. Requests to the Publisher for permission should be addressed to the Permissions Department, John Wiley & Sons, Inc., 605 Third Avenue, New York, NY 10158-0012, (212) 850-6011, fax (212) 850-6008, e-mail: permreq@wiley.com.

Substantial discounts on bulk quantities of Jossey-Bass books are available to corporations, professional associations, and other organizations. For details and discount information, contact the special sales department at Jossey-Bass Inc., Publishers (415) 433-1740; Fax (800) 605-2665.

Jossey-Bass Web address: http://www.josseybass.com

Manufactured in the United States of America. Nearly all Jossey-Bass books and jackets are printed on recycled paper that contains at least 50 percent recycled waste, including 10 percent postconsumer waste. Many of our materials are also printed with either soy- or vegetable-based ink; during the printing process these inks emit fewer volatile organic compounds (VOCs) than petroleum-based inks. VOCs contribute to the formation of smog.

Designed and produced by Publishing Professionals, Eugene, Oregon

Library of Congress Cataloging-in-Publication Data

Caffarella, Rosemary S. (Rosemary Shelly), date.
    Planning programs for adult learners : a practical guide for educators, trainers, and staff developers / Rosemary S. Caffarella — 1st ed.
      p.   cm.— (The Jossey-Bass higher and adult education series)
    Includes bibliographical references and index.
    ISBN 0-7879-0033-8
    1. Adult education—United States—Administration. 2. Adult education—United States—Planning. I. Title II. Series.
LC5225.A34C34   1994
374'.973—dc20
                                              94-21355
                                               CIP

FIRST EDITION
PB Printing 10 9 8

The Jossey-Bass Higher and Adult Education Series

Consulting Editor
Adult and Continuing Education

Alan B. Knox
University of Wisconsin, Madison

This book is lovingly dedicated to Ed Caffarella, my husband, and Christy Caffarella, my daughter, for their care, support, and incredible patience in this project.

Contents

List of Tables, Figures, and Exhibits

Foreword

Welcome to the exciting world of program planning for adults—exciting because this book makes it so.

In it Rosemary Caffarella, one of the most effective scholar-practitioners of our era, explores the existing program planning models, which are mostly based on a linear, step-by-step process, extracts the best features of each, and incorporates these features into an essentially new model. This new model transforms program planning from a fundamentally mechanistic operation of following the steps to a creative operation of designing adventures in learning.

Because this new model involves cooperation between and among the planners, the organizational sponsors, and the participants in planning and implementing the program, Caffarella calls it an "interactive" model. I think of it also as a "dynamic" model, in contrast to a "static" or "routine" model.

You will find this book firmly grounded in clearly expressed concepts and principles derived from research-based theories of adult learning and loaded with practical suggestions for strategies and methods for applying these principles.

Whether you are new to the field or an old-timer, you will have one happy adventure.

July 1994   Malcolm S. Knowles

Preface

Planning and evaluating educational programs for adults is like trying to negotiate a maze. Sometimes we manage to get through the maze quickly and feel a real sense of satisfaction that we could do it with such ease. Other times we constantly run into dead ends and have to retrace our steps and find new paths, which can be frustrating yet challenging. So it is with program planning. Some programs run smoothly from beginning to end. Other programs have minor but fixable glitches, such as presenters being sick or equipment not being delivered to the right place. Still other programs seem to wander all over the place, with lots of revisions and changes along the way. Often, when the norm is an evolving and ever-changing planning process, many of the alternative avenues that must be explored cannot even be anticipated. Rather, new or reconfigured pathways will be added to the maze while you are still in it, with differing kinds of walls and openings along the way. For example, new staff may have very different ways of planning programs than what has been accepted practice; program budgets may be cut with little or no warning; or senior management may ask for proof of learning transfer, while most of the available evaluation data focus on program delivery and content knowledge rather than application. Yet when these seemingly unmanageable programs have successful endings, we feel a real sense of accomplishment and satisfaction with our work. I wrote this book to assist people who take on this challenge of "running the maze" of planning educational programs for adults, whether the maze is simple, complex, and/or ever-changing.

Numerous models of planning educational programs for adult learners exist—ranging from conceptual and data-based studies on program planning to how-to handbooks, guides, and pamphlets. Some of these planning models are considered seminal works, such as Cyril Houle's *The Design of Education* (1972) and Malcolm Knowles's *The Modern Practice of Adult Education* (1980). Other authors have provided very useful, but often brief and/or incomplete descriptions of the planning process. And most models of program planning for adults—especially those published more recently—have limited their application to very specific contexts, such as training in business and industry or staff development in schools.

Planning Programs for Adult Learners is distinctive for two major reasons. First, the program planning model presented in this book both captures and reconfigures classical and current descriptions of the program planning process. The result is a comprehensive eleven-component model of planning programs for adults that draws on the best content and practice knowledge from across a variety of contexts—business and industry, public schools, colleges and universities, health care, the Cooperative Extension Service, government, community action programs, the military, religious institutions, and so on.

Second, *Planning Programs for Adult Learners* provides both a concrete framework for program planning and a how-to guide and resource book for practitioners. This eleven-component framework can be applied in many ways. Program planners are asked, for example, to choose which component or components of the model they should work on first; the model does not assume that there is only one place to start or end the planning process. They may also choose to use the entire model, or only those parts that are applicable to their specific planning situation. Program planning for adults, within this framework, becomes an interactive and action-oriented process in which decisions and choices are made about learning opportunities for adults; thus flexibility is a fundamental norm of the planning process.

The how-to part of *Planning Programs for Adult Learners* serves as a practical guide and provides hands-on resources for staff who are constantly in the middle of planning one program or another. The many exhibits, tables, figures, and lists presented throughout the text give the reader substantial information in a concise and easily usable format. Many of these could be used by planning staff as handouts related to specific tasks they must complete. In addition, there are Applications Exercises at the end of most chapters to help readers apply the material addressed in the chapters to their own program planning situations.

This book is intended for people who plan educational programs for adults in a variety of settings. It is targeted primarily at people who either have or aspire to obtain positions as adult educators, trainers, or staff developers. These people already have (or will have) major responsibilities related to planning and evaluating educational programs as all or part of their job. Their work settings are diverse. They may be employed, for example, by the corporate sector, public schools, voluntary agencies, colleges and universities, government, and health care organizations. In addition, there are two other audiences for whom *Planning Programs for Adult Learners* could be helpful. The first is paid staff who plan educational programs as one part of what they do, whether or not planning is a part of their official position descriptions. For example, many line staff, such as principals, division directors, and managers, are expected to provide educational opportunities for their staff; and in many cases, they take leadership roles in and/or actually produce educational activities. The second audience is the legion of volunteers who develop programs for adult learners—from committee and board members of social service agencies to community action groups. The commonality among all of the many audiences for this book is that they are all responsible in some way for planning and evaluating programs for adult learners, whether these learners be colleagues, other staff, clients, customers, or the general community.

Overview of the Contents

Planning Programs for Adult Learners is organized into two major parts. The first three chapters of the book lay the groundwork for the rest of the volume by introducing what program planning is all about—in other words, the model of program planning that provides the framework for the remainder of the book. More specifically, Chapter One describes the purposes and outcomes of educational programs, who plans these programs, how they are planned, and what constitutes a program planning model or guide for action. Chapter Two presents an overview of the interactive model of program planning for adults, the basic assumptions on which the model rests, and the sources on which the model was built. The eleven-component model, discussed in more detail in Chapters Four through Fourteen, is presented as a guide to practice, to assist educators, trainers, and staff developers in navigating the maze of people, ideas, organizational contexts, and administrative trivia (which is not trivial) that are part of the program planning and evaluation process. Chapter Three addresses three important topics related to using the model in practice: identifying personal beliefs about program planning, developing up-front assumptions about each planning situation, and determining both what parts of the model are needed and the alternative ways the model can be applied. The chapter closes with a challenge to program planners to be ethical in their practice.

The second part of the book makes the eleven-component model come alive—the framework becomes a working guide for practice. Each component of the framework is explained, and practical tips and ideas related to concrete tasks within each of the components are given. The eleven components are reviewed as follows:

Chapter Four. Establishing a basis for the planning process
Chapter Five. Identifying program ideas
Chapter Six. Sorting and prioritizing program ideas
Chapter Seven. Developing program objectives
Chapter Eight. Preparing for the transfer of learning
Chapter Nine. Formulating evaluation plans
Chapter Ten. Determining formats, schedules, and staff needs
Chapter Eleven. Preparing budgets and marketing plans
Chapter Twelve. Designing instructional plans
Chapter Thirteen. Coordinating facilities and on-site events
Chapter Fourteen. Communicating the value of the program

Applications exercises are provided to assist the reader in applying the material covered in each chapter to his or her own program planning situation.

# *Acknowledgments*

Planning Programs for Adult Learners is a book for people who spend all or part of their time developing educational programs for adults. The book was inspired by those practitioners, both my students and many others I have worked with from field settings, who wanted a sound model—but one that is grounded in practice and has usable and practical guidelines and tools.

Many of those practitioners have provided invaluable assistance at various stages of the process. Sharan Merriam and Margaret Bradley, both of the University of Georgia, were instrumental in getting and keeping me moving to update an earlier version of this material. Ann Richardson, Gale Erlandson, and Alan Knox worked well as a team to facilitate the book's publication. Student colleagues enrolled in my Fall 1993 class in staff development at the University of Northern Colorado (UNC) provided very helpful feedback on my first draft of the manuscript, as did the outside reviewers. A special thanks here to Ron Cervero, University of Georgia, for making a nonlinear model not look linear any more. Special thanks also to Cheryl Schneider, my manuscript typist, for all her patience and fine work; to Bill Boyd and Jack Scott, graduate assistants, for tracking down references; to Lynn Zinn for her careful proofreading; and to my UNC colleagues, who offered me continued support throughout the process. To all of you, I say a heartfelt thanks. Finally, I wish to say an extra special thanks to my husband, Ed Caffarella, and my daughter, Christy Caffarella, who managed to survive yet another one of my major projects. It is great to have family like you! It goes to show how important for some of us the links are between the worlds of work and family. For me, they are intertwined.

July 1994

Rosemary S. Caffarella
Greeley, Colorado

The Author

Rosemary S. Caffarella is a professor in the Division of Educational Leadership and Policy Studies at the University of Northern Colorado. She received her B.A. degree (1968) in community leadership and development from Springfield College, her M.A. degree (1973) in rehabilitation counseling from Michigan State University, and her Ph.D. degree (1978) from Michigan State University in adult and continuing education. Before coming to the University of Northern Colorado, she served on the faculties and in administrative positions at the University of Maine and Virginia Commonwealth University.

Caffarella's research and writing activities have focused on adult learning and development and on program planning. More recently, she has expanded her work to include the area of women and leadership. She is coauthor of *Learning in Adulthood* (1991, with S. Merriam) and has coedited (with L. Jackson) a forthcoming New Directions for Adult and Continuing Education volume, *Experiential Learning: A New Approach*. Her other books and monographs include *Psychosocial Development of Women: Linkages to Teaching and Leadership in Adult Education* (1992), *Self-Directed Learning* (coauthored with J. O'Donnell, 1989), and *Program Development and Evaluation Resource Book for Trainers* (1988).

Caffarella has served on the steering committee for the annual North American Adult Education Research Conference and the Commission of Professors of Adult Education and on the board of directors for the American Association for Adult and Continuing Education, the Virginia Adult Education Association, and the Maine Association for Public School Adult Education. She has been a Kellogg Fellow at the University of Montana and Faculty Fellow for the Project for the Study of Adult Learning at Illinois State University. In addition, she is currently a consulting editor for *Adult Education Quarterly* and *Adult Learning*.

PLANNING PROGRAMS
FOR ADULT LEARNERS

One

The Program Planning Enterprise

Educational programs for adults come in all shapes, sizes, and formats. They vary from information or skill sessions lasting only an hour or two to day-long conferences and workshops to highly intensive residential study at corporate training centers and universities. Programs may be individualized, through such mechanisms as professional or personal growth plans, or be designed for small or large groups of learners (or even whole communities). Program participants may need to come to one location to attend a program, as in the case of annual meetings and conferences hosted by many professional associations, or they may be able to participate in an educational program from their home or office through teleconferencing and computer-assisted instruction. Some programs are planned for a small, select group of people, such as senior managers from a given organization; others, such as classes and activities sponsored by community recreation programs or senior centers, are open to whoever signs up.

Planning and evaluating educational programs for adult learners is both an organized and a haphazard endeavor. On the surface, the planning process appears to be a fairly logical and orderly process, progressing from identifying ideas to program design and implementation to evaluation and follow-up activities. Yet for those persons who actually develop and coordinate educational programs, the process seems to be more a mass of decisions, details, and deadlines than precise and clear steps of what should be done, when, where, by whom, and how.

The purpose of this chapter is to introduce the reader to what planning educational programs for adults is all about. Discussed are the purposes and primary outcomes of these programs, who plans these programs and how they are planned, and what constitutes a program planning model or guide for action.

Understanding the Purposes of Educational Programs

Educational programs for adults are conducted for five primary purposes and a variety of audiences, as illustrated in the following examples (Caldwell, 1989; Merriam and Cunningham, 1989; Richey, 1992; Merriam, 1993):

Program Purpose	Program Examples
To encourage continuous growth and development of individuals	Continuing education course on Chinese art and culture of the 19th and 20th centuries
	Session hosted by the local library: "Using the Library as a Lifelong Learning Resource"
	Workshop: "How to Use Your Home Computer to Tap into 101 Data Bases"
To assist people in responding to practical problems and issues of adult life	Seminar on ways to cope with life transitions
	Combination information/support group for newly diagnosed cancer patients and their families
	Series of preretirement seminars offered for all interested employees
To prepare people for current and future work opportunities	New-worker orientation program
	Formal apprenticeship and college and degree programs
	Workshop on applications of new software packages to daily work activities
	Seminar on alternative job and career options
To assist organizations in achieving desired results and adapting to change	Two-day seminar for all employees of an organization on total quality management
	Workshop offered by the Council of Economic Development: "Changing Demographics Through the Year 2020: Implications for the Workplace"
	In-house seminar for all supervisors and managers on "downsizing" the organization
To provide opportunities to examine community and societal issues	Action workshop on developing skills for site-based management for teachers, administrators, and parents
	Community Earth Day celebration consisting of numerous learning opportunities and events
	Nationwide teleconference on AIDS, with the focus on health, economic, and social issues

Educational programs often serve more than one purpose. For example, workplace literacy programs are usually designed to assist individuals to develop their language and computation skills while at the same time meeting organizational and societal needs for competent workers.

Primary Outcomes of Educational Programs

Implicit in each of these five purposes for conducting educational programs is the expectation of change as an outcome or result (Laird, 1985; Loucks-Horsley, 1989; Brockett, 1991; Rothwell and Kazanas, 1993; Welton, 1993). Educational programs foster three kinds of change: individual change related to acquisition of new knowledge, building of skills, and examination of personal values and beliefs; organizational change resulting in new or revised policies, procedures, and ways of working; and community and societal change that allows for differing segments of society (for example, members of lower socioeconomic classes, women, ethnic minorities, the business sector) to respond to the world around them in alternative ways. Sample program outcomes in all three categories are outlined below:

Sample Outcomes: Individual Change

- Individuals who attend the workshop on "How to Use Your Home Computer to Tap into 101 Data Bases" will be able to (1) describe at least five different data bases they could use in their daily lives and (2) demonstrate that they know how to use at least two of the five data bases they have identified.

- Teachers will individually examine, with the assistance of a peer coach, how they interact with boys versus girls in their classrooms (for example, in terms of how often children of both genders are called on, how they themselves respond to behavior). Based on this examination, each teacher, as needed, will develop an individual action plan to explore both behavioral and attitudinal changes.

Sample Outcomes: Organizational Change

- Supervisors of staff who attend the training sessions on the use of two new software packages will allow time on the job for program participants to practice using the software packages. Then, within a six-month time period, these same supervisors will implement new operational guidelines that require the use of these software packages for particular functions within the organization.

- Except for people who can demonstrate proficiency in Spanish, all new and current staff in the Division of Motor Vehicles who are responsible for providing information and services to the public will be required to enroll in an intensive Spanish language program. The end result of the program will be that staff will be able to effectively communicate verbally with customers in both English and Spanish. As part of this organization-wide training initiative, the personnel system will be modified to provide incentives for current staff who are able to demonstrate or achieve language proficiency. In addition, one of the requirements for all new hires who work directly with customers will be demonstrated language proficiency in both Spanish and English.

Sample Outcomes: Community and Societal Change

- A cancer survivorship organization will sponsor an action workshop on how to affect state and national policies related to cancer prevention, treatment, and education. One of the major goals of the workshop is to develop local networks of people who will lobby for legislative action in their districts.
- School personnel who have demonstrated knowledge and commitment to equality issues in classroom teaching will be given time to attend, as both presenters and participants, statewide and national conferences and action workshops related to gender equality in schools. In addition, they will be responsible for assisting at least one other school district in changing its current practices.

Although a desire for change underlies all educational programs, the reality of most educational and training programs is that planning for change—that is, preparing concrete and workable transfer-of-learning plans—has not often been an integral part of the planning process (see Chapter Eight). Rather, people responsible for planning programs have assumed that somehow this transfer of learning would happen as long as their programs were well designed and executed.

Who Plans Educational Programs?

Educational programs for adults are planned and coordinated by many different kinds of people. While some staff have clearly defined roles and responsibilities as program planners and carry official titles such as training specialists, staff developers, or continuing education staff, many people who plan educational programs for adults do not (Nadler, 1985; Hentschel, 1990; DuFour, 1991). For example, line managers and supervisors are often expected to serve as staff developers through such mechanisms as the supervisory process, coaching, and mentoring. Yet their job descriptions may not reflect these responsibilities and tasks, and some supervisors are not rewarded or even recognized for their efforts. In addition, many people also give countless hours as volunteer program planners for community groups, professional associations, and nonprofit organizations. This broad spectrum of responsibility for program planning is shown in Figure 1.1. This idea of the centrality of doing program planning as part of one's job is further illustrated in the following three scenarios.

Scenario 1: Program Planning as a Primary Responsibility

Robert B. is employed as a training specialist for the Blackwell Corporation. His office is located at the Corporate Training Center, and he reports to the associate vice president for human resource development. He is one of three training specialists employed at the corporate level. His major responsibility is to design educational programs for both staff and customers of the company. These programs range from one-hour modules to three-week intensive seminars. Though at times he may actually serve as the instructor for one of the programs, his major job is to

Figure 1.1. Centrality of Responsibility for Educational Programs.

More Responsibility

Centrality of Responsibility	*Examples of Job Titles or Roles*
Educational programs are defined as the primary responsibility	Program developers Training specialists Conference coordinators Instructional designers Program evaluators
Defined as one of multiple responsibilities	Managers of training Directors of staff development Managers of human resources Deans of continuing education Directors of continuing medical education
Secondary or tertiary responsibility (may or may not be a defined part of responsibilities)	Supervisors Managers Directors Administrators Division heads Volunteer planners

Less Responsibility

develop and coordinate the various programs offered by the organization. In essence, Robert's major role is that of program developer. He functions as a program design specialist and is responsible for planning, coordinating, and evaluating training programs requested by the various divisions within the company, and for ensuring that transfer of learning happens (Rothwell and Kazanas, 1992; Richey, 1992; Piskurich, 1992). He rarely works alone. Instead, he works in tandem with content specialists—usually company personnel from the division that has requested the program and/or outside consultants. In addition, he may work with the training center's production group on the development of the instructional materials to be used in the program (or, if the program is to be housed at the center itself, with the center's conference coordinator).

Scenario 2: Program Planning as One of Multiple Responsibilities

Betty W. serves as director of staff development and training for a large metropolitan school district. She reports to the director of personnel for the district. Betty has a staff of five people: three training specialists, one teacher on special assignment, and one secretary. In reviewing her calendar for the next day, Betty has made the following notations beside her commitments:

9:00 A.M.   Staff meeting
              (Note: review the district staff development calendar
              for the next six months.)

10:30 A.M.   Joe C.
              (Note: lay out the final plans for the districtwide needs
              analysis of administrative personnel.)

Noon	Lunch with Susan M. [her boss]
	(Note: stress the importance of the upcoming statewide conference on developing curriculum standards, which is being hosted by the district.)
2:00 P.M.	Bill Q. [maintenance supervisor]
	(Note: he wants some assistance with problems of absenteeism and staff morale.)
3:00 to 5:00 P.M.	Conduct workshop on cultural diversity for all assistant principals in the district
	(Note: make sure all handouts are ready.)

On that one day, Betty will assume four different roles: manager of staff development, program developer, consultant, and instructor (Nadler, 1985; Bradley, Kallick, and Regan, 1991; Diegmueller, 1992; Sparks, 1992). If you were to examine her calendar on successive days, how much time she devotes to each role would change, depending on her own plan of work. Therefore, although Betty is involved in program planning, it is only one of many primary roles that she assumes.

Betty's function as a program planner varies from actually designing full programs to serving as a consultant on program planning for her own staff and other district personnel (including both principals and central office staff). She may take charge of parts of the program planning process when she believes this is important or when her expertise is especially relevant. For example, Betty may direct an organization-wide needs analysis if she believes obtaining accurate data is crucial to the success of her operation. At other times, she will choose to be involved in only a peripheral way, perhaps as a program coordinator or informal sounding board for program ideas.

Scenario 3: Program Planning as a Secondary or Tertiary Responsibility

John S. is the director of nursing of a medium-sized metropolitan hospital. He has a nursing staff of 300, including both full- and part-time employees. He reports directly to the associate executive director of the hospital. He has learned that in about two months a new charting system for patients will be installed in the hospital. His job is to ensure that all his nursing staff will be able to use the new system in an effective and efficient manner. He has called a meeting of selected supervisory nurses to assist him in determining how he can get all the nurses trained to use this new system in such a short period of time. Meanwhile, he is having major problems in other areas, including the recruitment of new staff, the settlement of a two-year labor contract, and the resignation of one of his best assistant directors.

John is also involved in program planning for ongoing staff training, but only as a part of his job responsibilities. He knows the task has to be done, and although it is not in his official job description, it is clearly a part of his responsibilities. Yet it is a task to which both he and his manager have assigned fairly low priority. Most of what John has chosen to do in this area is to send staff to programs run by other departments in the hospital or by other organizations. He has invited a few university people to give "clinical updates," but he has delegated all the work on those activities to two of his supervisory nurses. He knows he has to pull this latest training effort off himself, however, because the director of the medical staff and the director of the hospital have made it a priority item.

How Educational Programs Are Planned

Some educational programs are carefully planned, while others are literally thrown together. The following scenarios illustrate this point:

Scenario 1

George S., the director of continuing education at a community college, has been asked to coordinate a half-day workshop for all part-time instructors teaching adults. Somehow the date slips his mind, and a week before the workshop he realizes that he has no instructor for the workshop. He calls the local university, hoping he can get one of the adult education professors to come for the morning. He is in luck, or so he thinks. Professor Bland gives a three-hour lecture on how to teach. Not only is the material old hat to most of the instructors, but the professor, well versed in literacy education, uses examples primarily from that arena to illustrate his points. The workshop receives very low marks from all the participants.

Scenario 2

Marie J., a teacher on special assignment, has been asked to develop a half-day districtwide workshop on peer-coaching skills as a staff development strategy. She calls together five teachers who are well respected in their buildings to ask them what they think the teachers need to learn about this area. Based on the information she gleans from these teachers, and on some discreet observations of current practice in some of the schools in the district, she determines that a one-hour overview and demonstration of basic peer-coaching skills is needed, followed by a two-hour practice session. She asks three teachers from another school division, who are known for their ability in peer coaching, to assist in putting on the workshop. She also makes sure that a good lunch is served, at the district's expense, at the end of the morning. The workshop is well received by all participants.

Careful planning of educational programs does not guarantee their success, but it increases their probability for success. It also gives planners better data on which to evaluate their successes and failures. What is helpful for many program planners is to have a guide or roadmap of program planning to assist them in getting from the start to the finish of any program. A model (or models) of program planning can provide this needed guide.

Program Planning Models

Program planning models consist of ideas of one or more persons about how programs should be put together and what ingredients are necessary to ensure successful outcomes. These models come in all shapes and sizes. Program planning models may be simplistic in their orientation—with steps 1 through 5, for example— or very complex, using highly developed flowcharts to depict a comprehensive array of decision points (for example, Knowles, 1980; Harris, 1989; Sork, 1990; Tracey, 1992).

A program planning model is usually conceived of as an "open" or "closed" system (Nadler, 1982; Sork and Caffarella, 1989). In a closed system, all inputs to the system can be identified, and the outcomes can be both predetermined and ensured. An open system recognizes that outside factors exist, that these factors have an impact on the program planning process, and that many of these factors are beyond the control of the planner. Very few educational programs can be built based on a closed-system model. Simple things (such as snowstorms and late airplanes) and more complex happenings (such as an unplanned but severe budget reduction) can affect both the substance and the outcomes of planned programs.

Some models of program planning are linear. In these, the educator is expected to start at step 1 and follow each step in sequential order until the process is completed. This type of model may be helpful to newcomers; but it soon loses its appeal, because it does not represent the day-to-day working reality of most program planners. An alternative to the linear approach is to conceptualize program planning as a process that consists of a set of interacting and dynamic elements or components and decision points (Houle, 1972; Caffarella, 1985; Murk and Wells, 1988; Sork and Caffarella, 1989; Cervero and Wilson, 1991, 1994). This type of model allows the program planner to address a number of the components simultaneously, to rearrange the components to suit the demands of different planning situations, and/or to delete unneeded parts of the process.

Why Program Planning Models Are Useful

A systematic planning process can be a "powerful tool for designing effective, efficient, relevant, and innovative educational programs" (Sork and Caffarella, 1989, p. 235). Five major reasons why program planning models are useful are discussed below.

Resources Can Be Used More Effectively. Program planning models can assist people to better use their planning resources of people, time, and money. For example, a model can help clarify what program developers need to do to get a program up and running. This is especially true for novice planners and/or those who do not do program planning as a regular part of their job responsibilities. These people can save time by not having to figure out all the essential ingredients by themselves and by not having to go back and do or redo parts they forgot and/or did not realize were important.

Daily Work Is Made Easier. The daily work of program planners can be made easier with a model, because most models provide a continuing guide for action. Because a model helps planners lay out beforehand tasks that must be done, they need not haphazardly limp along and then play catch-up at the last minute. This is especially true of those program elements that can realistically be preplanned, such as conducting a formal needs analysis and preparing program brochures.

For example, the chair of a program committee for a major conference on preventing violence, to be hosted cooperatively by the police department, area churches, and a community action group, could—based on a comprehensive model of program development—prepare a checklist of tasks to be done, including a column in which to write deadline dates and the person or persons responsible for getting each task accomplished (as in Exhibit 1.1). This could then be used by those persons responsible for developing the conference as a practical guide for getting certain tasks done in a timely manner.

Exhibit 1.1. Sample Program Checklist.

| Task to Be Accomplished | Person(s) Responsible | Timetable | |
		Immediate Deadline	Final Deadline
Identify theme and program objectives	Committee as a whole	Draft: Oct. 1	Oct. 15
Determine program format	Committee as a whole		Oct. 15
Prepare program budget	Susan M.	Draft: Oct. 1	Oct. 15
Identify possible presenters and session topics	John C. Bob R. Joyce H.		Oct. 15
Line up major presenters	Joyce H.		Nov. 15
Finalize all sessions, topics, and presenters	Bob R. John C. Kathy W.		Nov. 15
Prepare publicity	Joyce H. Bob R.	Draft: Nov. 15	Dec. 1
Plan evaluation and transfer of learning	Joyce H. Bob R.	Draft: Nov. 15	Jan. 5
Program delivery			Mar. 1, 2

Teamwork Is Fostered. Teamwork among people responsible for planning a program can also be fostered by using a specific program planning model. A model can provide a means for clarifying roles and responsibilities for all involved, which can lead to a better spirit of team cooperation and less fighting over who was supposed to do what. The two scenarios below, both descriptions of the same situation, illustrate this benefit. The scene is a mid-year planning meeting of a regional conference committee of the American Association for Adult and Continuing Education (AAACE). The chair has asked each person to review his or her assignments for the upcoming conference to be hosted by the association in three months.

Scenario 1

Sue responds to the chair's request by asking if the chair can review again what each of the committee members is to do. She does not remember the specifics, nor does a colleague of hers who is not present and whom Sue has been asked to represent. (A second member is missing but unrepresented.) The chair fumbles through his notes of the last meeting trying to figure out just what was said. Meanwhile, two of the members fume—they have already completed their responsibilities and are ready to report on them.

Scenario 2

Each person at the session describes what he or she has accomplished. The chair then gives a report for the two missing members. The group as a whole reviews the next set of tasks as described on the conference planning checklist they developed three months earlier. Due to some last-minute changes, some minor modifications need to be made to their plan of work, but all agree they are right on target in their planning of the conference. They agree to meet via a conference call in one month to ensure that all the final arrangements are completed.

Basis for Control Is Provided. Using a program planning model can benefit not only planners but also people who supervise those planners. Having a detailed and clear planning procedure can provide a basis for control over both the process and the subordinate's role in that process. This gives supervisors an opportunity to coach their staff in areas in which they appear weak and to reward them for those tasks they complete effectively and efficiently.

Better Programs Are Developed. A better program usually results when planners use a model of program planning as a guide. Most models dictate that a close look be given up front to the problems or ideas presented. This focus helps planners move beyond just reacting to day-to-day crisis situations and requests for programs to analyzing carefully those problems and requests and making informed choices about possible courses of action. For example, a manager may request that the training department conduct a seminar on time management for his or her employees. In investigating the request, the educational specialist determines that the problem is not poor management of time by employees but a severe overload of work. Thus a program on time management would not solve what the manager had originally perceived as the problem unless other changes were made in how the division functions.

In addition, using a program planning model helps prevent people from forgetting to address essential tasks of the program planning process. When these tasks are not done, holes are left in the planning process itself and in the final product of that process. For example, the checking of facilities and equipment for an upcoming program is of prime importance. Failure to complete such checking can lead to disastrous results, as illustrated in the following example.

Scenario

Warren P. had the responsibility for making all final arrangements for a continuing professional education conference. Although he had seen diagrams of the rooms to be used, he did not have the chance, nor did he really see the need, to visit the facilities himself. The hotel staff had assured him that the room space would be adequate and that they had an excellent sound system for the main banquet room. When he arrived on the morning of the conference, Warren discovered, to his horror, that not only was the sound system inadequate but a major remodeling project was under way in areas that the conference would be using.

Using a program planning model also alerts staff to the need for sound evaluation procedures. These ensure that the planners know whether the program actually produces the results that were proposed and also provides data for improving future program offerings.

Why Program Planning Models Are Not Routinely Used

There are four major reasons why people involved in developing educational programs do not use program planning models: time pressures, inclement organizational climate, lack of knowledge, and the belief that models are not useful (Pennington and Green, 1976; Brookfield, 1986; Cervero and Wilson, 1991; Munson 1992). Let us look at each in turn.

Time Pressures. Personnel responsible for educational programs often find themselves with too much to do just responding to requests for educational activities and coping with the daily workload. It is difficult for many staff to develop the formal plan called for in program planning models, let alone find the time to adequately address each step of the plan. The reality is that planning takes time. There just may not be enough white space in a day's calendar to allow for adequate time to do it.

Scenario

Sharon R., an adult education specialist in state government, has been in one meeting after another this week. She has been working on the strategic plan for her division, due in two weeks. She has also conducted two half-day in-house seminars and has managed to fit in a workshop for herself conducted by a continuing education unit of a local university. She has three requests sitting on her desk for future educational programs, which she has not had time to respond to, and she needs to develop three others that are slated for next month. In addition, her supervisor has just asked her if she would serve on a special task force recently set up by her division.

Organizational Climate. Some organizations are conducive to planning and therefore encourage the use of program planning models. Other organizations seem to run on a crisis mentality, always trying to solve the day's problems before the day is over. These organizations may be short-staffed, and/or their staff may not be well organized. Trying to introduce a program planning model, which calls for forward planning and thinking, may be almost impossible in such a climate.

Lack of Knowledge About Available Models. Often persons responsible for planning programs are not aware that there are models of program planning available for their use. This is not surprising, because many adult educators and trainers are content specialists first and have not been exposed to materials related to program planning. (Even content specialists who seek out planning information may be defeated, finding few materials readily available in their specialty area.) Other people, both paid and volunteer staff, who have only a peripheral involvement in planning programs have little time (and may not see the need) to become knowledgeable in this arena. In addition, many of the models are difficult to interpret and to use in any practical sense because of the way they are presented. Most practitioners—especially volunteers—just do not have the time or motivation necessary to plod through a more formal academic text, no matter how good the proposed model may be.

Belief That Models Are Too Confining to Be Helpful. The idea of using a program planning model is rejected by some educators because they view it as too confining to be helpful. In particular, many experienced program planners find that they do not develop programs in any one way—at least not as defined by any one author. There are too many realities that get in the way, from resource problems to political maneuvering by individual staff, special-interest groups, and organizations as a whole. Rather, what these planners see as central to what they do is making "defensible judgments about what to do in terms of what is possible . . . and what is desirable" (Cervero and Wilson, 1991, p. 41) within a specific set of circumstances. Therefore, models of program planning—especially the lock-step models—are viewed as neither useful nor practical. For example, Sally S., a knowledgeable and experienced adult educator, has tried over the years to adapt two distinct models into her everyday work activities. She has found, however, that they do not fit her situation. Because she was spending more time trying to rework the models themselves than on planning the actual programs, she is back to her "using her experience as a guide" planning style—one that has worked well for her in the past.

Chapter Highlights

Educational programs for adults are conducted for five primary purposes: to encourage ongoing growth and development of individuals, to assist people in responding to practical problems and issues of adult life, to prepare people for current and future work opportunities, to assist organizations in achieving desired results and adapting to change, and to provide opportunities to examine community and societal issues. Change is the driving force and underlying theme that links together all types of educational and training programs for adults. People who are responsible for planning these programs include staff, both paid and volunteer, who carry such titles as adult educator, staff developer, and trainer. Yet often this role of program planner comes with other roles that adults play and is not considered a major or even secondary part of what they do. In planning educational programs for adults, it is helpful for program planners to have a model or guide to get them from the start to the finish. One such guide for action, the subject of this book, is the interactive model of program planning. It is described in the next chapter.

Applications Exercises

This chapter's Applications Exercises will help you define the purpose of your educational programs (Exhibit 1.2) and understand your role as a program planner in an organizational setting (Exhibit 1.3).

Exhibit 1.2. Defining the Purpose of Educational Programs.

1. Within the framework outlined, list examples of educational programs you have participated in and/or planned within the last two to three years.

The Purpose of Educational Programs	Programs You Have Participated in and/or Planned
To encourage continuous growth and development of individuals	
To assist people in responding to practical problems and issues of adult life	
To prepare people for current and future work opportunities	
To assist in achieving desired results and adapting to change	
To provide opportunities to examine societal and global issues	

2. Highlight the positive points of these experiences as either participant and/or planner and indicate what problems and disappointments you encountered.

_____

_____

_____

Exhibit 1.3. Understanding the Role of Program Planners in Organizational Settings.

1. List your present title and give a brief job description.

_____

_____

2. Is the role of program planner a *formal* part of your job description? ❑ Yes   ❑ No
If yes, briefly describe what you do in that role.

_____

_____

If no, what role, if any, do you play as a program planner?

_____

_____

3. Outline, on the following chart, the personnel in your organization (or a specific subunit of your organization) who are responsible for planning and conducting educational programs. Indicate whether this responsibility is a formal or informal part of their jobs. Then outline the tasks each person does as part of this work.

Position, Name and Program	Formal or Informal Responsibility?	Tasks Related to Educational Programming
1.		
2.		
3.		
4.		
5.		
6.		

4. How might those who do program planning in your unit and/or organization be supportive of each other's efforts? List specific suggestions below.

_____

_____

_____

—— ∞ ——

An Interactive Model
of Program Planning

TWO

Numerous models of program planning for adult learners exist, as I noted in Chapter One. Among the most often discussed and used are the models proposed by Houle (1972), Knowles (1980), Laird (1985), Cervero (1988), Harris (1989), and Tracey (1992). The commonalities among these frequently used models are the attention paid to the learner and/or the organizational needs as central to the program planning process, the importance of the context in which programs are planned, and the idea that there are identifiable components and tasks that are important to the planning process.

In building the interactive program planning model for adults that I introduce in this chapter, I drew many ideas from these previously proposed models of program planning (for example, Houle, 1972; Knowles, 1980; Sork and Caffarella, 1989; Tracey, 1992). Therefore, the model, on the surface, appears similar to other models of program planning. What is different about this model is the combination and comprehensiveness of the components and tasks that are included, the suggested ways the model can be used by practitioners, and its focus on practical ideas for making decisions and completing program planning tasks for each component of the model. In addition to describing the model itself, with its components and key tasks, in this chapter I also discuss the assumptions within which the model is grounded and the sources and ideas upon which the model is constructed.

The Interactive Model of
Program Planning for Adults

The interactive program planning model for adults is presented here as a guide, not as a blueprint for practice. Persons responsible for planning programs for adults are encouraged to use the relevant parts of the model in the planning process (see Exhibit 2.1).

As many experienced program planners have found, planning programs is not a linear, step-by-step process. Rather, program planners often work with a number of planning components and tasks at the same time and not necessarily in any standard order. For example, in the planning of a major national or regional conference, the logistics of the meeting (such as place and date) often need to be handled before the theme or the objectives of the conference are determined. Figure 2.1 represents one way in which

Exhibit 2.1. Eleven Components of the Interactive Model.

Establishing a basis for the planning process
Identifying program ideas
Sorting and prioritizing program ideas
Developing program objectives
Preparing for the transfer of learning
Formulating evaluation plans
Determining formats, schedules, and staff needs
Preparing budgets and marketing plans
Designing instructional plans
Coordinating facilities and on-site events
Communicating the value of the program

Figure 2.1. One Application of the Interactive Model of Program Planning.

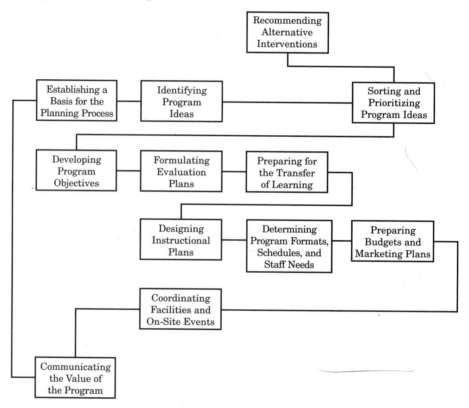

Note: Graphic representation of the model was prepared with the assistance of Kathy Schaefer, Regis University, Denver, Colorado.

planning staff could use the model. Additional illustrations of how the components of the model could be used are given in Chapter Three.

In addition, experienced practitioners have found that the process of planning programs is essentially a negotiated activity between and among educators, learners, and organizations (Brookfield, 1986; Cervero and Wilson, 1992, 1994). Rarely is a program produced by a single planner. Rather, most programs for adult learners "are produced by people with multiple interests working in specific institutional contexts that profoundly affect their content and form" (Cervero and Wilson, 1992, p. 27). Therefore, the key to using this model of program planning is *flexibility*. In essence, the use of the model should be tailored to meet the demands of a specific planning situation.

Tasks Within Each Component of the Model

Each program component of the model includes a set of tasks and decision points. As noted earlier, not all of the components—and therefore not all of the tasks—need to be addressed in developing every program. For example, once the context for an educational program is identified, program planners do not need to address that task for each new program as long as the context remains relatively stable. However, review of policy statements and support systems is helpful at specified intervals. The same could be said for the process of compiling a list of ideas, needs, and problems for possible educational programs. One well-conceived and -executed needs analysis can provide data pointing to a number of needed educational programs and activities.

The tasks that make up each component are presented in the list below. Each of the tasks is then discussed more fully in Chapters Four through Fourteen.

Establishing a Basis for the Planning Process

- Become knowledgeable about the internal and external contextual factors for planning, including the structural aspects, the people, and the cultural milieu of the planning situation.
- Build and maintain structural supports for planning (for example, mission statements, standard operating policies and procedures, information systems, and financial resources).
- Ensure support from program participants, organizational staff, and external constituencies through such mechanisms as active participation in planning and conducting educational activities, transfer-of-learning strategies, and formal and ad hoc committee work.
- Provide a supportive organizational culture in which continuous learning and change are valued.

Identifying Program Ideas

- Decide what sources to use in generating ideas for educational programs (for example, former and/or current program participants, employers, organizational and community leaders, personal issues, governmental regulations and legislative mandates, societal problems).
- Determine the best way or ways to identify these ideas (for

example, formal needs assessments, observations, interviews, conversations with colleagues, job analysis, review of written materials).

Sorting and Prioritizing Program Ideas

- Determine whether an educational program, one or more alternative interventions, or a combination of both is the best way to respond to the ideas generated.
- Develop a process for prioritizing those ideas for which educational programs should be planned. The critical ingredient in this process is the establishment of clear criteria for making decisions about each of the ideas.
- Become knowledgeable about alternative interventions and create networks of people who will listen and act when these alternative interventions are needed.

Developing Program Objectives

- Write program objectives that reflect both what participants will learn and the resulting changes from that learning, as well as the operational aspects of the program.
- Ensure that both measurable and nonmeasurable program outcomes, as appropriate, are included and that a way for revising the objectives is in place.
- Check to see that program objectives are written clearly so that they can be understood by all parties involved (for example, participants, sponsoring organizations).
- Use the program objectives as an internal consistency and "doability" checkpoint (for example, do the transfer-of-learning and evaluation plans match the objectives?).

Preparing for the Transfer of Learning

- Decide when the transfer-of-learning strategies should be employed.
- Determine the key players who need to be part of the transfer-of-learning process (for example, participants, program planning staff, instructors, work supervisors, community leaders).
- Choose transfer strategies that will be the most useful in assisting participants to apply what they have learned (for example, developing individualized learning plans, providing mentors or peer coaches, self-help or support groups, organizational development interventions).

Formulating Evaluation Plans

- Specify the evaluation approach or approaches that will be used (for example, objectives-based or quasi-legal approaches), including the use of informal or unplanned evaluation opportunities.
- Determine how the evaluation data will be collected (for example, through observations, questionnaires, product reviews).
- Think through how the data will be analyzed, including how

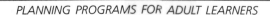

to integrate the data that were collected through any informal evaluation processes.

- Describe how judgments will be made about the program, using predetermined and/or emergent evaluation criteria for program success.
- Develop recommendations for current and/or future programming directions based on the judgments that were made and suggest ideas for how to address these recommendations, including what resources would be needed.

Determining Formats, Schedules, and Staff Needs

- Choose the most appropriate format or combination of formats for the learning activity (for example, individual, small-group [face-to-face], large-group [face-to-face], distance-learning, or community-learning formats).
- Devise a program schedule that best fits the format(s) chosen and the participants' personal and/or job commitments.
- Identify staff needs (that is, program designers, program coordinators, instructors/facilitators, and program evaluators).
- Determine whether internal staff (paid or volunteer) can plan and conduct the program or whether external consultants need to be hired instead or in addition.

Preparing Budgets and Marketing Plans

- Estimate the expenses for the program, including costs for the development, delivery, and evaluation of the program (for example, staff salaries, participant expenses, facility rental charges, outlays for instructional materials, transfer-of-learning costs).
- Determine how the program will be financed (for example, participant fees, organizational subsidy, government funding).
- Conduct a target population analysis to help determine the background and experience of the potential audience as one of the foundational pieces of the marketing plan.
- Select and prepare promotional materials (such as brochures, electronic mail, flyers) that "tell the story well" of the who, what, where, why, and how of the program.
- Prepare a targeted and lively promotional campaign, paying careful attention to the target audience, the type of promotional material you want to use, the time frame, and the cost.

Designing Instructional Plans

- Develop clear and understandable learning objectives for each instructional session.
- Select and sequence the content based on the participants' knowledge and experience, the nature of the content itself, and instructor preference.
- Choose instructional techniques that match the focus of the proposed learning outcomes and that you are capable of us-

ing (for example, lectures, case studies, role playing, story-telling, games, and metaphor analysis).

- Select and/or develop instructional materials that will enhance the learning effort.
- Choose an evaluation component for each instructional unit that will enhance participant learning and assist in ascertaining whether the instructional event actually produced the desired result.

Coordinating Facilities and On-Site Events

- Obtain suitable facilities that will provide a good environment for learning and arrange for instructional equipment that works.
- Oversee all of the on-site program arrangements (for example, those dealing with facilities, instructors and other staff, equipment, program schedule).
- Create a positive climate for learning from the moment the participants arrive (with, for example, a user-friendly registration system, participant orientation, and introductions).
- Provide a system for monitoring the program and making sound (but quick) decisions when program changes are needed.
- Gather data for the program evaluation and provide incentives, when needed, for completing the on-site evaluation process.
- Give recognition to program participants (for example, certificates, mugs, celebrations) and thank both staff and participants for being a part of the program.
- Tie up all loose ends after the program is completed (such as storing equipment, completing administrative forms, conducting staff debriefings).

Communicating the Value of the Program

- Prepare a program "report" (for example, a journalistic-style report, media presentation, poster, product display) that addresses well the function, scope, and audience for the program.
- Ensure that the report is done in a format that will reach appropriate individuals, groups, organizations, and/or the general public.
- Be proactive in how you time the release of the report.
- Follow up as needed with appropriate individuals and groups to clarify any questions or concerns about the program.

Assumptions on Which the Model Is Grounded

The interactive model of program planning rests on six major assumptions. The assumptions have been drawn primarily from the work of Houle (1972), Knowles (1980), Brookfield (1986), Sork and

Caffarella (1989), Sork (1990), and Cervero and Wilson (1992, 1994).

- Assumption 1: Educational programs should focus on what the participants actually learn and how this learning results in changes in participants, organizations, and/or societal issues and norms. Program planners must have a clear understanding of why they are doing what they are doing. They should be able to articulate what change will or could come about as a result of the educational program. These changes may be work-related or focused on other practical issues and problems of adult life, on organizational adaptation, and/or on alterations in societal norms and practices. Some of these changes can be demonstrated almost immediately, such as learning a specific job skill; while other changes, such as abolishing discriminatory practices, may take years of continuous effort on the part of educators.

- Assumption 2: Program planning involves both systematic, preplanned tasks and "on-your-feet" (sometimes last-minute) decisions. Persons responsible for planning programs can never know all the variables in the planning process. Even when the planning parameters and tasks are explicitly defined, they are often subject to change. For example, major presenters may cancel at the last minute, expected numbers of program participants may not show up, and weather conditions may prevent a specific event.

- Assumption 3: The development of educational programs is a complex interaction of institutional priorities, tasks, people, and events. Developing educational programs very rarely works in a logical fashion. Planners tend to spend a great deal of time formulating and then reformulating the many facets of the process. In addition, the more organizations and persons you add to the planning process, the less logical the process tends to be. For example, when different people representing a number of organizations are responsible for different parts of a program, some people may make every planning deadline while others make none. The latter can be a planning coordinator's nightmare, especially if the delinquent person's tasks are an essential element in getting the program off the ground. The key to keeping oneself sane as a program planner is to maintain flexibility throughout the process.

- Assumption 4: Developing educational programs is a cooperative rather than "operative" endeavor. There must be cooperation between and among the planners and the organizational sponsors of programs in the development and implementation of successful programs. Such cooperation may take several forms, from informally screening a proposed program or specific instructional plan through a group of potential participants and sponsors to involving those parties in all or part of the formal planning process.

- Assumption 5: Designing educational programs is a practical art. There is no single method of planning educational programs that will ensure success. Rather, program planners are very much like orchestra conductors. They must be able to bring together diverse players and pieces in a harmonious and balanced effort. This task may not be easy: some of the pieces may be much more difficult than anticipated, and some of the players may not be as adept at their parts as was hoped.

- Assumption 6: Individuals, using one or more planning models as guides, can learn to be more effective program planners through practice. Effective program planners are not born that way. Through trial and error, they become more skilled at balancing the various components and tasks of the process. It is important for planners to evaluate their planning efforts to see where they have been effective and where they can improve.

Sources for the Model

The interactive program planning model is derived from three major sources: classical and current descriptions of program planning, principles and practices of adult learning, and practical experience.

First, then, building on Tyler's (1949) original description of the curriculum development process, eight process descriptions for planning programs provided the primary source to frame the model (Houle, 1972; Knowles, 1980; Laird, 1985; Caffarella, 1985; Sork and Caffarella, 1989; Sork, 1990; Tracey, 1992; and Rothwell and Kazanas, 1993). In addition, eight other sources (Boyle, 1981; Nadler, 1982; Cervero, 1988; Harris, 1989; Bradley, Kallick, and Regan, 1991; Munson, 1992; Richey, 1992; Cervero and Wilson, 1994) provided some very useful material.

Second, as foundational material in building and using this model, it was important to consider how adults learn and change. Highlighted below are the major principles and practices of adult learning that were used in developing the model:

- Adults can and do want to learn, regardless of their age.
- Adults have a rich background of knowledge and experience. They tend to learn best when this experience is acknowledged and when new information builds on their past knowledge and experience.
- Adults are motivated to learn based on a combination of complex internal and external forces. We need to understand the nature of those forces and how they interact to inhibit and/or encourage adult learning.
- All adults have preferred styles of learning, and these differ.
- For the most part, adults are pragmatic in their learning. They tend to want to apply their learning to present situations.

- Adults are not likely to willingly engage in learning unless the content is meaningful to them.
- Adults come to a learning situation with their own personal goals and objectives, which may or may not be the same as those that underlie the learning situation.
- Adults prefer to be actively involved in the learning process rather than passive recipients of knowledge. In addition, they want the opportunity to be supportive of each other in the learning process.
- Adults learn both in independent, self-reliant modes and in interdependent, connected, and collaborative ways.
- Much of what adults learn tends to have an effect on others (for example, on work colleagues and family).
- Adults are more receptive to the learning process in situations that are both physically and psychologically comfortable.
- What, how, and where adults learn is affected by the many roles they play as adults (for example, worker, parent, partner, friend, spouse), their gender, their ethnicity, and their social class.

More in-depth discussions about learning in adulthood can be found in Belenky, Clinchy, Goldberger, and Tarule (1986), Brookfield (1986), Levine (1989), Mezirow (1991), Merriam and Caffarella (1991), Caffarella (1992, 1994), and Merriam (1993).

Consider these examples of how specific principles and practices of how adults learn and change have been incorporated into the interactive model of program planning:

- Identifying program ideas. Because adults are not likely to willingly engage in learning activities unless the content is meaningful to them, collecting ideas for programs from participants enrolled in current educational programs is a good way to generate ideas for future programs.
- Designing instructional plans. Instructors should design their learning objectives in such a way that participants, whenever possible, can incorporate their own learning agendas. The instructional content should build on the past knowledge and experiences of the participants and be, where appropriate, problem-oriented and practical. Teaching techniques should permit active learner participation and provide opportunities to apply newly learned knowledge and skills. Learning activities should encourage participants to assume responsibility for their own learning and allow for both independent and collaborative activities.
- Formulating evaluation plans. Because adults want to give and receive feedback on their learning experiences (both from a personal and programmatic standpoint), opportunities for individual evaluation by both the instructor and the learner should be part of the evaluation plan.
- Coordinating facilities and on-site events. To ensure that the

learning climate makes adults feel respected, accepted, and supported, instructors should provide opportunities for the participants to modify the learning activity's objectives, content, and/or methods). Evaluation data should be collected in a way that does not interfere with the learning or rights of participants.

The third source used in developing the model was practical experience—my own and that of other professionals in the field. The importance of this source is demonstrated by the work of Pennington and Green (1976), Brookfield (1986), and Cervero and Wilson (1991, 1992, 1994). Pennington and Green (1976) were among the first to challenge the assumption that program planners always follow specific models of planning and include all the steps in those models. Although they found that planners could identify a clear set of tasks and decision points, they saw major discrepancies between what planners did and what popular models of program planning said they should do. For example, comprehensive needs assessments were rarely conducted as the basis for program development, and often those designing the actual instructional activities did not take into account the background, characteristics, and experiences of the particular group of learners who were to attend the program. Further, Brookfield (1986) and Cervero and Wilson (1991, 1992, 1994) have observed that experienced program planners are often unable to recognize, in many program planning models, what they actually do. In other words, program planning is an interactive and action-oriented process in which decisions and choices must be made that do not necessarily fit what the various models prescribe.

Among the major variables in how decisions are made in the program planning process is the experience that planners bring to the table. Therefore, in deciding on the components and tasks included in the model presented in this book and determining how the model should be used, I sought—and received—very helpful ideas and feedback from experienced practitioners: my graduate students (most of whom are practicing professionals in adult and continuing education, training in the public and private sectors, and public school and postsecondary education), participants in workshops I have conducted on program planning, and many practitioners (both paid and volunteer) I work with in the field who are engaged in planning programs as part of their responsibilities. The ideas from these various constituents were incorporated in the many revisions of the model that brought it to its present form.

Chapter Highlights

The interactive model of program planning for adult learners consists of eleven components, with each component containing a series of tasks and decision points:

- Establishing a basis for the planning process

- Identifying program ideas
- Sorting and prioritizing program ideas
- Developing program objectives
- Preparing for the transfer of learning
- Formulating evaluation plans
- Determining formats, schedules, and staff needs
- Preparing budgets and marketing plans
- Designing instructional plans
- Coordinating facilities and on-site events
- Communicating the value of the program

Program planners often work with a number of components and tasks at the same time and apply the model in different ways; and they rarely work alone. Therefore, the key to using the model is remaining flexible in its application throughout the planning process.

The model is grounded on six major assumptions. Among those assumptions, the following two are the most critical for those using the model: educational programs should focus on what the participants actually learn and how this learning results in changes in participants, organizations, and/or societal issues and norms; and, the development of educational programs is a complex interaction of institutional priorities, tasks, people, and events.

In constructing the model, I used three major sources: classical and current descriptions of program planning, principles and practices of adult learning, and the day-to-day experiences of educators, trainers, and staff developers. Although frameworks of earlier models and knowledge about learning in adulthood were helpful in building the model, without the voices of the practitioners the interactive model of program planning would be neither as rich nor as practical in its applicability.

Three

Using the Interactive Program Planning Model

A program planning model is meant to be *used* rather than simply tucked in a file folder or left on a bookshelf. Thus, before deciding to try any program planning model, program planners should examine their own beliefs and values about planning programs for adults to determine whether the model fits with who they are and how they prefer to practice. If, for example, they prefer to work solo, the interactive program planning model will not work for them. (Remember that one of the basic assumptions of the model is that collaborative planning is a given in most planning situations.) Once planners have decided to use a particular model, they need to make some preliminary assumptions about the planning situation so that initial decisions about the planning process can be made. Developing these planning assumptions will, among other things, assist staff in determining whether they need to use all or only parts of the planning model. Finally, making decisions about how and what programs to plan requires more than just knowing how to plan programs effectively; it often involves making decisions that have moral and ethical consequences for the participants, the planners, and the program sponsors. Each of these important topics related to the use of the interactive program planning for adults—identifying personal beliefs about program planning, developing up-front planning assumptions, determining what parts of the model are needed, and ethical issues of program planning—is discussed in this chapter.

Identifying Personal Beliefs Related to Program Planning

In applying the interactive program planning model, program planners need to know what they stand for as educators and trainers. More specifically, they need to be able to identify their beliefs and values and determine working philosophies about the program planning process (Apps, 1973, 1991; Boyle, 1981; Zinn, 1990b). By articulating these beliefs and values, program planners can determine whether or not the interactive model fits what they believe and how they work. (If it does not, perhaps they might be willing to reflect on their present practice and modify or change their beliefs so that the model could be a useful resource and enhance their practice.) For example, do they see the program planning process as sequential or as a highly flexible and interactive process in terms of what planners do first, second, and so on? Do they believe in the basic assumptions of the model, such as the assumption that program planning is a cooperative endeavor involving complex interactions among institutional priorities, people, and events? And do they believe that adults can and do want to learn, regardless of their age, and that adults tend to learn best when their experiences and prior knowledge are incorporated into learning activities?

Boyle (1981) and Apps (1991) have provided useful categories to assist educators and trainers in articulating and examining their working philosophies on program planning. The various categories, as illustrated below with sample belief statements, incorporate ideas about what people believe about the purpose of education, the program planning process, adults as learners, and the process of learning.

The Purpose of Adult Education

- The purpose of educational programs is to promote changes in the way workers behave so their job performance is enhanced.
- The purpose of educational programs is to encourage the growth and development of individuals.
- The purpose of educational programs is to assist adults to bring about change in societal norms and values.

The Program Planning Process

- Program planners should act as content experts and/or managers of the planning process, making sure that all necessary tasks are completed.
- Program planners should serve as coordinators and facilitators in the planning process, enabling all parties (such as participants, supervisors, funding sources) to have an active role. They also may be content experts.
- Program planners should act as the negotiators between and among the various groups involved in the planning process. They also may be content experts.

Adults as Learners

- Adults can and do want to learn regardless of age.
- Adults have a rich background of knowledge and experience that should be used in the learning process.
- Adults, for the most part, are pragmatic in their learning. They want to apply their learning to present situations.

The Learning Process

- Participants learn best when new information/skills build on past knowledge and experience.
- Participants are more motivated to learn when a variety of teaching methods are used.
- Participants learn both in independent, self-reliant modes and in interdependent and collaborative ways.

One instrument that is useful in assisting planners to determine their underlying beliefs about program planning is Zinn's (1990a) Philosophy of Adult Education Inventory. The purpose of that instrument is to help educators identify their personal philosophy of education as related to the categories described by Boyle and Apps. The inventory is self-administered, self-scored, and self-interpreted, which makes it easy for planners to use in clarifying their personal beliefs about areas important to the program planning process.

Rarely do persons involved with planning programs ever fully articulate their personal beliefs about program planning; yet a system of beliefs and values guides their actions. Contrast, for example, two different people responsible for developing educational activities.

Scenario 1

Bob C. involves as many people as possible in designing the educational activities for which he is responsible. He has a very active education committee and uses a variety of ad hoc groups in the planning of new programs and other educational initiatives. He strongly advises his instructors to use participatory methods in their program delivery and to gear their material to what would be useful to the participants back on the job. He ensures that all participants receive prompt feedback on what they have learned (whether it be information, skills, or changes in attitudes and values), both during the sessions and when they try to apply the material to their specific work situations.

Scenario 2

Wanda R., on the other hand, prefers to plan educational activities by herself, although she occasionally hires outside consultants to assist. She finds working with committees and with staff outside her unit very cumbersome. She does not like her instructors to waste any time in class and requests that they stick strictly to the topic at hand and make sure the participants know the content. Wanda requires pre- and posttests for each session, but no follow-up training or evaluation is done once the program is completed. Wanda believes that follow-up activities are a waste of time and money. If the participants did not get the material the first time (she believes), they did not really want to learn it in the first place. Wanda also assumes that it is the participant's responsibility to be able to apply the material, not hers.

Although most program planners do not take the time to spell out clearly and precisely their working philosophies, being cognizant of and acting on one's beliefs about program planning is critical in planning programs for adults. Adult learners and program sponsors are usually quick at making judgments about planners who espouse one set of beliefs and then act in opposition to those beliefs. For example, if potential program participants are asked for ideas for future programs, they want to see those ideas used; and if their ideas are not used, they want to know why. Likewise, if organizational sponsors expect certain outcomes (and have been promised that all of those outcomes will be addressed), they do not like the planners of the event to respond to only some of their expectations. And when program planners say they are interested in fostering change in participants, organizational practices, and the like, administrators and participants expect them to take this charge seriously and not simply assume that the changes will happen through the good intentions of participants and/or sponsors. In essence, adult learners and sponsors of educational and training programs expect program planners to plan and deliver what they say they will deliver. For program staff to do otherwise often results in angry—or even worse, indifferent—participants and the attitude that educational and training programs are a waste of time and money.

Developing Up-Front Assumptions

Developing up-front assumptions about any planning situation is a very helpful starting point for applying the interactive program planning model. Although stating these planning assumptions is a generally useful practice, it becomes especially critical when large programs, with their increased complexity and staffing, are being launched. In addition, formulating these preliminary assumptions can assist planners in determining whether all or only parts of the model are necessary to a given program. Four major factors need to be considered in developing these initial planning assumptions: current program commitments, organizational context, planning personnel, and available resources (Forest and Mulcahy, 1976; Boyle, 1981; Sork, 1990; Cervero and Wilson, 1994). Each of these is discussed briefly below.

Current Program Commitments

When deciding whether to initiate a program, those responsible for the planning process must have a clear understanding of both the new ideas that have been identified and the present priorities and commitments for educational programs. These commitments may include carryover programs and activities that must be repeated.

Interpreting new ideas in terms of present activities can be handled in three ways. The first is to consider the present commitments as possible priorities, "along with other emerging and new concerns. Selecting this option means some present commitments eventually will be rated a lower priority" (Forest and Mulcahy, 1976, p. 17). A second approach is to recognize that prior or ongoing commitments will take time, and therefore time must be set aside to meet them. Third, the past priorities and commitments can be ignored. This alternative will not be very popular, of course, because commitments are often made to get or keep the support of others. Whatever approach is used, all current programs and ongoing activities and commitments, as well as the emerging ideas, must be considered when deciding whether to initiate a new program.

A sample assumption in the area of current program commitments reads as follows: *All present commitments, along with new ideas and concerns, will be considered as possible priorities on an equal basis.*

Organizational Context

Planning assumptions must be made in light of the sponsoring group's or organization's mission and goals. For example, does the organization expect that educational programs will result in greater productivity (and thus cost savings)? Is it expected that the educational unit will be a profit-making operation? Will innovative programs, along with those that have stood the test of time, be supported? Is the organization primarily interested in serving one major audience, or is a broader clientele accepted?

In addition, it is necessary to consider the politics of the organization (Bolman and Deal, 1991). How are decisions made, and who makes them? Are there power coalitions, both formal and informal, that program planners need to cultivate? How can staff wisely use the political structure to enhance their programs? "If planners are not politically astute, they surely will be ineffective" (Cervero and Wilson, 1991, p. 45).

A sample assumption in the area of organizational context reads as follows: *It is expected that educational programs will result in increased productivity and effectiveness of employees. One measure of this must be demonstrated through cost-benefit analysis.*

Planning Personnel

Program planners rely on their own values, perceptions, and experiences in making planning assumptions. Therefore, it is important to know who the people are who will be involved in making these decisions. What are their educational backgrounds? What kinds of work and/or volunteer experience have they had? Are they oriented more toward service, organizational goals, social issues, or the growth and development of self and others? What are their perceptions of the value of education?

The influence of program planners as educational leaders within the organization is important, but it should not take precedence over the opinions and experiences of other people who are key stakeholders. Yet in the final analysis, the programs selected—whatever they are—must become the personal agendas of the program planners, because it is they who are responsible for getting the job done.

A sample assumption in the area of planning personnel reads as follows: *A team of three people, composed of two teachers and the principal, will determine what kinds of staff development options will be extended to staff during the next academic year.*

Resource Availability

In determining program assumptions, the type and amount of resources available for educational programs must be spelled out. Resources include time, money, personnel, facilities, equipment, material, and supplies. Boyle has outlined three key questions that need to be answered about resources in setting program assumptions: "Do we have the quality and quantity of resources necessary to affect change through a program? Are they the right kind of resources? Are we employing new personnel to coincide with changing program priorities?" (Boyle, 1981, p. 174).

A sample assumption in the area of resource availability reads as follows: *No new financial resources will be available to the Human Resource Division. The division may choose to reallocate present resources, however (including staff time and funds available for current programs).*

Determining Which Components
of the Model to Use

Depending on the planning situation, people responsible for planning programs may choose to use all or only selected components of the interactive model of program planning. Program planners developing comprehensive programs for adults would generally use all of the components of the model. Examples of such programs include

- National, regional, or state professional and trade conferences
- Adult degree programs in colleges and universities
- Comprehensive community education or development programs
- Regional job training and retraining programs
- Districtwide staff development programs

Even when program planners determine that they need to use all of the components of the model, they may apply the model in different ways, however. They may, for example (as discussed in Chapter Two), start the program planning process at any one of a variety of different points; they may focus on only one component at a time or work on a number of components simultaneously; they may choose to give some tasks more emphasis than others in the planning process; and they may need to revisit a component more than once during the planning process. Two differing applications of the model are illustrated in Figure 3.1.

Figure 3.1. Two Sample Applications of the Program Planning Model.

Example 1: Adult Off-Campus Degree Program

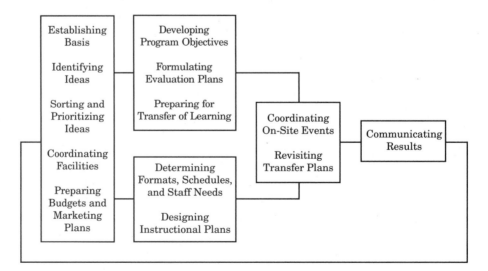

Example 2: Annual Conference for Professional Association

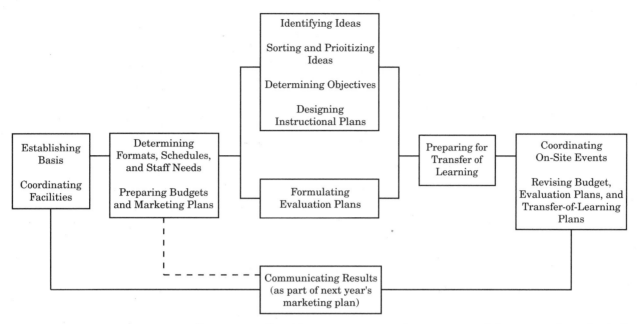

In many situations, program planners need to use only selected parts of the model. Examples of such situations are listed here:

Planning Situations	Components to Be Addressed
Programs that are limited in scope and time and have set audiences, budgets, and places to meet	Identifying program ideas Developing program objectives Determining program format and staff needs Designing instructional plans
Already developed programs being repeated in different locations with participants who have similar backgrounds and experiences	Coordinating facilities and on-site events Preparing for transfer of learning at the various locations Communicating program value
Already developed programs being repeated for different audiences in the same location	Formulating marketing plans Coordinating on-site events Communicating program value
Programs in which the delivery and content are being changed	Determining program format Designing instructional plans Formulating evaluation plans Preparing for transfer of learning
Programs where attendance is mandatory and the goals, format, content, and evaluation are set	Determining program staff Coordinating facilities and on-site events Designing instructional plans Preparing for transfer of learning
Programs for which logistics and on-site coordination are handled by staff of the facility where the program is being held	Identifying and prioritizing ideas Developing program objectives Determining staff and format Designing instructional plans Formulating evaluation plans Preparing for transfer of learning

Like program planners who use the whole model, planning staff who use only selected components may choose to address one component at a time or simultaneously work with two or more components.

Sometimes program planners, whether they are using all or only selected components of the model, have the freedom to apply the model in deliberate, methodical ways. Often, though, outside forces (such as budget cuts, the weather, and/or other unforeseen changes during a planning cycle) dictate what component or components must be addressed to get a program up and running or keep it functioning. A sampling of these program planning "interruptions" is listed below:

- A major new program initiative was announced on the assumption that start-up funds were available to get the new program up and running (after which it would be self-sufficient). Now, however, unexpected budget cuts have eliminated that start-up funding. The question is whether alternative funds can be found or the program should be canceled.

- A very popular program for volunteers of an organization has been oversubscribed. The instructors know that if all of the people who have registered in advance actually come, what they have planned in terms of format and teaching methods will not work. The organizers do not want to tell some of the participants not to come, because they are afraid they would lose some good volunteers. The question is whether (1) they can redesign the instructional part of the program and find additional instructors so a larger number of people can be accommodated or (2) they should offer the program a second time and give people the opportunity to choose one of the two times.

- A fire has destroyed the headquarters hotel two days prior to the opening of a major national conference. The primary tasks to be addressed are housing participants who were to stay at this hotel and finding enough meeting rooms for the program sessions.

- An unforecast snow and ice storm has kept all the major program presenters stranded at a hub airport all day. The airport was supposed to reopen at noon, but now it has been shut down until morning—and the program is scheduled to begin at 8:00 A.M. It is now 7:00 P.M., and there are no other transportation options available. Many of the program participants are either on their way or already at the program site, as they are all within drivable distance and it is only raining where they are. The major issue is what to do with the participants until the presenters arrive.

What becomes readily apparent, as stressed in Chapter Two, is the need for flexibility and creativity on the part of all involved in the program planning process.

Making Ethical Decisions in Program Planning

One of the values on which the interactive program planning model rests is that using an ethical approach in making decisions about educational programs for adults should be of concern to all parties involved in the process of planning such programs. "To overlook ethical concerns is a blatant disregard for the value of human beings" (Apps, 1991, p. 113); in addition, it diminishes what we do as program planners and educational leaders. But acting in an ethical manner may be easier said than done. Common ethical dilemmas and issues encountered by many program planners as they try to meet deadlines, produce programs that will work, or (for some) simply stay in business are illustrated below as they relate to selected components of the interactive model of program planning (Apps, 1991; Brookfield, 1988; Sork, 1988):

Establishing a Basis for the Planning Process
- Asking people to serve on educational advisory committees and then repeatedly ignoring their advice
- Publicly stating the beliefs of the educational unit and then not modeling those beliefs in program planning and delivery

Identifying Program Ideas
- Conducting a formal needs assessment of potential participants knowing full well that senior management has already identified program needs
- Basing programs on needs or ideas not acknowledged by program participants

Developing Program Objectives
- Claiming that certain outcomes will happen as a result of the program when they cannot be demonstrated
- Agreeing to unwritten program goals that primarily enhance the stature of the educational unit rather than meeting either participant or organizational needs

Coordinating Facilities and On-Site Events
- Setting participant fees so that only "selected clientele" can attend
- Offering programs at major resort areas and then using sign-up as the only criterion for successful completion

Designing Instructional Plans
- Employing big-name presenters who can draw a crowd, even though staff believe that their presentations are usually of poor quality
- Continuing to use instructors whom participants consistently evaluate as ineffective
- Knowingly using out-of-date and/or inappropriate resources because they are cheap and easy to get

Formulating Evaluation Plans
- Providing evaluation data on participants to work supervisors of these participants without participants' prior knowledge or consent

- Changing the criteria for program effectiveness as a response to political pressure, even though the new criteria are much less stringent
- Reporting only agreed-upon evaluation findings when unethical or harmful practices have been observed

Having a framework for responding ethically to the many decisions that must be made in the course of planning programs for adults can be very helpful (Starratt, 1991; Brockett, 1988). A sample framework is given in Figure 3.2.

Figure 3.2. Sample Framework for Making Ethical Program Planning Decisions.

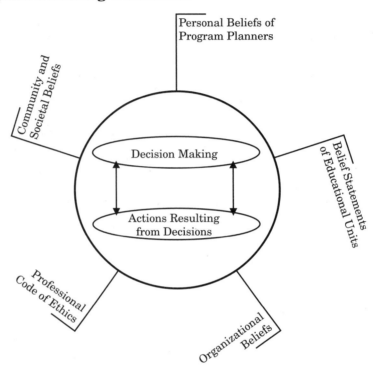

As this figure shows, there may be one or a multiple set of beliefs that must be considered in making and acting on program decisions that have ethical components. Obviously, the more comprehensive the scope of a program, the more difficult it becomes to respond in a way that all parties involved will agree is ethical. Framing responses is especially problematic when there is conflict between and among the belief systems of the different people, organizations, and/or communities. Thus responding to ethical dilemmas fostered by planning staff who are not modeling belief statements of their department is easier to do than coping with ethical dilemmas resulting from major differences in beliefs between and among program planners, funding agencies, and powerful community interest groups.

In using the above framework, program planners must first start with themselves: they must examine their own beliefs about program planning. Affirming their own beliefs and philosophies may be the only part of the equation over which planners are able to exercise any control. (The process of identifying one's beliefs was discussed earlier in this chapter.) The next step is to make public the belief statements of the educational unit or the organization as a whole related to educational programming. This means, as will be described in Chapter Four, developing very definitive statements of beliefs about developing educational programs for adults and then sharing them with program participants, colleagues, the leadership of the organization, and/or other appropriate groups, including the general public. Sample belief statements for a program unit might look like this:

- Human growth and development are lifelong pursuits.
- Organizational change will be a continuing phenomenon.
- Organizational needs and individual development are both important elements of the educational programs sponsored by this division.
- Validated knowledge and active inquiry form the basis of professional practice in this organization.
- Fostering collaboration in planning forms the cornerstone of how educational programs are developed.
- Being caring and ethical is fundamental to our practice of planning educational programs.

The third task is to identify any codes of ethics or statements of beliefs of professional groups or other groups and organizations that are part of the planning process. These statements and ethical codes should be brought into the planning process as warranted. The last operational step, and definitely the most difficult (in some cases, nearly impossible), is to identify the beliefs and values of the community and wider society in which program planners work. Although locating documents that explicitly outline community or societal beliefs can be a very difficult task, especially when there are competing and constantly changing belief systems, there are some planning situations where they are vital. Examples of such situations include planning educational programs on major social concerns (for example, health care or school reform) or for large numbers of people (for example, all state or federal employees, participants in national and international forums). Being able to tease out this information is especially critical when program planners find themselves in unfamiliar territory or in environments where change is the norm.

Chapter Highlights

In applying the interactive model of program planning, planners need to know what they stand for—their personal beliefs about the purpose of education, the program planning process, adults as learners, and the process of learning. Does the model (and the assumptions upon which it is grounded) fit with their implicit or explicit beliefs as portrayed in their actions as program planners? If not, is it because of the exigencies of the planning situation or because their beliefs and actions as planners are truly incompatible with the model? Knowing one's beliefs is one of the cornerstones of ethical practice.

In using the model in specific planning situations, planners benefit from making some preliminary assumptions about those situations. Explicitly stated assumptions about the organizational context, the backgrounds and experiences of planning personnel, how current program commitments fit in with new programs, and other available resources can be helpful guideposts throughout the planning process. These assumptions can and will change, but having people on the same wavelength at the start of the process can provide a solid foundation for open communication between and among the planning parties.

Depending on the planning situation, program planners may choose to use all or only selected components of the model. In many planning situations, only some of the components (and the tasks within those components) are needed. Whether all or only parts of the model are used, the key words in applying the model are *flexibility* and *creativity*. Experienced planners know that even the best programs rarely come together without a lot of juggling of ideas, strategies, resources, and people.

The remainder of this volume outlines in detail each of the components and corresponding tasks of the interactive model of program planning, starting with establishing the basis for planning. For those planners using one or many components of the model, a critical operating principle is that an ethical approach is fundamental to how we make planning decisions. Program planners often face ethical dilemmas as they move through the planning process—from questionable reasons for conducting programs to poor teaching and learning practices. In handling problems and issues of an ethical nature, it is helpful for program planners to have a framework for making these kinds of decisions, which are often complex and have no right or wrong responses (except in the eyes of the beholder).

Applications Exercises

The three Applications Exercises presented here will help you adapt the interactive program planning model to your own planning efforts. The first exercise will help you identify your personal beliefs related to program planning (Exhibit 3.1), the second will help you clarify preliminary assumptions about the specific planning situation (Exhibit 3.2), and the third will help you determine which components of the interactive model of program planning are appropriate for your situation (Exhibit 3.3).

Exhibit 3.1. Identifying Personal Beliefs Related to Program Planning.

1. First identify your own beliefs in the following four areas. Then outline specific actions related to what you do as a program planner that illustrate your belief statements and actions that appear to contradict those statements.

Beliefs	Personal Belief Statement(s)	Your Actions That Illustrate Your Beliefs	Your Actions That Appear to Contradict Your Beliefs
About the purpose of educational programs for adults			
About the program planning process			
About adults as learners			
About the process of learning			

2. Ask others you work with in planning programs to identify their beliefs. Where are your beliefs similar and where different? Have these similarities and differences enhanced the planning process; and if so, how? Have the differences created difficulties in program planning?

_____

_____

_____

_____

Exhibit 3.2. Developing Up-Front Assumptions.

1. Briefly outline a situation in which you have the responsibility for developing program planning assumptions.

_____

_____

_____

2. For the following four factors, list the assumptions you need to make before you initiate your program planning process. Be as specific as you can.

Current program commitments:_____

_____

_____

_____

Organizational context:_____

_____

_____

_____

Planning personnel: _____

_____

_____

_____

Available resources: _____

_____

_____

_____

Exhibit 3.3. Determining Which Components of the Interactive Model to Use.

1. Describe briefly an educational program you anticipate being involved with as part of the planning effort.

_____

_____

_____

_____

2. Indicate with a check mark those components of the interactive model of program planning that you believe will need to be addressed. Place a second check by those that should receive special emphasis for this program (and briefly note why).

  ❑ ❑ Establishing a basis for the planning process

  ❑ ❑ Identifying program ideas

  ❑ ❑ Sorting and prioritizing program ideas

  ❑ ❑ Developing program objectives

  ❑ ❑ Preparing for the transfer of learning

  ❑ ❑ Formulating evaluation plans

  ❑ ❑ Determining formats, schedules, and staff needs

  ❑ ❑ Preparing budgets and marketing plans

  ❑ ❑ Designing instructional plans

  ❑ ❑ Coordinating facilities and on-site events

  ❑ ❑ Communicating the value of the program

3. Using Figure 3.1 as your guide, prepare a flowchart indicating which components you would choose to address when.

————— ∞ —————

Four

Establishing a Basis for the Planning Process

Two major elements emerge as essential in identifying and establishing a basis for program development: (1) knowing the context for planning and (2) establishing a solid base of support for educational activities. The way that educational and training personnel tackle each of these elements will differ, depending on whether the educational function is centralized or disbursed among organizational units and staff and whether education is viewed as a critical part of the mission of the organization, a secondary, or sideline activity. In addition, who the educational programs are designed for makes a difference in what kind of support is needed. Are the programs for persons associated with the organization in one way or another (that is, as staff, volunteers, clients), or are the programs for a wider audience (as are university continuing education programs and community action ventures)? Do program participants come on a voluntary basis (as do, for example, participants in a library discussion group or a professional association conference), or are participants mandated to attend (as are, for example, participants in a program on a new organizational initiative such as quality service or a Saturday driving school)?

Addressed first in this chapter is the planning context—the internal and external institutional and environmental factors within which program planners function. Discussed next is the need to establish a solid base of support for planning programs. More specifically, strategies are outlined for building and maintaining structural support; ensuring the support of program participants, organizational staff, and external constituencies; and providing a supportive organizational culture.

The Context for Planning

People who develop educational programs do not work in a vacuum, as can be seen in the following scenarios:

Scenario 1

Lisa M., the staff development coordinator for School District 10, has been asked to develop, in cooperation with a team of teachers and administrators from the district, a districtwide program on working with diverse student populations. This program is the direct result of three recent incidents in the district—fights and other acts of violence—between and among the various ethnic groups within the school system.

The district superintendent and the school board chair have made some sweeping promises about how this behavior will be stopped, and a number of parent and student groups have been extremely vocal about wanting changes in the way district personnel work with minority students; in addition, a series of articles in the local paper on the poor management by school personnel of these incidents included the accusation that the responses to the problems have been racially biased.

Scenario 2

John P. has been asked to plan a similar program for his district, but the situation there is entirely different. Learning new ways to work positively with diverse students has been set as a major objective for the district for this school year. This objective was targeted as a result of both observations made by school improvement teams in six of the eight schools and the concerted effort of two community groups whose major mission is to promote ethnic understanding. District administrators and the teachers' governing body also support this thrust by the district.

Program planners need to have a basic understanding of the context within which they are functioning (Sork and Caffarella, 1989; Bradley, Kallick, and Regan, 1991; Cervero and Wilson, 1994). *Context* is defined as the situational and environmental factors that affect decisions planners make about programs. These factors include both the milieu of the organization in which program planners work (the internal factors) and the wider community in which the organization or group functions (the external factors).

Internal Contextual Factors

Internal contextual factors are broadly categorized under three headings: structural, people, and cultural (Deal and Kennedy, 1982; Bolman and Deal, 1991; Merriam and Caffarella, 1991).

Structural factors include the mission, goals, and objectives of organization, standard operating policies and procedures, the system of formal organizational authority, information systems, organizational decision-making patterns, financial resources, and physical facilities. *People factors* include program planning staff, program participants, top-level management and administrative personnel, supervisory personnel, program "stakeholders," and boards of directors. *Cultural factors* include the history and traditions of the organization, organizational beliefs and values, and organizational rituals, stories, symbols, and heroes. Illustrations of selected factors from each category are given below:

Structural: Standard Operating Procedures

- Staff at all levels will be given the opportunity to attend the equivalent of three days of educational programs per year at the organization's expense.

- Before participating in an educational program, a person must receive permission from a specified person (such as work supervisor or executive director) and/or department.

Structural: Organizational Decision Making

- Decisions about educational programs within the organization are made primarily through a formal, hierarchical chain of command.

- Decisions about educational programs are made in a collaborative and democratic manner, with each staff member having an equal voice.

People: Program Planning Staff

- The program planning staff consists of a manager, two instructional designers, and six people who coordinate and conduct training programs.
- Planning educational programs for staff is considered to be among the functions of every line administrator (for example, division heads, principals, directors).

People: Supervisory Staff

- Those who supervise staff are all very supportive of the educational opportunities afforded people in the organization.
- There is a large percentage of supervisory personnel who view educational programs for their staff as a useless waste of time.

Cultural: History and Traditions of the Organization

- Offering educational programs for adults has had a long history at this institution, with an emphasis on quality and service to the participants.
- This organization has a strong tradition of viewing education for job advancement as the responsibility of the individual worker.

Cultural: Organizational Symbols

- The organizational logo includes the words "learning for life," visualized in the symbol of a continuous circle.
- Persons who complete the Senior Management Institute are given pewter mugs engraved with the organization's symbol; they are expected to display these in their offices.

External Contextual Factors

It is also important that program planners address external factors—those that involve the wider community and the interactions between the primary sponsoring organization and that wider community—when planning programs. Of particular concern to educators and trainers are these factors:

- Relationships with organizations and groups that have major influence and/or control (including regulatory and/or funding responsibilities) over the programs being planned (for example, professional associations, regulatory bodies, governmental and quasi-governmental agencies, private nonprofit entities, and grass-roots community groups)
- The nature of interactions (for example, competitive or cooperative) between and among the sponsoring organization and other providers of similar educational and training programs
- How the organization or group is perceived by potential program participants who are themselves not members of the sponsoring group (that is, the issues of credibility, applicability)

- The more general economic, political, and social climate (Belsheim, 1988; Sork and Caffarella, 1989; Cohen, 1990; Sork, 1990)

This final factor is increasingly becoming more important. This can be seen, for example, in how specific topics such as diversity in the workplace, AIDS education, and delivery of health care have become more and more politicized; they are seen as major economic and social issues that must be addressed not only by organizations but by society in general.

Information on the Internal and External Planning Context

Where can information about the planning context be found? Four basic sources are accessible to program planners in most organizations: *written documents* (for example, annual reports, organizational descriptive material, policies and procedures manuals, strategic planning reports, newspapers, magazine articles, government documents), *people* (for example, colleagues, supervisors, key managers, program planners from other organizations, professional networks), *formal group sessions* (such as boards and committees, work teams, community meetings), and *electronic data bases*. In addition, planners may have access to more informal sources of information: they may be invited to eat in the executive dining room, to attend meetings with senior management personnel, or to go to a ball game with a group of people "in the know."

The level and depth of the information that people need to have about the context for planning varies, depending on the role of the planner, the planner's background and experience in this context, and the educational programs being planned. Let us consider two very different situations.

Scenario 1

Fred C. has just been appointed as a training specialist for computer operations in the commercial division of the Jones Bank. A new operating system is to be brought on line within the next six months. Fred will be responsible both for developing the user manuals and for conducting the actual training of employees. He has been promoted through the ranks to his present position and has a clear understanding of how the unit presently functions.

In addition, his supervisor has briefed him on the proposed changes and their importance to both the commercial division and the general operation of the bank. The supervisor has also explained to Fred the evolving nature of commercial banking—especially how their bank is changing. Fred has obtained for review a copy of the last two annual reports and some in-house reports on the commercial division to better understand his particular situation.

Scenario 2

Mary D. has just assumed the position of corporate vice president for human resource development and training for the Jones Bank. Though familiar with the banking industry, she was hired from the outside. Mary did her homework prior to her interview, however. She has a very clear "outsider's understanding" of the overall mission and expected future direction of the bank, based on written materials and her interviews. Now she needs to convert that data to an insider's perspective. Mary has decided on five basic strategies to achieve those ends: she intends to review all available in-house documents related to the present and future operations of the organization; interview members of the senior management team, key middle managers of each major division of the bank, and her own staff; attend all strategic planning meetings at both the corporate and division levels; join the regional chapters of the American Society for Training and Development and the American Management Association; and scan whatever material she can locate related to how her organization and the banking industry in general are viewed in political, economic, and social terms. Mary hopes through her efforts to gain an in-depth understanding of her new organization and how her unit fits into that organization.

Both Fred and Mary needed to gain a basic understanding of the context in which they would be planning and/or managing educational programs. But the type and level of information that each person needed to effectively function was quite different.

Building a Solid Base of Support

It is important to establish a firm base of support for planning and conducting educational programs. Nadler (1982) stresses that this support must take the form of both commitment and action. *Commitment* is viewed as a recurrent promise, which usually comes in the form of written and/or verbal statements. For example, the chief executive officer might emphasize, in her annual "state-of-the-union" address, that continuing learning is foundational to the mission of the organization. *Action* involves having people at all levels in the organization respond to that commitment in the form of budgetary and other resource allocations and actual involvement in the educational function. In building this organizational support, as in analyzing the internal contextual factors, program planners must pay attention to the structural, people, and cultural factors.

Building Structural Support

Because the type of structural support that program planners need to build depends primarily on how central the educational function is to the organization, planners need to evaluate the role of that function within their own organization. The ways in which educational programs are incorporated into organizations vary widely, of course, but most organizations fall into three general categories:

- Organizations that sponsor educational programs for adults as their primary mission (such as corporations that provide only educational and training services and schools for adult students only)
- Organizations that have as a major function of their operations a centralized educational and training unit charged with managing educational programs (such as colleges of continuing education in universities, staff development departments in public schools, and training divisions in business and industry)

- Organizations that provide educational programs as one of their services but do not have separate units charged with managing or coordinating functions (for example, organizations offering programs in which nurses teach patients in primary-care settings, principals plan in-service programs, and managers are asked to be mentors and coaches)

Let us turn now to a sampling of specific ways to build organizational support around three structural factors—organizational mission and goals, standard operating procedures, and the organizational authority of educational programs—within each of the three organizational frameworks.

Organizations Whose Primary Mission Is Adult Education. If you are part of an organization dedicated to adult education, you might build structural organizational support as follows:

- *Mission and goals of the organization.* The mission and goals statements should clearly define the main focus of the organization as developing and providing educational programs for adults. The language of the mission statement needs to be clear to all organizational personnel, potential program participants, and key external organizations, groups, and individuals.

- *Standard operating policies and procedures.* All staff should be expected to respond to requests by program participants in a timely and helpful manner; and all management systems related to the program (systems for registration and for obtaining instructional materials, for example) should be designed for the convenience of the participants.

- *Organizational authority for educational programs.* The chief executive officer of the organization should serve on the governing board, and all top-level administrators should serve as either ex-officio or staff to the board.

Organizations with a Centralized Educational Unit. If you are part of an organization that has a centralized educational or training unit, you might build structural organizational support as follows:

- *Mission and goals of the organization.* The mission and goals statements should refer to the importance of continued individual and organizational learning as a function of the organization. In addition, the educational unit should have its own mission statement and clearly communicate it to all appropriate parties internal and external to the organization.

- *Standard operating policies and procedures.* The operating procedures of the educational unit (and any changes in these procedures) should be clearly communicated to all other parts of the organization. Each department in the organization should keep the staff of the central educational unit informed of its educational needs on a quarterly basis.

- *Organizational authority for educational programs.* The

manager of the educational unit should be part of the organization's executive council and serve on the strategic planning committee. In addition, the unit should have its own advisory council composed of representatives from all departments that receive services.

Organizations That Provide Education Noncentrally. If you are part of an organization that supports and offers education, although it has no specific educational unit, you might build structural organizational support as follows:

- *Mission and goals of the organization.* The mission and goals statements should refer to the importance of continued individual and organizational learning as a function of the organization.
- *Standard operating policies and procedures.* Participants who complete a certain number of educational programs should be recognized by their supervisors and given either bonuses or pay increases. All staff should be allowed an equivalent of at least three days per year of paid leave to attend educational programs.
- *Organizational authority for educational programs.* The manager or administrator for each department should be given the authority for planning educational opportunities for staff as part of his or her official job description. In addition, there should be an organization-wide advisory council on educational programs composed of staff from all levels and units of the organization and staffed by the Human Resource Department.

Ensuring People Support

In building people support for educational programs, one or more of the following types of people should be included in the planning process:

- Potential participants
- In work situations, supervisors of potential participants
- Senior management of the sponsoring organization(s), sometimes including the members of the board
- Other groups who have a stake in either the planning process or the results of the educational program (such as grassroots community groups, funding agencies)

In many organizations, there are certain key people who should continually be tapped for support, especially when planning educational programs is part of a centralized unit or the major mission of the organization. For example, in securing people support for an adult education program housed within a public school system, it is important to gain support from the superintendent, the principal of the building in which the program is housed, the participants, and the various organizations and community groups that the program impacts (such as specific businesses and industries or other literacy programs).

Although there will, in all likelihood, be a fairly set group of people who support educational programming within an organization, the supporters may need to change for different programs, depending on the goals and objectives of new programs, the potential audiences, and the organizational sponsors. For example, if the public school adult education program described earlier were asked to extend its operations to deliver, in cooperation with the local community college and literacy volunteers, a new program for adults who need to learn English as a second language, an expanded network of people support would be needed. This network might include the president and other key opinion leaders at the college, the leaders and volunteers of the literacy organization, and the leaders of groups that have regular contact with the potential participants for this program (such as local churches, the migrant worker association).

There are numerous ways to gain support from key people for planning educational programs. Outlined below are ideas for obtaining support from participants, immediate supervisors in work situations, and senior-level managers and administrators.

Support from Participants. Support from program participants is best produced by providing meaningful and useful programs (Munson, 1992). Most participants will spread the word if a program was well presented and helpful to them. And if they perceive an educational program as poor or ineffective, they will probably be even more vocal about it. Therefore, attendance at future programs, especially for those programs where participation is voluntary, is definitely influenced by former participants. But even in programs where participation is mandatory, former participants can and do affect the support of those participants who must attend. For example, if the word is passed around in a work situation that a particular program is a waste of time, participants are more apt not to pay attention, to bring other tasks to do during the sessions, and to come late and leave early. This kind of behavior is especially prevalent when the immediate supervisors of the participants also believe that the program and the time away from the job are not worth it.

A second strategy for building participant support is to actively involve participants in planning and conducting the program.

Before the Program, Planners Can
- Ask participants what they want to learn about and how they prefer to learn
- Invite selected participants to assist in planning the program
- Ask participants who have been involved in previous programs to help recruit new participants

During the Program, Planners Can
- Invite participants to serve as instructors and/or resource persons
- At specified intervals ask participants how they feel the sessions are going and make changes, as appropriate, based on their suggestions

- Pair experienced practitioners with novices, asking them to serve as helpers in the learning process

After the Program, Planners Can

- Encourage participants to serve as peer coaches to each other in applying what they have learned
- Ask selected participants to assist in collecting and reviewing evaluation data
- Invite previous program participants to serve as mentors, assisting participants to apply what they have learned

Support from the Immediate Supervisors of Participants. In programs for work settings, whether for paid or volunteer staff, support from the immediate supervisors of participants and potential participants is crucial at all points in the educational cycle, from planning to follow-up. To illustrate, consider the following case:

Scenario

The enrollment for Corporation X's training seminar on working with difficult employees is always good. But on the day of the training session, there is always a high percentage of both no-shows and attendees who wander in and out of the session. Despite this, participants consistently rate the program very high, especially in usefulness for on-the-job activities. In investigating this problem, program staff discover that for a period of six months, the no-shows and leave-earlys have all come from four of the ten departments involved in the program. They also discover that the supervisors in two of these four departments have complained loudly and often about the enormous amount of time that their people spend on training activities.

As can be seen in this scenario, supervisors exert considerable influence over staff attending educational programs. Supervisors also play a very important part in whether or not any of the knowledge, skills, and attitudes/values acquired in these programs can actually be used on the job. If supervisors understand and support the goals and objectives of the educational efforts, it is easier for staff to change their behavior and attitudes (and for supervisors to reinforce that change positively).

As with participant support, support for educational activities from immediate supervisors of paid and volunteer staff can best be gained by providing worthwhile programs and involving the supervisors at various times in the programming cycle (Nadler, 1982; Broad and Newstrom, 1992; Munson, 1992). The opportunities for supervisory involvement are many.

Before the Program, Planners Can

- Invite supervisors to assist in assessment of the learning needs of staff, including asking staff what they perceive their needs to be
- Encourage supervisors to assist in scheduling educational activities and choosing staff for these activities
- Invite supervisors to work with participants to help them prepare for the upcoming session, with a focus on how the material can be integrated back into what they do

- Ask supervisors to assist in collecting baseline evaluation data

During the Program, Planners Can
- Invite supervisors to attend parts of the program that would be helpful to them in carrying out their supervisory responsibilities
- Ask supervisors to avoid calling participants out of sessions to handle work-related problems
- Encourage supervisors to serve as instructors or resource persons for specific programs
- Urge supervisors to help participants make connections between what they are learning in the program and what they actually do on the job
- Ask supervisors to provide informal feedback on how the program is being received by staff

After the Program, Planners Can
- Ask supervisors to provide feedback to the planning staff and instructors on whether programs are addressing adequately the needs that were identified
- Urge supervisors to provide time for participants to share their learning with fellow staff and encourage participants to serve as peer coaches to each other in applying what they have learned
- Request that supervisors work with participants to assist them in integrating the knowledge, skills, and attitudes/values learned in actual work or volunteer activities
- Ask supervisors to assist in collecting data for evaluation and follow-up

Although the support of supervisors is crucial to all aspects of the educational process, it is especially important that planners seek the active involvement of supervisors before and after the programs. Special assistance should be given to supervisors on the transfer of learning into actual work activities (a subject that will be addressed in greater detail in Chapter Eight). This can be a time-consuming activity, but it is very beneficial to all parties involved—program planners, participants, and supervisors.

Support from Senior Management. Senior management support for educational programs is reflected in individuals' style and practice as leaders and managers, their budgetary commitment to educational programs, and their public support of the educational function in organizational publications and key organizational meetings. Their support can be gained in a number of ways, a sampling of which is listed below (Nadler, 1982; Munson, 1992).
- First and foremost, do good work! Set specific goals and objectives for the educational activities and then meet them. Provide documentation, in an easily understood form, of the successful results and benefits of the program.
- Demonstrate that you know the business of the organization. Whatever the business of the organization is, from computer

technology to educating children, know well what the mission, goals, products, and services of the organization are.

- Request that senior management issue formal policy and procedural statements concerning the educational activities of the organization.
- Ask selected top managers and administrators to become actively involved in the design and evaluation of highly visible programs. For example, a manager could serve as a consultant to a planning group designing a program in an area of his or her competence; or a group of managers could serve in an ad hoc capacity to preview proposed educational programs that have organization-wide impact.

Munson (1992) warns that it is easy to get discouraged trying to gain the support of senior managers and administrators—an effort that can take a considerable investment of time yet offer few initial concrete results. Yet time may be one of the keys in gaining managerial support. Because educational programs for adults are not the primary focus of most organizations, it will, in most cases, take longer for senior executives to take note of such activities and to give them more than nominal support. Therefore, it is important to develop a consistent track record of successful educational programs.

Internal and External People Support via Committees. Using committees can be a helpful way to build both internal and external people support for educational programs. These committees may be permanent, or they may be put together on an ad hoc basis as needed. Whatever the form chosen, the purpose, function, and authority of an educational program committee must be understood by all involved. Guidelines for operating successful committees include the following (Knowles, 1980):

- Committee members should clearly understand what they are supposed to do and what the parameters are for making decisions and taking actions.
- Committee members should have a working knowledge of the program.
- Staff should ensure that committee members have real tasks to do and that they are responsible for decisions that are still in the "idea stage"; they should not be asked merely to rubber-stamp decisions already made by others.
- Committee meetings should be well planned. Operating norms and procedures for meetings should be clear and either applied consistently or, if they are not working, modified.
- Individual and group tasks accepted by committee members should be clear, specific, and definitive. A tracking system should be used to ensure that all assignments are carried out in a timely and effective manner.
- Committee members should be kept informed about how their decisions and actions have been incorporated into the work of the sponsoring unit or organization.

Committees, whether they be permanent or ad hoc, should not outlive their usefulness. When committee members feel that they are wasting their time—or even worse, know that they are nothing more than names on a piece of paper—it is time to refocus or disband the committee.

One common type of committee is a formally constituted *education committee*. Education committees may be given a variety of formal titles, such as steering committees, advisory boards, coordinating committees, and planning committees (Hopfengardner and Potter, 1992; Rothwell and Kazanas, 1993). Although these committees are often advisory and therefore not empowered to make decisions that must be followed, committee members can nonetheless influence staff and affect the direction and form of the educational function in an organization.

It is essential, as noted earlier, that members of education committees have real tasks to do. Knowles (1980) and Hopfengardner and Potter (1992) have outlined sample tasks appropriate for such committees:

- Identifying problems and issues for which educational programs might offer solutions
- Assisting in conducting a needs analysis
- Helping to define program objectives
- Reacting to initial drafts of program design and content
- Interpreting past achievements and efforts for key individuals and groups, such as senior management, potential program participants, and community groups
- Ensuring that program ideas, especially ones that are potentially controversial, are considered by staff
- Identifying and recruiting program participants
- Serving as talent scouts for instructors and other program staff
- Helping to locate and secure other resources (for example, money and space)
- Assisting in program review and evaluations

Choosing members for the education committee requires careful deliberation. The three major factors to be considered are the following:

- Individual characteristics of potential members (for example, age, gender, ethnic background)
- Types of people needed on the committee (for example, content and process experts, organizational leaders, program participants)
- Geographic location of potential members, especially for regional and national programs

One way to ensure that these specific factors are taken into account when choosing members is to use the two-way grid portrayed in Table 4.1.

Table 4.1. Two-Way Grid for Selecting Committee Members.

Criteria	Existing Committees, Current Committee Members						Potential Committee Members			
	1	2	3	4	5	6	a	b	c	d
Age										
Under 30 years of age	x			x						
From 30 to 45 years of age		x	x							
Over 45 years of age					x	x				
Gender										
Men	x				x	x				
Women		x	x	x						
Ethnicity										
Caucasian			x		x	x				
African-American	x									
Hispanic/Latino										
American Indian		x		x						
Other										
Social Class										
Upper middle	x			x	x					
Middle		x				x				
Lower			x							
Types of People Needed										
Content experts		x		x						
Process experts	x		x							
Organizational leaders					x	x				
Program participants						x				
Community leaders	x				x					
Geographic Location of Members										
Local area				x	x	x				
Regional area	x									
National		x								
General community			x							

Source: Adapted from Houle, 1989, p. 40. Reprinted by permission of Jossey-Bass Inc., Publishers.

In addition to these three major factors, program planners should address other criteria as well. Knowles (1980) and Rothwell and Kazanas (1993) stress that care must be taken to select individuals who have an interest in the program and its goals; a willingness to voice their opinions and follow up with actions; competence, credibility, and time to do the work of the committee; the ability to work collaboratively with other members of the committee; and a position of influence with significant elements of key organizations and/or community groups.

Ad hoc committees (also termed task forces, project teams, and self-managing teams) are usually constituted for short time periods (Rothwell and Kazanas, 1993). Their role is generally limited to accomplishing specific tasks, with very clear and explicit responsibilities. One of the most common tasks given ad hoc committees is developing specific educational activities. Consider the following example:

Scenario

Sally J., director of human resources, is asked to develop a program for secretarial staff on organizing one's work. Although "canned" programs are available, she has not been impressed with those she has reviewed. Therefore, she decides to develop an in-house training program. Although she has already conducted secretarial training in various content areas, she feels that she would like some assistance in planning this particular program. She asks four people to join an ad hoc planning committee to help her: two office managers, a secretary at grade 3, and a secretary at grade 5. All of her committee members are well respected by their fellow workers and are known as top-notch personnel. Sally has requested that the group meet at least three times to discuss program content and structure. All the committee members are delighted by the invitation and receive permission from their supervisors to be on the committee.

Another reason for constituting ad hoc committees is to support large educational programs within an organization. Committee projects may range from conducting an organization-wide needs assessment to instituting a major new instructional method, such as computer-based instruction. It is mandatory for such ad hoc committees to enlist the support of key line personnel (including senior management, when desirable). For example, an ad hoc committee appointed to oversee a statewide needs analysis of all family practice physicians should include the following types of people (titles, of course, vary among organizations):

- Assistant dean of the medical school
- Director of continuing medical education
- Assistant chair, family practice
- Three family practice physicians (representing different experience levels and geographic areas)
- An adult educator (with experience in conducting formal needs assessments)

In addition, continuing medical education staff should be ex officio members, serving as staff support for the committee.

Such a variety of personnel ensures that different perspectives on ideas for continuing education programs for family physicians will be heard and that programs developed in response to identified ideas and needs will be well received. The actual committee members, representing the best and the brightest, must, of course, be chosen with care.

Providing a Supportive Organizational Culture

Promoting an organizational culture or climate that supports continuous learning and educational programming as part of the organization's basic values and actions can be a difficult and often frustrating task. It is especially challenging when a climate that fosters learning and development has not existed before or exists in name only. For example, even in units or organizations whose major focus is educating adults, such as continuing education divisions in universities and proprietary schools, the major outcome expected may be revenue generation. If this means shortchanging students and staff and creating a less than favorable environment for learning, so be it; generating a 20 or 30 percent profit margin is the major focus of any programs offered.

Just as there are numerous ways to build structural and people support for educational programs, so too are there numerous ways to build favorable organizational climates for learning and for planning educational programs (Apps, 1988; Schlossberg, Lynch, and Chickering, 1989; Hiemstra, 1991; Watkins and Marsick, 1993). Most of these strategies have been reviewed earlier in this chapter, in the discussions of building structural and people support, because developing these kinds of support is often critical to ensuring a positive culture or climate for learning. In all support efforts, a strong commitment in words and action from top-level management or administration is often stressed, including active endorsement of policies and procedures that support quality educational activities (Munson, 1992; Rothwell and Kazanas, 1993).

Apps (1988) has suggested a more global way—a process of transformational action—by which organizations can become more supportive of programs for adult learners. The center of this transformational process focuses on questioning the basic assumptions and values about how the organization perceives programs for adults. The process includes five phases: (1) developing awareness—recognizing that something is fundamentally wrong with the way we are planning and delivering educational programs; (2) exploring alternatives—searching for new beliefs and ideas from other institutions and acknowledging that changes are needed in how, when, where, and by whom educational programs are planned and delivered; (3) making a transition—leaving the old system of values, beliefs, and approaches behind (or dramatically changing them) and adopting a different set of beliefs and ways of operating related to planning educational programs; (4) achieving integration—putting the pieces from the transition back together; and (5) taking action—putting the new ways of planning and conducting educational programs into actual practice. This type of process would need the backing of senior-level personnel and the involvement of all key players in the program planning process (such as staff, participants, other stakeholders).

In organizations where the primary purpose is to deliver educational programs for adults or where program delivery is decentralized, one result of the above-described transformational process could be a revision of both the overall mission of the organization and the policies and procedures related to educational programs. In organizations where a centralized unit for managing educational programs exists, in addition to changes in the overall mission and policies, that unit itself might also revise its mission or, if none exists, draft one. Mission or policy statements for educational units should clearly and precisely outline the "why, what, who, where, and how" of the unit (Nilson, 1989; Munson, 1992; Rothwell and Kazanas, 1993).

- *Why?* Outlines the basic values and beliefs of the unit and the end results to be accomplished, in terms of overall purpose and goals
- *What?* Describes the broad functional areas with which the educational unit will be concerned (such as management development, technical training, organizational development, volunteer training, community education)
- *Who?* Identifies the potential audiences with whom staff in the educational unit work
- *Where?* Defines the parameters within which the educational unit will function (that is, the whole organization or specific departments, divisions, or sites within the organization)
- *How?* Describes the major delivery modes that will be used in educational programs (such as classroom instruction, on-the-job training, computer-based instruction, off-site programs and conferences, community action projects)

A sample mission statement of an educational unit is shown in Exhibit 4.1.

Exhibit 4.1. Sample Mission Statement for a Corporate Department Of Education and Human Resource Development.

Purpose
The purpose of the Department of Education and Human Resource Development is threefold: (1) to prepare people to enter the workplace, improve their present job performance, or advance and/or change their chosen occupation; (2) to assist the overall organization to adapt to changing markets, products, and ways of operating; and (3) to assist people in the organization to respond to and cope with both work and personal problems and issues that they encounter.

Values and Beliefs
The staff of this department believe that the purpose of educational programs is to encourage the growth and development of the organization and individuals within the organization. They view continuous learning, diverse forms of inquiry, and collegiality as fundamental values of the organization. The staff believe that all adults and organizations can (and want to) learn and continue to grow and change. The role of the staff is to serve as both

process and content experts in the program planning process.

Functions
The staff of this department are responsible for four primary functions:

1. To coordinate all existing educational activities within the XYZ Organization
2. To develop and manage all educational activities for supervisory and administrative personnel
3. To serve as consultants to senior management on issues related to organizational change and development
4. To provide educational programs that address both the work and personal development needs of individual employees

Audience and Parameters of Programs
The audience includes administrators and others working throughout the XYZ Organization. This includes central office staff and personnel located within all divisions and locations of the organization. The staff of this department work primarily with the educational personnel located within each unit of the organization and with administrative and supervisory personnel. Only the senior staff serve as consultants to senior-level administrators.

Primary Ways Educational Programs Are Delivered
Educational programs are delivered both through in-house programs (such as seminars, workshops, and computer-based instruction) and off-site programs (such as conferences and institutes). Both formally designed educational programs and self-directed learning activities are considered legitimate ways for participants to learn.

A new or revised mission or policy statement should be approved by senior management prior to its circulation among organizational personnel. Once it is approved, care should be taken that all appropriate individuals (for example, division directors, supervisory personnel, union representatives) receive a copy. This will ensure that key people in the organization have at least some basic information about the overall scope and responsibilities of the educational unit.

Chapter Highlights

In establishing the basis for program planning, program planners should concentrate on four major tasks:

- Becoming knowledgeable about the internal and external contextual factors for planning, including the structural aspects, the people, and the cultural milieu of the planning situation
- Building and maintaining structural supports for planning (for example, mission statements, standard operating policies and procedures, information systems, and financial resources)

- Ensuring support from program participants, organizational staff, and external constituencies through such mechanisms as active participation in planning and conducting educational activities, transfer-of-learning strategies, and formal and ad hoc committee work
- Providing a supportive organizational culture in which continuous learning and change are valued

These tasks, if viewed as an ongoing and integral part of the planning process, often need to be revisited in a more formal way only at the start of major new program initiatives, when people take on new positions or additional planning responsibilities, and/or on a scheduled periodic basis. The importance of establishing a sound basis for the planning process will become apparent in subsequent discussions of the other components and corresponding tasks included in the model (Chapters Five through Fourteen). Unless the tasks within this first component are done well, it will be difficult, if not impossible, to complete the other parts of the planning process.

Applications Exercises

The three Applications Exercises presented here will help you lay the groundwork for program planning. The first exercise is designed to assist you in analyzing the context for planning (Exhibit 4.2), the second will help you build structural support (Exhibit 4.3), and the third addresses building people support (Exhibit 4.4).

Exhibit 4.2. Analyzing the Context for Planning.

1. Describe briefly an organizational setting—either your present one or one in which you worked previously—where part of the function is planning educational programs for adults.

   _____

   _____

2. Identify, within the framework outlined below, key internal contextual factors that could affect the program planning process within that organization.

   Structural factors: _____

   _____

   People factors: _____

   _____

   Cultural factors: _____

   _____

3. Identify key external contextual factors that could affect the program planning process within that organization.

   _____

   _____

4. List sources you could use to investigate further the internal and external contextual factors within this organization. Be specific as to what documents you would want to review and whom you would want to interview.

   Documents to review: _____

   Persons to interview: _____

   Other strategies: _____

5. Review this material with a colleague and add additional ideas as needed.

Exhibit 4.3. Building Structural Support for Educational Programs.

1. Describe briefly your current organizational setting or one that has as all or part of its function planning educational programs for adults.

_____

_____

_____

2. Indicate whether planning educational programs is
   - ❑ The primary mission of the organization
   - ❑ One of the functions of the organization, with a centralized unit to manage that function
   - ❑ One of the functions of the organization, but with no centralized unit to manage that function

3. Identify, within the organizational framework you have indicated above, how you would build structural support for planning educational programs within that organization.

Structural Factors	Specific Examples of Ways to Build Support
Mission Statements	
Policies and Standard Operating Procedures	
System of Formal Organizational Authority	
Organizational Decision Making	
Financial Resources	
Physical Facilities	

Exhibit 4.4. Building People Support for Educational Programs.

1. Complete the chart with ideas for how you could involve participants and supervisors in your organization's educational activities. Be as specific as possible in naming the persons and/or types of personnel you would like to include.

	Before the Program		During the Program		After the Program	
	Activities	*Potential Players*	*Activities*	*Potential Players*	*Activities*	*Potential Players*
What Participants Could Do						
What Supervisors Could Do						

2. Review your ideas with a colleague and/or your planning committee and revise as needed.

Five

Identifying Program Ideas

John B., director of computer training, is not quite sure why the training activities he has been coordinating are, as his boss terms it, "not overly successful." He has hired what he believes are top-flight instructors and includes a free lunch as part of each program's events. Overall, though, the enrollments are low, and a small but noticeable number of participants leave at the morning coffee break. Participant evaluations (at least for those programs John remembers to have participants evaluate) praise the presenters and the food but are critical about the lack of usefulness and immediate transferability of the information presented. John cannot understand this reaction, because the programs are exactly like those run by one of his close friends, a training specialist at a similar organization, and his friend's sessions have received rave reviews. Perhaps, John thinks, he should reevaluate how he decides what the content of the programs should be, but he is unsure how to go about doing this. He has just assumed, based on his previous experience as an expert computer operator and programmer, that what is successfully working in one organization should work in another, providing you can get the operating systems (in this case, the training programs) properly installed and up and running.

Identifying relevant ideas—the program content—is one of the major tasks of people involved with planning educational programs (Houle, 1972; Robinson and Robinson, 1989; Bennett and LeGrand, 1990; Sork, 1990; Bradley, Kallick, and Regan, 1991). Although some educational programs may be "borrowed" from other organizations, as John has done in the above scenario, this is not the only, or necessarily the best, way to generate ideas for educational programs. For example, program ideas may come from such diverse sources as personal observations and hunches and data-based needs assessments and research studies.

In most program planning models, this component of identifying ideas would be called a *needs assessment* or *needs analysis*. "Although needs assessment can be a powerful tool to justify and focus the planning effort" (Sork, 1990, p. 78), conducting a formal needs assessment, as noted above, is only one of many ways ideas are formulated for educational programs; and in actual practice, a formal needs assessment may not be necessary or even useful in terms of either time or money spent ("Employee Training in America," 1986; Sork, 1990). For example, when an educational program is mandated as part of federal or state regulations, conducting a needs assessment to see whether either the organization or the staff desire such a program is a waste of time.

Likewise, if an organization installs a new computer system or other new equipment, whether staff like it or not they will need to become knowledgeable about this system in order to keep their jobs.

This chapter will first address what planners are looking for in this phase of the planning process. That discussion is followed by a description of the many sources from which program ideas are derived. Finally, alternative ways for generating program ideas are outlined, with the caveat that whatever methods are used, planners still have to make choices between and among possible ideas, all or most of which are viable but cannot practically be addressed at the same time.

Knowing What You Want to Accomplish

A number of concepts or descriptors have been used to define what program planners are looking for in generating ideas for educational programs—educational needs, performance problems, new opportunities, changing conditions, areas for improvement, research-driven practice, societal issues, client demands, resource availability, and images of ideal practice (Kaufman, and Stone, 1983; Rossett, 1987; Bennett and LeGrand, 1990; Bradley, Kallick, and Regan, 1991). No matter what term is used, however, program planners are seeking to respond to what they and the people, organizations, and/or communities they work with are perceiving as important topics for people to know more about.

The term *educational need* is by far the most often used descriptor in the literature and rhetoric of practice as the focal point for identifying ideas for educational programs. An educational need is usually defined as a discrepancy between what presently is and what should be (Kaufman and Stone, 1983; Witkin, 1984; Rothwell and Kazanas, 1993). This discrepancy can appear in many forms. For example, an unemployed individual may enroll in a workshop on job-seeking skills because he wants to know how to look for another job in this economic climate. An organization might offer "outplacement" seminars for employees being laid off in hopes that the seminars can help these employees learn to sell themselves elsewhere. Or a community or adult education program might believe that a job-skills training program is needed to address the high rate of unemployment in the community. In each case, a gap in knowledge and skills is recognized either by an individual, an organization, or the community.

According to Sork and Caffarella (1989), it is not enough just to identify an educational need or problem; descriptions of the need "should be presented in a format that makes both the present and the more desirable condition as explicit as possible" (p. 237). Samples of such descriptions follow:

What Presently Is	What Should Be
Adults who are unemployed do not know how to describe the present economic climate and the employment opportunities that exist in their community. They are also unaware of job-seeking strategies and skills that are most likely to work at this point in time.	Adults who are unemployed are able to describe in lay terms the factors that affect the economic climate in their community. In addition, they are able to list at least five specific job opportunities that are available to people with their background and skills and the three job-seeking strategies that are most likely to work for those particular types of positions at this time.
Twenty-five percent of adult residents in XYZ community have neither earned a high school diploma nor passed the equivalency exam.	Ninety-five percent of adult residents in XYZ community should have a high school diploma or have passed the equivalency exam.

Although the concept of educational need is often used and can be helpful in identifying ideas for educational programs, it can also be limiting. This limitation stems primarily from the negative connotation inherent in seeing "need" as a "discrepancy"—the perception that because there is a need, something is missing or *wrong* with a person, an organization, or society and has to be *fixed* (Nilson, 1989). For example, the implementation of total quality management programs by fiat from above is sometimes interpreted by staff and clients as an administrative statement that services and/or products are of less-than-acceptable quality and that only with this new training will staff perform in ways that are truly oriented to quality products and service. If staff believe that the organization is already producing quality products and service, they may resent both the implication that their operations are not up to standard and the intrusion on the successful way they are currently doing business. Likewise, previously satisfied clients may be frustrated that staff are not as available as they were before (since they always seem to be in training sessions!) and that procedures they liked and trusted are changing; they may also fear that their costs will escalate because of this new way of doing business.

Responding to needs as a way to justify program planning also implies that developing educational programs is primarily a *reactive* versus a *proactive* process (Cross, 1979); the trainer or educator is viewed as the person asked to help put out organizational or community fires rather than one who tries proactively to initiate innovative changes. For example, community organizations and schools often sponsor educational programs on AIDS as a response to parents' and other community members' fears rather than proactively using the educational process to assist in changing people's negative stereotypes about AIDS.

Developing programs on identified educational needs of learners, organizations, or communities may have nothing to do with programs being successful (Sork and Caffarella, 1989; Sork, 1990). For example, opportunities for good programs might just present themselves. Perhaps a well-known content expert is in town—one who is recognized as an excellent, on-target presenter with cutting-edge material—and all you have to pay is a speaker's fee. Perhaps the organization has new facilities (such as a new conference center) that the board expects to be used. Perhaps program ideas just "feel right" based on a hunch, a chance conversation with friends or colleagues, or recent experiences.

To further complicate program planning, individual, organizational, and/or community ideas for what is needed or wanted are not always in sync. Although organizational needs often drive educational programs, they are frequently at odds with what individuals in the organizations believe they need or want to know more about. For example, senior management may decide that decision making should be a collaborative endeavor between and among departments and ask the training department to implement programs to train staff in this decision-making style. Those members of the staff who do not believe that this is the way organizations should function do not want any part of the training or the proposed changes. Other staff see the content of the training as too theoretical and out of touch with what they do on a daily basis; they want practical, hands-on material they can use to make collaborative decision making a workable process (tips, for example, on how to get departments that have been at odds for years to collaborate in a meaningful way). Also, and with more frequency, the voices of groups external and often not directly connected to an organization are asking that their ideas be heard. Ideas from these external parties often come in the form of changes that they request, or in some cases demand, through legislative action and the like. As an added dynamic for these messages sent by external groups, the ideas and needs identified may be in conflict with each other, which then creates some difficult questions and issues. Can program planners realistically respond to these conflicting ideas? If not, which group or groups should be listened to, and why? How do staff respond to those groups whose ideas were rejected?

Sources of Ideas for Educational Programs

Ideas for educational programs surface in a number of ways, as described in the previous section—from identified needs to specific problems and opportunities. These ideas stem from four primary sources: people, responsibilities and tasks of adult life, organizations, and communities and society in general. Examples of specific sources, drawn primarily from the work of Knowles (1980), Nadler (1982), and Tracey (1992), are given below:

Sources	Specific Examples
People	Potential participants Educators, staff developers, and trainers in other organizations Employers Colleagues Friends and family Content experts Consultants
Responsibilities and tasks of adult life	Being a spouse/partner Being a parent Being a volunteer Being a friend Jobs and careers Living in a community Personal development Leisure activities Health and fitness Spiritual life

Organizations	Changes in the mission of the
	  organization
	Changes in policies, procedures,
	  and/or structure
	New products or services
	Identified problems (for example,
	  absenteeism, low employee
	  morale)
	Government regulations
	Legislative mandates
	Recommendations from
	  professional associations

Communities/society	Identified problems at
	  community, state, and
	  national levels
	International issues and problems
	Political climate/changes
	Social issues (for example,
	  gay rights, health care, violence)
	Technological innovations

Often the first sign that an educational program might be warranted surfaces as a specific need, problem, or opportunity from one of these four primary sources, as illustrated below:

People

- Teachers comment to their principal that they are not receiving telephone messages in a timely fashion, which is affecting their relationships with parents.
- Program participants are very vocal about how difficult it is to register for programs and how unhelpful staff are in answering their questions.

Responsibilities and Tasks of Adult Life

- Balancing work and family has become problematic for a number of women and men, especially those who are committed to time-consuming careers.

- Coping effectively with life events (such as the illness of parents, job changes, returning to school, parenting teenagers) is a major challenge for many adults.

Organizations
- There is a higher rate of absenteeism for Division X than for Divisions Y and Z.
- On an organization-wide basis, supervisors appear to be having trouble interpreting to their subordinates the new set of policies and procedures concerning benefits, overtime work, and sick leave.

Communities/Society
- Violence in schools and the community has become a major issue.
- Issues related to acceptance of diversity (for example, ethnicity, gender, sexual preference, social class) continue to surface on a national and international level.

At this point, the job of educators is to define the idea in more depth. This process of problem clarification and analysis, which can be done in a number of ways, often occurs during the gathering and assessment of program ideas.

Generating New Program Ideas

Ideas for educational and training activities can be generated in a number of ways, as illustrated by the following scenarios:

Scenario 1

Matt C., a staff member in the College of Continuing Education, attended a teleconference on "Gender Issues and Leadership Development." Because he believed the ideas presented would be very helpful to the administrative staff of his unit, he reviewed the materials he had received (including two suggested videos he had not previously seen). He then tried out the idea over lunch with three key staff members, including the associate dean for continuing education, and they were enthusiastic about the proposed program.

Scenario 2

Joyce R., a training specialist for a large paper company, has been informed that the level of productivity on two pieces of newly installed equipment has been steadily declining, even though there was an initial production rise a month after the machines were fully operating. After closely examining the analysis of efficiency indexes (data on downtime, repairs, and waste, for example), she decides, in consultation with two of her line supervisors, to do a formal job analysis to get a better handle on the problem. Joyce forms an ad hoc task force to assist her.

Scenario 3

The director of education for a large metropolitan hospital has been asked to conduct an organization-wide needs assessment related to planning a program on sexual harassment in the workplace. She convenes a committee of five people to assist her in planning and conducting this effort. The committee is charged with spelling out the specific purposes for this assessment, what data collection methods will be used, how and to whom the results will be reported, and how and by whom the results will be used.

These three scenarios illustrate the broad range of ways to collect ideas for programs, from observations based on personal experiences to more formally structured needs assessments. Let us turn now to key methods used by program planners to get a sense of what potential program participants might want or have to know. That discussion is followed by a description of a sample model for conducting a formal needs assessment.

Key Methods   Eight of the most widely used methods (termed *techniques* by some authors) for generating ideas for educational programs are outlined below. A description of each method is given in Table 5.1, along with a list of basic operational guidelines.

Table 5.1. Methods for Generating Ideas for Educational Programs.

Method	Description	Operational Guidelines
Observations	Watching people doing actual or simulated tasks and activities. Individuals and/or groups of people can be observed.	Can use observations that are open-ended or structured (with specific variables to investigate). Examples of specific types of observations include time-motion studies, task listings, behavioral frequency counts, and the recording of critical activities or events.
Written questionnaires/ surveys	Gathering opinions, attitudes, preferences, and perceptions by means of written questionnaires (such as climate and attitude surveys).	Should pretest and revise the questions and format as needed. Can use a variety of question formats (open-ended, ranking, checklists, and forced choice, for example), and be administered through the mail or given to individuals or groups to complete.
Interviews	Conversing with people individually or in groups, either in person or by phone.	Can use interviews that are open-ended, nondirected, or formally structured (with specific questions to ask). Should pretest and review interview questions as needed.
Group sessions	Identifying and analyzing ideas, problems, and issues in group sessions.	Start with an idea, problem, or issue known to be of concern to group members. Use one or more group facilitating techniques— brainstorming, nominal group techniques, focus groups, consensus ranking, or general group discussion. Provide for competent leadership and group members who are both knowledgeable and willing to participate.

(continued on next page)

Method	Description	Operational Guidelines
Job and task analysis	Collecting, tabulating, grouping, analyzing, interpreting, and reporting on the duties, tasks, and activities that make up a job. Tasks may be cognitive and/or motor (action) in nature.	Be sure the analysis is of a current job and performance. Provide for data collection from all knowledgeable parties (for example, job incumbents, supervisors, managerial personnel, volunteers, and/or clients/customers). Use a variety of techniques to collect data, such as questionnaires, task checklists, individual and group interviews, observations, a jury of experts, work records, and analysis of relevant technical publications.
Written and performance tests	Using paper-and-pencil tests, performance exercises, and/or computer-based items to measure a person's knowledge, skill, and/or attitudes/values.	Know what the test measures (knowledge, skills, attitudes, values) and use it as a diagnostic tool for only those areas. Choose a specific test carefully. Be sure that what the test measures is relevant and important to the particular situation in which it will be used. (For example, do not use a test for knowledge if you are really interested in a hands-on skill.) Check to see if the test is both reliable and valid.
Written materials	Gleaning information from written materials in a variety of forms: strategic planning reports, policies and procedures manuals, performance evaluations, minutes of meetings, employee records, job efficiency indexes, monthly and annual reports, research and evaluation studies, curriculum reviews, statements of professional standards and competencies, books, professional and trade journals, legislation, and contents of file drawers.	Maintain an up-to-date, active file of written materials that pertain to your educational activities. Use the materials as sources of information in conjunction with other methods.
Conversations with colleagues, friends, family, and acquaintances	Talking informally with people about ideas for educational pro- grams. These conversations take place over coffee, at lunch, in the hallways, in meetings, and so on.	Record ideas in a "tickler file" for current and future reference. Use a variety of ways to check out these ideas.

In addition to the methods described in Table 5.1, there are numerous other techniques for eliciting program ideas. Some of these other methods, such as network analysis, are quite technical in nature and are primarily used by the corporate sector and selected government agencies (Scott, 1991). Other methods, such as reviewing prepackaged educational programs, using computer-based data sources, and bringing back ideas from various conferences and trade shows, are more generally applied. Especially helpful resources for more in-depth descriptions of methods and techniques for generating program ideas include material by Knowles (1980), Zemke and Kramlinger (1982), Rossett (1987), Tracey (1992), and Rothwell and Kazanas (1992, 1993).

No one method for generating ideas for programs is better than another. Each method has its own strengths and weaknesses, depending on the situation and the data required. How, then, do program planners determine which method or combination of methods is best for their situation? The following six criteria, extracted primarily from the work of Newstrom and Lilyquist (1979), are helpful to those selecting methods:

- Level of involvement wanted by current or potential program participants
- Level of involvement wanted by other people, groups, and/or organizations
- Time requirements for gathering information
- Cost of using the method
- Type and depth of data required
- Ability of planning staff to use the method

Observations, for example, normally require a low level of involvement by current or potential participants, while interviews and group sessions require a higher level of involvement. Costs and time requirements for written questionnaires and job analyses are usually high; in contrast, costs and time requirements for conversations with colleagues and friends and for reviewing written materials are generally low or moderate.

There are no hard and fast rules for rating a specific method, because situational variables may greatly alter how each method is viewed. For example, although administering a written questionnaire is usually costly and time-consuming, using an already developed instrument, administering the questionnaire to a group, and standardizing analysis procedures can cut down greatly on both the time and expense.

One additional factor should be considered in choosing methods for generating ideas in relationship to paid work and/or volunteer tasks: the nature of the job itself. Some methods are better suited for particular kinds of work than others, as shown in Table 5.2.

This evaluation of the appropriateness of various methods for particular job types is not ironclad, but it generally reflects the experience of practitioners.

Conducting a Formal Needs Assessment

Although conducting a formal needs assessment is not the major way by which ideas are identified for educational programs, it is a process that has had wide acceptance in the literature on program planning and in practice. A formal needs assessment is defined as a systematic way to identify educational gaps or problems. The focus of the assessment is not on *solutions* for specific problems but on clarifying and defining the problems.

Table 5.2. Appropriateness of Methods for Particular Job Classifications.

Method	Manual	Technical	Clerical	Professional
		Job Classifications		
Observations	x	x	x	
Written surveys/questionnaires				x
Interviews		x	x	x
Group sessions			x	x
Job and task analysis	x	x	x	
Written and performance tests		x	x	
Written materials		x	x	x
Conversations	x	x	x	x

There is no one accepted process for conducting a formal needs assessment. Rather, a number of models or descriptions of procedures have been developed (Caffarella, 1982; Witkin, 1984; Kaufman, 1987, 1988; Rossett, 1987; Sleezer, 1991; Tracey, 1992). A nine-step revised version of the Caffarella (1982) model, incorporating many features of other descriptions, is given here to illustrate the process, along with specific examples of how to carry out each step for an organization-wide needs assessment.

Steps	Examples
1. Make a conscious decision to complete a needs assessment with a commitment to planning.	The president's executive council has issued a formal request to the Department of Human Resources (HR) to conduct a needs assessment.
2. Identify individuals to be involved in planning and overseeing the needs assessment.	A steering committee of six people is appointed, composed of members of the HR department and midlevel and entry-level managers.
3. Develop focus and specific objectives for the needs assessment (to ensure that it answers the questions one really wants to know).	The steering committee decides to focus the needs assessment on the following questions: (1) What major skills, values, attitudes, and knowledge do midlevel managers need to perform effectively and efficiently in their present positions? (2) In two years, how might this list of needs change, based on future forecasts and trends?
4. Determine the time frame, budget, and staff.	The steering committee determines that it needs to complete the needs assessment in six months. Three members of the HR department are named as staff for the project, and $1,000 is allocated for expenses.
5. Select data collection methods.	The methods chosen for data collection include a written survey, key informant interviews, group meetings, and a review of written materials and documents.

6. Collect data.	The survey is developed in consultation with the steering committee and administered by staff members from the HR department. These same staff conduct the group sessions with selected midlevel managers and their subordinates and review all written materials. The steering committee conducts the key informant interviews with twelve people: two top managers, six midlevel managers, three subordinates of these managers, and one outside consultant.
7. Analyze data to determine (a) the basic findings in terms of quantitative (numerical) and qualitative descriptions, (b) points of agreement and disagreement, and (c) agreed-upon findings concerning identified needs.	An analysis of the data that includes an in-depth description of each major need area (what presently is and what should be) is completed by the HR staff. The steering committee then reviews and critiques this analysis. Changes are made based on group consensus.
8. Sort and prioritize each of the identified needs and indicate (a) which needs should be responded to first, second, and so on, and (b) needs for which alternative interventions are more appropriate.	The steering committee puts aside those "need descriptions" that in their judgment call for other interventions. They then, using a priority rating instrument followed by group discussion, arrive at a consensus of what needs should receive priority rankings.
9. Report the results of the needs assessment to appropriate individuals and groups within the organization.	A full report of the needs assessment process, findings, and conclusions is submitted to the president's executive council. An executive summary of the report is given to all midlevel managers after the report has been approved by the executive council. In addition, members of the steering committee meet with key individuals from senior and midlevel management to discuss preliminary ideas for management development programs.

One of the most important outcomes of a formal needs assessment is a commitment by those involved in the process to ensure that the ideas from the needs assessment are actually used in the program planning process (Cross, 1979; Bradley, Kallick, and Regan, 1991). According to Bradley, Kallick, and Regan (1991), "This may seem self-evident, but we would be wealthy if we had one dollar for every needs-assessment process that was undertaken and the data not used. Don't raise false hopes in those who contribute to the needs assessment" (p. 168). This means making sure at the outset that those who have the authority to implement the findings of such assessments are willing to listen to the voices of those who respond and that they will actually implement programs based on those findings. One helpful way to let respondents know that they have been heard is to inform them (through newsletters, bulletin boards, meetings, and the like) how the results have been translated into upcoming programs and why some of the ideas have not yet been implemented.

What to Do with Program Ideas

There are no magic formulas for deciding which program ideas are the best, whether these ideas are generated through a formal needs assessment or through one of the many other methods described. This is because often there are too many good ideas that "must" be addressed and/or problems that "must" be solved. However, developing an educational or training program may not be the best, or even a viable, way to respond to the ideas and problems that have been identified. In addition, ideas for programs may contradict each other, be unclear, or be unrealistic in terms of time, staff expertise, and cost. So even with armloads of data and/or long lists of good ideas, program planners must figure out ways of making decisions about what ideas are important, affordable, necessary, and the like.

Therefore, program planners at this point have to translate the ideas that have been identified into clear statements of priority needs for programs and set aside those ideas for which an educational program, in their judgment, is not warranted (see Chapter Six). Planners often seek assistance with these decisions, both through official channels (such as program committees and advisory boards) and by more informal ways (such as running ideas past colleagues and learners and paying attention to the local press).

Chapter Highlights

Identifying relevant ideas for programs demands a lot of time and effort on the part of people who plan programs. These ideas take the form of educational needs, performance problems, new opportunities, client demands, images of ideal practice, and so on. Program ideas surface from a number of sources—people, responsibilities and tasks of adult life, organizations, and communities and society in general—and are generated in both formal and informal ways. It is important to address the following tasks in idea identification:

- Decide what sources to use in generating ideas for educational programs (for example, former and/or current program participants, employers, organizational and community leaders, personal issues, government regulations and legislative mandates, societal problems).

- Determine the best way or ways to identify these ideas (for example, formal needs assessments, observations, interviews, conversations with colleagues, job analysis, review of written materials). Program planners should remain open to gathering program ideas in a wide variety of ways, including methods that may not have been predetermined or even thought about.

The next step in the identification of program ideas—sorting and prioritizing those ideas—is described in the following chapter.

Applications Exercises

This chapter's Applications Exercises are designed to help you describe your organization's educational needs (Exhibit 5.1), identify appropriate sources of ideas for educational programs (Exhibit 5.2), and select the best method or methods by which to solicit program ideas from those sources (Exhibit 5.3).

Exhibit 5.1. Describing Educational Needs.

1. When presenting ideas for programs in the form of educational needs, the way you present those needs should be as explicit as possible. Based on a program you are or have been involved in, either as a participant or a planner, outline two or three major educational needs you believe the program was built upon. Use the following format in describing these needs.

   What presently is or was? _____

   _____

   _____

   What should be as a result of the program? _____

   _____

   _____

2. In your judgment, were these needs addressed, and if not, why not?

   _____

   _____

   _____

Exhibit 5.2. Identifying Sources of Ideas for Educational Programs.

1. Outline on the following chart what sources of ideas you could use in planning educational programs. Be as specific as possible in naming those sources, whether they are individuals and groups or titles of reports and documents, and indicate where the sources can be located.

   People:_____

   _____

   Responsibilities and tasks of adult life:_____

   _____

   Organizations: _____

   _____

   Communities/society: _____

   _____

2. Based on the material you outlined in response to the previous question, make a list of those sources you would use first, second, and third. Are there any you would choose not to use at this time?

   Sources you would use first: _____

   _____

   _____

   Sources you would use second:_____

   _____

   _____

   Sources you would use third: _____

   _____

   _____

   Sources you would choose not to use at this time: _____

   _____

   _____

Exhibit 5.3. Generating Ideas for Educational Programs.

1. Briefly describe an organization or group you work with, in either a paid or volunteer capacity:

   _____

   _____

   _____

2. Suggest alternative ways this group or organization could generate ideas for educational programs and indicate why these might be useful:

   _____

   _____

   _____

3. Of those methods you listed in response to the previous question, which ones do you prefer to use, and why?

   _____

   _____

   _____

—— ∞ ——

Sorting and Prioritizing Program Ideas

Christy C. has just been appointed as the statewide director of staff development for the Cooperative Extension Service. She has been with the Cooperative Extension for twelve years, eight of those years as a county agent and four as an extension specialist. Because the position has been vacant for six months, there is already a pile of requests for staff development activities sitting on her desk. In addition, her predecessor had conducted a statewide needs assessment, but none of the recommendations has yet been implemented. Christy decides she should get some programs up and running fast.

In reviewing all the program requests and the needs assessment data, she comes to two major conclusions: some of the items appear not to be problems that can be addressed by an educational program (for example, the problem of staff being repeatedly asked to take on too many assignments), and there are too many good program ideas to start up all at once. Christy first, after consultation with her staff, puts aside those items for which an educational intervention is clearly not appropriate. She plans to talk with the assistant director about how to best recommend alternative ways to tackle those issues. Second, she decides to plan, with a quickly constructed ad hoc committee, a series of workshops on volunteer leadership development. She knows that this topic of improving volunteer leadership addresses one of the major goals of the statewide strategic plan, was cited as a major problem in the needs assessment report, and is viewed by county boards as a critical issue. In addition, Christy decides to respond to three of the many requests she has on her desk that seem amenable to an educational intervention. It just so happens that these three requests are from colleagues whom she knows she can count on to get people to the programs, and they deal with issues that the Extension Service needs to demonstrate to the county and state government officials that they are doing something about.

As can be seen from the above scenario, generating ideas for educational programs is usually not enough. People involved with program planning also need to sort through these ideas to determine which of them make sense in terms of planning an educational program. Then, from the pool of ideas considered appropriate for educational activities, they need to decide which idea or ideas should have priority in the planning process. Discussed first in this chapter is what the sorting process is all about. Next, the what, who, and how of priority setting is addressed, and one systematic process for determining program priorities is highlighted. The chapter concludes with a description of some of the most often used alternative interventions to educational and training programs.

Sorting and Analyzing Ideas

Planning educational activities is not the only, or necessarily the best, way to respond to various ideas, problems, and opportunities that have been identified. Therefore, program planners need to make decisions about whether alternative interventions—options other than educational and training activities—might be a more useful response (Laird, 1985; Shroyer, 1990; Rothwell and Kazanas, 1992). Sometimes these decisions are clear-cut: the idea fits well in either the alternative interventions pile or the educational programming pile. Other ideas are not as easy to sort. For example, some ideas may not lend themselves to clearly defined interventions. For others, a combination of strategies, including a formal education program, may be the best way to go. In sorting through ideas, it is wise to err on the side of keeping ideas that are not easy to categorize in the educational pile.

As with other planning tasks, asking for assistance with this sorting process is usually a good idea, especially when large numbers of ideas have been generated from diverse sources. This assistance could come from colleagues, education committee members, other groups internal to the organization, external parties, and/or a combination of the above. Personnel who have experience in human resource management or personnel issues are often especially helpful in this sorting process.

Three major factors, alone or in combination, can be used to make judgments about whether an educational program should be developed based on an identified idea or problem: people, environmental conditions, and cost. The *people factor* centers on the knowledge and skills of individuals and groups (Laird, 1985). Is the content being proposed something people already know or can do but either choose not to demonstrate or are blocked from demonstrating by other people? For example, a secretary may be knowledgeable about how to respond in a positive manner to phone inquiries, but fails to use that knowledge because she does not want to be bothered, especially when calls interrupt other tasks she considers to be more important. Another secretary may want to respond in a helpful way to those who call for information, but has been told repeatedly by his supervisor that she believes he is spending far too much of his time on the phone, answering what she considers to be unimportant questions. The problem in these cases is not that the secretaries need more information or skill development; they need another intervention so that they and/or their supervisors can change their actions and responses. Examining the people factor, which is often the most ticklish and yet critical factor, is illustrated in Figure 6.1.

Figure 6.1. Making Decisions About Alternative Interventions Based on What People Know and/or Can Do.

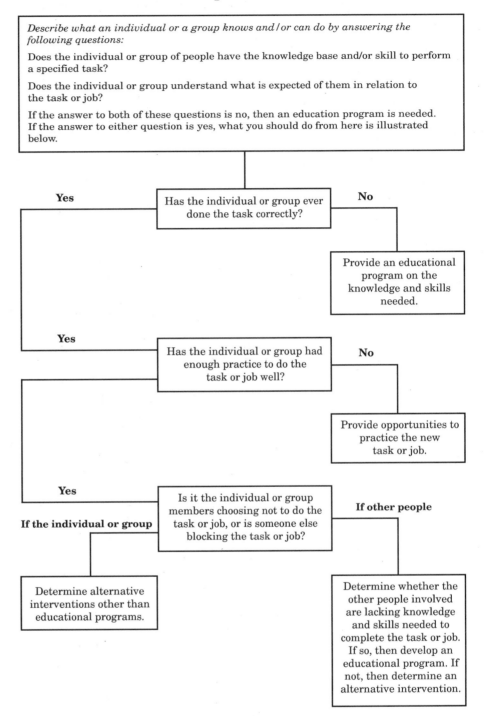

Describe what an individual or a group knows and/or can do by answering the following questions:

Does the individual or group of people have the knowledge base and/or skill to perform a specified task?

Does the individual or group understand what is expected of them in relation to the task or job?

If the answer to both of these questions is no, then an education program is needed. If the answer to either question is yes, what you should do from here is illustrated below.

Yes — Has the individual or group ever done the task correctly? — **No**

Provide an educational program on the knowledge and skills needed.

Yes — Has the individual or group had enough practice to do the task or job well? — **No**

Provide opportunities to practice the new task or job.

Yes — Is it the individual or group members choosing not to do the task or job, or is someone else blocking the task or job? — **If other people**

If the individual or group

Determine alternative interventions other than educational programs.

Determine whether the other people involved are lacking knowledge and skills needed to complete the task or job. If so, then develop an educational program. If not, then determine an alternative intervention.

Source: Adapted from Dugan Laird, *Approaches to Training and Development* (Revised), Second Edition (p. 85), © 1985 by Addison-Wesley Publishing Company, Inc. Reprinted by permission of the publisher.

The *environmental factor* focuses on conditions external to the person (Rothwell and Kazanas, 1992). Types of environmental or situational conditions that may need to be altered in lieu of offering an educational program include communication systems, personnel practices, physical environments, organizational norms and expectations, equipment, and the nature of the task or job itself. For example, an educational program on how to live with a continually stressful work environment might be much less effective in assisting staff to cope than making changes in the work environment itself (for example, ensuring adequate physical facilities and equipment and/or altering the unwritten work ethic from sixty or seventy hours a week to forty or fifty hours).

The third factor for consideration is the *cost factor,* which includes time, money, and staff. When the costs of a proposed educational program are more than the benefits it provides, it is time to consider other alternatives to get at the same issue or idea (Rothwell and Kazanas, 1992). One way to do this is through a cost-benefit analysis, which is discussed more fully in Chapter Eleven.

What is done with those ideas that are not included in the educational planning pile depends on the role and function of the planning staff. Some personnel involved with program planning are responsible for determining alternative interventions and ensuring that they are used. These people usually have specialized training in such areas as organizational development, instructional design, or human resource management. More often, though, program planners pass program ideas more appropriate for alternative interventions along to other units or groups, which then decide what should be done. This means, as stressed in Chapter Four, that people who plan educational programs must have good networks of people, know their organization and communities, and have access to sources outside of their immediate environment. In addition, they should have a working knowledge of alternative interventions, because they are often asked to help define more specifically the ideas or problems and what might be done about them. (A description of some of the most often used alternative interventions is given at the end of this chapter.)

Determining Priorities for Educational Programming

Rarely can personnel involved with educational programs design programs for *all* of the ideas identified as appropriate for educational programs, as I noted earlier. Therefore, they must have a system for determining which ideas will take priority in the planning of actual activities and events. What constitutes a priority idea in the context of program planning? A priority idea is often thought of as one that is among the most important or among those that it is most urgent to address. Depending on the specific planning situation, however, other factors must be considered, such as the number of people affected and availability of resources. As Sork states, "What is being done in determining priorities is to assign preferential ratings to needs which are in competition for available resources so that judgments can be made about how those resources will be allocated" (Sork, 1982, p. 1). Depending on the planning context, any combination of the following people may be involved in setting program priorities (Boyle, 1981; Kaufman and Stone, 1983):

- Current and potential participants
- Staff involved with the educational program
- Supervisors of potential participants
- Key management/administrative personnel
- Education committee members
- People from outside the sponsoring organization(s) (for example, community leaders and/or consultants).

Those responsible for planning programs may consult with these people on an individual basis and/or involve them in group discussions. Group meetings may be of an informal nature, or they may be formally organized committees (such as a formally constituted education committee).

For example, John A., the director of management development, might first talk informally with selected key managers in the organization concerning a report he has prepared on the major educational needs of entry-level managers. He might then ask a group of entry-level managers and their supervisors to form an ad hoc committee to review the material and develop priorities for management development programs based on the same report. His final step might be to have the education committee, using the priorities generated by both key management personnel and the ad hoc committee, make the final recommendations on what specific programs should be offered for entry-level managers.

The process of how final priorities are set is also tied to the context within which the decisions are being made (see Chapter Four). For example, do those responsible for planning programs have the authority to make decisions about priorities, or must all such decisions be cleared with someone higher up? Are planners expected to use a collaborative style of making decisions; and if so, is collaboration a genuine operational norm or one that senior staff just parrot, with the real expectation being quick results or an ever-increasing number of program participants? Can the planners make decisions within the confines of their own organizations, or must they form decision-making networks with external groups? Again, flexibility is the byword, because contexts for program planning can change overnight. For example, major budget cuts or public infighting between and among the leadership of an organization could drastically change how decisions are made about future programs.

In choosing who should be involved and how the priority-setting process should work, planners should bear in mind that the more systematic the process, the greater the likelihood that the resulting educational activities will reflect the most important ideas of the potential participants, the organizational sponsors, and/or the wider community. Yet people involved in planning educational programs often ignore the participative part of the decision-making process; they tend to think that the most urgent issues and ideas will be obvious to everyone involved (and thus will be handled first). Even worse, some program planners simply accept the fact that part of the program planning business is being "overwhelmed" with too much work, and they use that as an excuse for not being responsive to why ideas have or have not been translated into educational activities.

A Systematic Process for Determining Priorities

The following four-step process, based primarily on the work of Sork (1979, 1982), can help planners systematically determine priorities among identified ideas for programs. The key element is establishing (early in the process) clear criteria for making decisions about each of the ideas.

Step 1

The first step in this process is to identify the people who should be involved in setting priorities. As mentioned earlier in this chapter, depending on the situation, a number of different types of people could be involved in setting priorities for educational programs, from potential participants to key administrators or managers to influential community leaders. "Included should be those who are in a position to allocate resources and who are interested in employing a systematic procedure for determining priorities" (Sork, 1982, p. 9).

Step 2

The second step—selecting or developing appropriate criteria—is the key element in determining priorities, as I noted earlier. These criteria provide not only the basis on which priorities are judged, but also serve as the justification for the eventual choices. "No one criterion or set of criteria fits all situations and there are no formulas or guidelines for selecting criteria" (Sork, 1982, p. 2).

Kaufman and Stone (1983) have suggested two different criteria systems based on specified categories. The first set of criteria might look like this:
- Critical (must be resolved in the next six months)
- Very important (must be resolved in the next year)
- Important (should be resolved within two years)
- Minimal (should be dealt with, but only if enough time and resources are left over from higher-priority needs)
- Not important (not necessary to deal with)
- Not a need

Another set of criteria might look like this:
- Highest 5 percent of all ideas
- Highest 20 percent of all ideas
- Middle 50 percent of all ideas
- Lowest 20 percent of all ideas
- Lowest 5 percent of all ideas

Sork (1982) has approached criteria development in a somewhat different way. He has suggested that criteria generally fall into two major categories: those dealing with importance and those dealing with feasibility. An overall judgment about an idea could be made by rating program ideas only on their relative importance, only on their relative feasibility, or on both importance and feasibility. Sork then elaborates further by adding specific criteria for each category:

Importance Criteria	Description
Number of people affected	An estimate of how many people would be involved if a specific idea were addressed
Contribution to goals	The degree to which addressing the idea will contribute to the attainment of organizational goals
Immediacy	The degree to which each program idea requires immediate attention
Instrumental value	The degree to which one idea will have a positive or negative effect on addressing other ideas
Magnitude of discrepancy	The relative size of the gap between the present state of affairs and a more desirable future state of affairs
Feasibility Criteria	**Description**
Educational efficacy	The degree to which an educational intervention (program or series of programs) can contribute to addressing the idea, need, or opportunity
Availability of resources	The degree to which the resources necessary to address the idea would be available if it is decided that the idea should be addressed (for example, personnel, financial, equipment, facilities)
Commitment to change	The degree to which those with vested interests (for example, participants, administrators, community groups) are committed to addressing the idea or opportunity. This commitment may be positive or negative.

Source: Adapted from Sork, T. J. *Determining Priorities.* Vancouver: British Columbia, Ministry of Education, 1982, pp. 2–4.

Step 3		Sork explains that these eight criteria are only a partial set of guidelines on which decisions about priorities can be made. Other criteria might be more appropriate, depending on the planning context.

Step 3

The third step is to record the ideas, along with the criteria, on a priority rating chart. Assign, where appropriate, weighting factors to each criterion. Priority rating charts are especially helpful when priorities are determined by a number of individuals. The charts can be completed individually and then the ratings compiled, or they may be completed by a group as a whole. The size and complexity of the chart depends on how many criteria have been chosen and whether all the criteria should be rated equally or whether some criteria should have greater impact on the decision than others. (Sample priority rating charts are given in Exhibits 6.1, 6.2, and 6.3, somewhat later in this discussion.)

When the decision makers believe that some of the criteria should have more impact on the decision than others, weighting factors need to be assigned to each criterion. "One straightforward way to carry out this task," says Sork, "is to first identify the criterion which should carry the least weight in priority decisions. This criterion is assigned a weighting factor of '1.' All other criteria are then assigned weighting factors based on the desired weight they should carry in relation to the first criterion" (1982, p. 5).

Step 4

As the fourth step, apply each criterion to each idea using the priority rating chart. Combine individual values to yield a total priority value for each need. When applying criteria that are weighted equally, two alternative systems are suggested. The first is to do a simple ranking of each item on each criterion from "1" (lowest) to "N" (highest). The rankings are then totaled, and the one receiving the highest number is considered the top priority. An example of this system is pictured in Exhibit 6.1.

Exhibit 6.1. Sample Priority Rating Chart (with Criteria Weighted Equally).

Items to Be Prioritized: Program Ideas	Number of People Affected	Contribution to Goals	Immediacy	Availability of Resources	Total Score
Dealing with Ethical Dilemmas	4	4	4	4	16
Communicating Effectively (in Speech or Writing)	4	3	2	3	12
Attracting Women and Minorities into Leadership Roles	5	4	5	5	19
Coping with Conflict Situations	2	1	1	2	6
Motivating People	3	4	2	2	11

The top priority in this example would be attracting women and minorities into leadership roles, with dealing with ethical dilemmas a close second.

An alternative way to assign priorities when criteria are equally weighted is to assign each item a rating, such as high, medium, and low (see Exhibit 6.2). The results of this tabulation can then be discussed for points of agreement and disagreement, again with top priority given to those items receiving the highest ratings. It is important to specify what the ratings mean prior to completing the chart, however.

Exhibit 6.2. Sample Priority Rating Chart Using High, Medium, and Low (with Criteria Weighted Equally).

Items to Be Prioritized: Program Ideas	Number of People Affected	Contribution to Goals	Immediacy	Availability of Resources	Total Score
Dealing with Ethical Dilemmas	Medium	High	High	High	High
Communicating Effectively (in Speech or Writing)	High	Medium	Low	Medium	Medium
Attracting Women and Minorities into Leadership Roles	Medium	High	High	High	High
Coping with Conflict Situations	Low	Low	Low	Low	Low
Motivating People	Medium	Medium	High	High	Medium/High

If program planners use a priority system in which the criteria are not equally weighted, the process is more complex. Sork (1982, pp. 10–11) has suggested one way for completing this process:

1. For each criterion, rank all ideas from "1" (representing the lowest priority) to "N" (representing the highest priority).
2. Multiply the rankings by the weighting factors.
3. Add the weighted ranks for each idea (across the columns) and record the sum in the "Sum of Weighted Ranks" column.
4. Divide the sum of ranks by the number of criteria and record the result in the "Mean Weighted Rank" column.
5. Assign a final rank to each need based on the "Mean Weighted Rank," with the lowest score receiving a priority of "1" and the highest a priority of "N."

An example of a completed chart using this system can be seen in Exhibit 6.3. Again, Sork emphasizes that his suggested procedure is only one alternative for determining priorities when the criteria are not equally weighted.

**Exhibit 6.3. Sample Priority Ranking Chart
(with Criteria Weighted Differently).**

	Criteria						
	Number of People Affected	Contribution to Goals	Immediacy	Availability of Resources			
Items to Be Prioritized: Program Ideas	Wt. = 2	Wt. = 7	Wt. = 5	Wt. = 9	Sum of Weighted Ranks	Mean Weighted Rank	Final Rank
	Weighted Rank	Weighted Rank	Weighted Rank	Weighted Rank			
Dealing with Ethical Dilemmas	4 8	4 28	4 20	4 36	92	23	4
Communicating Effectively (in Speech or Writing)	4 8	3 21	2 10	3 27	66	16.5	3
Attracting Women and Minorities into Leadership Roles	5 10	4 28	5 25	5 45	108	27	5
Dealing with Conflict Situations	2 4	1 7	1 5	2 18	34	8.5	1
Motivating People	3 6	4 28	2 10	2 18	62	15.5	2

Alternative Interventions

As I noted earlier in this chapter, people who plan programs should know that educational and training programs are not always the answer to the ideas and problems identified. This may require a new way of thinking for some—especially for people who work with organizations and groups where using the educational process has always been the norm for solving problems or implementing new ideas. Although few program planners actually have the responsibility for developing and/or initiating these alternative interventions, it is important for staff to know what types of options are available. Having this knowledge can help planners do a better job with the initial sorting process, have a better sense of who they need to talk with about possible alternative interventions, and provide useful observations and suggestions to those who have the responsibility for implementing these different responses. A description of some of the most often used alternative interventions to educational and training programs are outlined below (Laird, 1985; Varney, 1987; Rossett and Gautier-Downes, 1991; Rothwell and Kazanas, 1992):

Alternative Intervention	Examples
Job aids. Mechanisms for storing information that is external to the user and provides guidance, direction, and/or support for doing work tasks and other activities.	Checklists Algorithms Procedures manuals Work samples Fold-out cards Charts Audio- or videotapes Memory joggers
Redefining the job or task. Changes in the content, activities, and/or responsibilities of a task or job.	Job enrichment Job enlargement Job rotation Performance standards
Feedback systems. A process for providing information to an individual and/or group about the task/activity being performed.	Individual meetings Memorandums Team meetings Quality circles Customer surveys
Personnel practices. Changes in the way people are recruited, screened, hired, trained, evaluated, and rewarded.	Recruitment practice Selection processes Staff training Appraisal/evaluation systems Job transfer Job termination System of incentives Flexible scheduling
Changes in work environment, facilities, and/or tasks. Alterations in the conditions where the job/task is performed and/or the tools used to do the job or task.	Effective heating and cooling units Good air quality Renovated facilities New equipment

Action research. Research that has as an end product a main goal of improving practice.	Testing of new techniques
	  or methods
	Examination of alternative
	  strategies
	Study of the culture of
	  the organization

Organizational development. A systematically planned change effort for the purpose of developing and implementing action strategies for organizational improvement.	Laboratory training
	Team building
	Total quality management
	Third-party facilitation
	Organizational redesign
	Redesign of
	  communication systems
	Changes in decision-making
	  processes
	Changes in reporting
	  relationships

In thinking through what alternative interventions might be the most useful, planners often find it helpful to focus on who or what the intervention is directed toward: individuals and/or groups, jobs or tasks, and/or whole (or part) organizations.

Individual/Group Alternatives

- Provide job aids (for example, checklists, charts, manuals, reference aids).
- Encourage regular feedback sessions.
- Transfer or terminate the individual.
- Host team meetings.
- Change the reward system (for example, allow for individual choice of schedule, provide educational opportunities at no cost to the individual).

Job/Task-Specific Alternatives

- Redefine the job.
- Encourage job rotation.
- Install new equipment.
- Change the environment in which the job is performed (for example, lighting, cooling, air quality).
- Change the performance standards.
- Communicate the performance standards differently.
- Eliminate the job.

Organizational Alternatives

- Improve the personnel system on an organization-wide basis.
- Conduct an action research project on the climate of the organization.
- Use an organizational development process to build trust levels among units in the organization.
- Change the organizational structure and/or patterns (such as who reports to whom within the organization).

The most frequently used alternatives to educational programs are individually oriented or job/task-specific. Job aids, for example, are standard items for many organizations. Examples of such aids are flowcharts on how to start up or shut down a piece of equipment and lists of key personnel with their office numbers and phone extensions. In recent years, there has also been more widespread use of organizational interventions—especially organizational development processes and techniques.

Chapter Highlights

Planning an educational or training program may not be the only, or even an appropriate, response to some of the ideas generated for programs; other interventions may be of more use in solving some of the problems and issues that surface. In addition, even for those ideas where conducting an educational program makes sense, there are often more ideas than program planning staff can handle. Therefore, planning staff have to decide which idea or ideas need to be acted upon first, second, and so on. In this sorting and prioritizing process, it is important to address the following tasks:

- Determine whether an educational program, one or more

alternative interventions, or a combination of both is the best way to respond to the ideas generated.

- Develop a process for prioritizing those ideas for which educational programs should be planned. The critical ingredient in this process is the establishment of clear criteria for making decisions about each of the ideas.
- Become knowledgeable about alternative interventions and work on creating networks of people who will listen and act when these alternative interventions are needed.

Once the program ideas have been sorted and prioritized, program planners can realistically move to finalizing program objectives for a given program or set of programs. Developing program objectives that are clear and understandable is the subject of the next chapter.

Applications Exercises

The Applications Exercises presented here will help you determine which of your potential program ideas to develop. The first should assist you in setting program priorities (Exhibit 6.4); the second should assist you in assessing when alternatives to educational programs are appropriate (Exhibit 6.5).

Exhibit 6.4. Setting Program Priorities.

Using the instructions given here, complete the following priority rating chart. (Instructions 3 through 7 are adapted from Sork, 1982, pp. 10–11.)

1. List the ideas identified by your organization as appropriate for educational activities.

2. Select appropriate criteria on which those activities should be judged.

3. Assign weighting factors to each of the criteria.

4. For each criterion, rank all ideas from "1" (representing the lowest priority) to "N" (representing the highest priority).

5. Multiply the rankings by the weighting factors.

6. Add the weighted ranks for each idea (across the columns) and record the sum in the "Sum of Weighted Ranks" Column.

7. Divide the sum of ranks by the number of criteria and record the result in the "Mean Weighted Rank" column.

8. Assign a final rank to each need based on the "Mean Weighted Rank," with the lowest score receiving a priority of "1" and the highest a priority of "N."

Priority Ranking Chart (with Criteria Weighted Differently)

Ideas	Criteria					Sum of Weighted Ranks	Mean Weighted Rank	Final Rank
	Wt. = __	Wt. = __	Wt. = __	Wt. = __	Wt. = __			

Source: Sork, T. J. *Determining Priorities.* Vancouver: British Columbia, Ministry of Education, 1982, p. 8.

Exhibit 6.5. Using Interventions Other Than Educational Programming.

1. Give a description of an idea or problem in your organization for which you believe developing an educational program might not be appropriate.

_____

_____

_____

2. List people who could assist you in deciding whether alternative interventions would be more appropriate than an educational program.

_____

_____

_____

3. Outline at least two reasons why you believe using a different intervention would be the best choice in this situation.

_____

_____

_____

4. Identify one or more possible alternative interventions (other than or in addition to an educational program) to the idea or problem you have described.

_____

_____

_____

—— ∞ ——

Seven

Developing Program Objectives

Carolyn C., the director of education for the Department of Human Services, is now ready to plan her first program on the department's new policies, services, and procedures related to child abuse cases. That subject is one of the top three areas for training that have been mandated by the state. Therefore, she knows that all staff who work with child abuse cases must attend. But where does she start? Carolyn knows she must address basic items, such as developing program objectives, finding instructors, estimating costs, locating facilities and equipment, and figuring out evaluation strategies, but which task should she do first? Carolyn decides some assistance from Pam R., a colleague who is an experienced educator, would be helpful. In talking over her dilemma with Pam, she discovers that there is no single order to the various tasks. Rather, each program planning situation she faces, and her own daily schedule, will influence which task or tasks she might do first. Pam stresses to Carolyn that three major elements should be addressed at this point in the planning process, however:

1. Where you want to go (program objectives, transfer of learning)
2. How you will determine if you have gotten there (program evaluation)
3. How you want to get there (formats, staffing, budgeting, marketing, instructional plans, and logistical details)

Logically, the first task seems to be to determine program objectives, based on the identified priority ideas; but in practice, as stressed in Chapters Two and Three, how programs actually get planned usually defies logic (at least it seems so to the external observer). What is important is that each of these elements is addressed in such a way that the final product has internal consistency and is doable. For example, does the program fit within the parameters of the overall mission and goals of the sponsoring organization(s) or group(s)? Is there a clear match between and among the program objectives, how these objectives will be evaluated, and how the learning activities are designed? Are the transfer-of-learning plans workable and consistent with the evaluation component, especially with any plans for follow-up evaluation? Does the "instructional" portion of the program actually reflect the program objectives and what has been said in marketing brochures? And does the budget allotment meet the requirements to implement the plan in all areas, from staffing to facilities to transfer-of-learning activities?

Each of the major elements of program planning highlighted above is discussed in turn in Chapters Eight through Thirteen. The focus of this chapter is on developing program objectives. Discussed first is how program objectives are defined. This is followed by a review of how program objectives are constructed and how planners can judge the clarity of these objectives. Explored in the final section of the chapter are ways program objectives can be used as the components in determining whether a program is internally consistent and/or doable.

Defining Program Objectives

Thinking through program objectives may be one of the most difficult tasks people who plan programs have to do. The difficulty stems from two sources. First, at the heart of formulating program *objectives* is defining program *outcomes*; and these are often elusive, especially at the beginning of the process. For example, those working in literacy programs know that one of the major objectives of these programs is that adults who are illiterate will be able to read and write. But what does being able to read and write mean? Does it mean reading at a specified grade level, having the reading and writing skills necessary to be a productive worker or member of society, or both of these outcomes and more? Second, in the actual writing of program objectives, the parameters are not always clear. The terms *objectives* and *goals,* for example, are sometimes used interchangeably in practice: what one organization terms a program *goal,* another may call a program *objective.* There is a useful distinction between the two terms, however.

Program *objectives* provide clear statements of the anticipated results to be achieved through an educational program. In addition, they can serve as concrete guidelines for developing transfer-of-learning plans (see Chapter Eight), as benchmarks against which programs are evaluated (see Chapter Nine), and as the foundation for instructional plans (see Chapter Twelve). In contrast, program *goals* usually refer to broad statements of purpose or intent for educational programs. For programs sponsored by organizations whose primary function is the education and training of adults (such as community-based literacy programs sponsored by community colleges), the major program goals are usually a part of the organizational mission statement (see Chapter Four). This is also true for organizations that have centralized units charged with the educational function; but in these organizations, the goals are usually a part of the *unit's* mission statement.

Program objectives focus primarily on what participants are expected to learn as a result of attending a specific educational or training program. This learning may result in changes in individual participants, groups of learners, organizational practices and procedures, and/or communities or segments of society. In addition, program objectives may outline how program staff will improve the quality and quantity of program resources and other basic operational aspects of the program. This second kind of program objective has also been termed an *operational objective* (Knowles, 1980). It is important to include, as appropriate, program objectives that focus on the learning outcomes as well as on outcomes related to improving the program operations. Examples of program objectives focused on participant learning and on program operations follow:

Program Objectives Focused on Participant Learning

- *Individual change.* To provide an educational support group for cancer patients with three primary outcomes. Participants will (1) gain knowledge about their disease, (2) have the opportunity to express their feelings about living with cancer, and (3) share ways they are helping themselves cope with cancer and ways they could help each other.

- *Organizational change.* To provide a training program on two new software programs for all staff who will be required to use them on the job within a six-month period. Two outcomes are expected as a result of this program: (1) staff will be able to demonstrate that they know how to use each new package, and (2) managers, in cooperation with the technology support staff, will develop operational guidelines that clearly define how these two packages are to be integrated into existing work systems.

- *Community change.* To provide a two-day workshop for leaders from all segments of the community (for example, police, government agencies, businesses, schools, social service agencies) on how to curb violence in their community. The major outcome expected is that an interorganizational team will be formed, which will then provide the leadership for future decisions and actions related to controlling and preventing violent acts of all kinds.

Program Objectives Focused on Program Operations

- To provide more adequate physical facilities for the educational program, including refurbishing three training rooms and adding an individualized instructional lab.

- To locate and equip five computer labs so that computer-assisted learning can become a more integral component of the program.

- To increase program revenues by 10 percent through higher participant fees, with the money used for innovative programming.

- To establish a volunteer pool of five to ten people who could assist program staff in planning and carrying out programs for low-income families.

People who plan programs often overlook those program objectives that are directed at improving the quality of the program operations. Yet if developing these kinds of objectives were included as a regular part of the process of constructing program objectives, the overall quality and efficiency of programming could, in many cases, be improved. In addition, although operational program objectives are probably more applicable to programs housed in formal educational organizations or units, these types of objectives may also prove useful to persons who conduct educational activities as part of their other job responsibilities. For example, a director of a community action agency responsible for the in-service training of her staff may note that she does not have adequate audiovisual equipment. Therefore, she may define as one of her program objectives to locate and secure by April 1 the following equipment: an overhead projector, a videotape player and monitor, and a hanging screen.

Constructing Program Objectives

Most people who plan programs agree that educational programs have some outcomes that are measurable and some that are not (Apps, 1985; Brookfield, 1986; Sork and Caffarella, 1989; Mehrens and Lehmann, 1991). Likewise, outcomes can be either intended or unanticipated, because it is almost impossible to know before-hand all the benefits a program could produce. Therefore, in constructing program objectives, it is important to state both measurable and nonmeasurable objectives and to be flexible in reshaping those objectives so that unanticipated but important achievements and outcomes of the program can be highlighted. This notion of measurable and nonmeasurable and intended and unanticipated results is illustrated in these examples of specific program objectives:

Measurable Achievements

- *Intended achievements (stated before the program is carried out).* To provide an educational program on time management for all new entry-level principals. As a result of the program, the principals will be able to demonstrate at least two ways they have restructured their day to save at least one hour of time per week. This must be verified by the assistant superintendent for instruction.

- *Unanticipated achievements (stated during the program or after it has been carried out).* About 50 percent of the secretaries for the new entry-level principals told them that it took them less time now to manage their calendars and monitor their telephone calls.

Nonmeasurable Achievements

- *Intended achievements.* To assist new administrators to feel they have more control over their daily work lives.

- *Unanticipated achievements.* A number of the new administrators remarked on the evaluation that they felt more confident to carry out their jobs.

Program planners should never develop program objectives in a vacuum. It is relatively easy to sit in one's office, carefully crafting program objectives, but there is always the risk of producing impractical and/or irrelevant projected outcomes. Instead, other people, such as program participants, work supervisors, and external stakeholders, should be asked to help in developing these objectives. This involvement can be handled in a number of ways. For example, educational staff could request that key supervisors of potential participants help draft and/or review program objectives for their people. They could also ask a sample of potential participants to help with this same process. Questions and comments from both these groups could be solicited on the relevance and usefulness of the objectives and on their understandability (especially concerning actual practical application and usefulness). In addition, if a formal education committee exists, this committee could serve as a review board and give advice and counsel in the initial writing and/or the redrafting of the objectives.

Program objectives "should be stated clearly enough to indicate to all rational minds exactly what is intended" (Houle, 1972, p. 149). Houle goes on to describe a number of properties that characterize clearly articulated program objectives; three of them are highlighted in the discussion that follows. *First, program objectives are essentially rational and thus impose a logical pattern on the educational program.* This does not mean that the objectives do, or even could, describe all the possible outcomes of educational programs over a specified period of time. For example, for large programs, no one set of objectives could be that comprehensive in scope. Nor will these objectives address the usually accepted, but often unstated, motives, aspirations, and objectives of those persons who plan and/or participate in educational activities.

Second, good program objectives are practical and concrete. As practical guides for action, program objectives should neither describe things as they ideally should be nor focus on esoteric problems that have no basis in reality. "The ultimate test of an objective is not validity but achievability" (p. 140).

Third, good program objectives are discriminative. By stating one course of action, another is ruled out. For example, if resources for the next calendar year are targeted at new personnel, for the most part all other staff will be excluded from educational activities. Whether this course of action is appropriate depends on a number of factors. For example, was an educational program for new staff seen as a priority need? Does senior management support this decision? Do the supervisors of the new staff believe the programs being planned meet the needs of their people?

More specifically, people who plan programs can ask themselves the following questions to help them judge the clarity of the program objectives they have developed (Boyle, 1981; Sork and Caffarella, 1989):

- Is there a clear relationship between the objective and the ideas, problems, and needs that have been identified as priority areas?
- Does the objective focus on a crucial part of the program?
- Is the objective practical and doable?
- Is the objective attainable in the time frame proposed?
- Does the objective clearly communicate the proposed outcomes or accomplishments?

- Is the objective meaningful, and will it be understood by all interested parties?
- Is the objective supposed to be measurable; and if so, is it?

Program objectives often need to be changed or reworked at some point (or points) in the life of a program. Practically speaking, this means program planners must be willing to eliminate, revise, and/or add program objectives as the situation warrants. This updating of program objectives should be done in a thoughtful way. Staff should not modify or eliminate certain objectives just because they do not want to do them or because those objectives cannot be met as proposed; rather, staff need to reflect carefully when revising or adding to initially agreed upon program objectives.

Using Objectives as Checkpoints

Clearly stated program objectives provide one of the major checks for ensuring that a program has internal consistency and is doable. As noted earlier, this does not mean these objectives will necessarily be constructed prior to working on or completing planning tasks. However, once these objectives have been developed, other aspects of the plan (for example, the transfer-of-learning activities, budget, and staffing) or the planning process itself can be revisited to see if what is being proposed really addresses the expected outcomes and can be done. The following scenarios illustrate this point.

Scenario 1

In planning a continuing education program for practicing physicians on a new on-line medical information system, the planning team at its third meeting reviews a draft of the program objectives. One of the major expected outcomes is that participants would be able to integrate this new system as part of their practice within the next six months. Three of the planning team members caution the team that the potential participants are probably at many different stages in integrating technology systems (such as this one) into their current practices and question whether this objective is realistic. Based on these observations, team members then decide to reexamine the activities planned for the program itself to determine whether they can develop a transfer-of-learning plan that addresses this issue.

Scenario 2

In reviewing a draft of a revised training program for new teachers, Cassie D., the director of the statewide literacy program, notices that what has been proposed is probably not doable, given some recently projected funding cuts in the training budget. She decides to ask the ad hoc committee that put the plan together to continue to meet and revise the plan in light of these projected budget shortfalls. In discussing with the committee chair how she might go about this task, Cassie suggests that the committee might start with reviewing the program objectives. For example, which of the objectives are more critical than others? Could some of the objectives be achieved in a different way—one that would require less cost? Might some of the objectives be scaled back in terms of the projected outcomes? The chair agrees that this would be a good starting point for revising the whole plan.

Using the program objectives as an internal consistency check can be especially helpful in matching transfer-of-learning and evaluation plans to what people want to see happen (see Chapters Eight and Nine). For some programs, the connections between and among the program objectives, the transfer activities, and the evaluation process may be readily apparent—the strategies and techniques for doing the transfer of learning and evaluation may overlap or be one and the same. For example, using the formal supervisory process may be the chosen strategy to ensure that participants use what they have learned on the job. In turn, the evaluation plan may include interviewing supervisors or staff who take the program as well as reviewing performance appraisal data. Therefore, checking to see that these components of the plan line up with one another and get at proposed outcomes may be relatively easy. In other programs, seeing that these components match may be more difficult. This is especially so, for example, when the sponsoring organizations or groups are not responsible for monitoring or evaluating the transfer-of-learning activities and outcomes.

Chapter Highlights

Program objectives provide clear statements of the proposed outcomes or anticipated results of a specific program. Although primarily focused on what participants will learn, they may also address the operational aspects of a program. The learning by participants may result in individual, organizational, community, and/or societal changes. In constructing program objectives, program planners should be cognizant of the following tasks:

- Write program objectives that reflect what participants will learn, the resulting changes from that learning, and the operational aspects of the program.
- Ensure that both measurable and nonmeasurable program outcomes, as appropriate, are included, and provide a way for revising the objectives.
- Check to see whether the program objectives are written clearly enough that they can be understood by all parties involved (for example, participants, sponsoring organizations).
- Use the program objectives as an internal consistency and "doability" checkpoint (to determine, for example, whether the transfer-of-learning and evaluation plans match the objectives).

The program objectives, in either draft or final form, often serve as the point of departure for preparing transfer-of-learning and evaluation plans, which are addressed respectively in the next two chapters of the book.

Applications Exercise

This Applications Exercise will help you develop and evaluate program objectives within your own organization.

Exhibit 7.1. Developing and Evaluating Program Objectives.

1. Develop two or three clearly written program objectives for a program area of your choice. As appropriate, include both objectives focused on participant learning and objectives focused on program operations. List each of those objectives on the chart provided.

2. Ask one or two of your colleagues to help you critique those objectives using the questions noted on the chart.

3. With the feedback they have provided, rewrite those objectives that need revising. (Please note that you may need or want to do this critiquing and revising process a number of times with the same and/or different colleagues.)

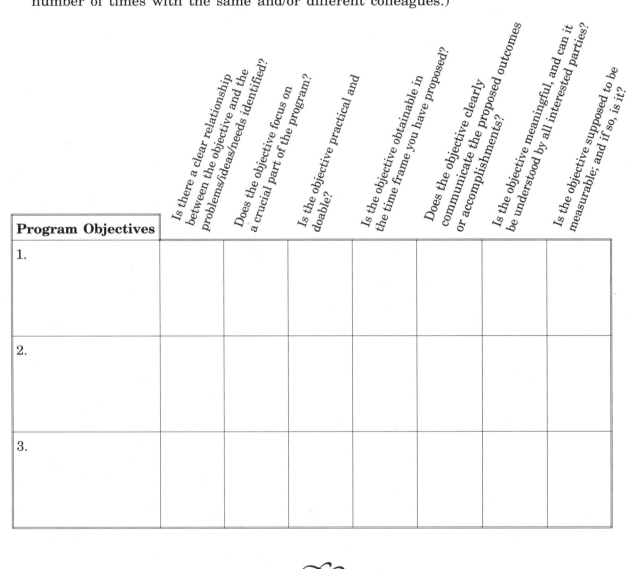

Program Objectives	Is there a clear relationship between the objective and the problems/ideas/needs identified?	Does the objective focus on a crucial part of the program?	Is the objective practical and doable?	Is the objective obtainable in the time frame you have proposed?	Does the objective clearly communicate the proposed outcomes or accomplishments?	Is the objective meaningful, and can it be understood by all interested parties?	Is the objective supposed to be measurable; and if so, is it?
1.							
2.							
3.							

Eight

Preparing for the Transfer of Learning

One of the basic tenets of people who attend, plan, and sponsor educational programs is that what has been learned is something participants can use after the program is completed. In the planning of most programs, until fairly recently, it was assumed that this transfer of learning would somehow just happen. Neither program planners nor instructors paid much attention to systematically planning for how program participants could integrate what they had learned back into their personal, work, and/or public lives. Rather, it was primarily left up to learners to apply, as they thought appropriate and needed, what they had learned.

In some cases, as illustrated in this scenario, leaving the application piece in the learners' hands makes sense:

Scenario 1

Dave R. has just completed a workshop sponsored by a local community recreation association on mountain biking. He has always enjoyed the out-of-doors and thought this would be an outdoor sport that might be fun and relaxing. One thing that he had not counted on is how expensive the sport is. Dave had hoped he could start riding on a regular basis right away but has decided, except for one short trip (for which he will rent a bike), that he will need a few months to save up so that he can buy the kind of bike he really wants. He also wants to entice one or two of his friends to join him in this venture, because it appears there is greater safety in numbers, especially for the longer rides into the back country of Colorado.

In other cases, as shown in the next scenario, program participants do need assistance in applying what they have learned:

Scenario 2

Susan J., the dean of continuing education, took an intensive three-week summer institute on leadership development four months ago. She is still very excited about what she learned in the program and about her plan (developed at the suggestion of the program facilitators) for putting into practice some of the key ideas. But reality set in on her first day back on campus as she faced a mountain of mail, phone messages, and meetings. Although the plan stayed in her "to do" file for the remainder of the summer and into fall semester, she never seemed to be able to get to it. And *still* she has no time. In addition, she now has a gut feeling that one of the major changes she wants to initiate would probably be blocked by the new vice president for academic affairs, even though she knows her staff would be supportive. As she reflects informally with a colleague about the summer experience, she comments that a more explicit follow-up component to the institute—including specific support from the institute staff—would have been very helpful.

This chapter first outlines a basic overview of what transfer of learning is all about and explains why it is important. Discussed next are the key factors that influence the transfer-of-learning process. The final sections then present a framework for planning the transfer of learning and highlight a number of strategies and methods that can be used prior to, during, and after educational programs to assist participants in applying what they have learned.

What Is the Transfer of Learning?

Transfer of learning is the effective application by program participants of what they learned as a result of attending an educational program (Silberman, 1990; Kemerer, 1991; Killion and Kaylor, 1991; Broad and Newstrom, 1992). It is often referred to as the "so what" or "now what" phase of the learning process. "So what does this all mean, and how can what was learned be applicable to my situation?" This is not a new component of the planning process (Michalak and Yager, 1979; Nadler, 1982; Fox, 1984). Rather, it is an element of the process that is currently receiving increased attention as both participants and sponsors of educational programs demand more concrete and useful results. Not all educational programs for adults need to have a plan for this part of the process, however. In fact, for some programs—a public lecture series or a weekend retreat for spiritual renewal, for example—a plan for how the transfer of learning should happen may be totally out of place. But for many programs, it is essential that a plan be developed for helping participants apply what they have learned.

Assisting people to make changes is what transfer of learning is all about—changes in themselves, other people, practices, organizations, and/or society (Rogers, 1983; Fox, 1984; Hall and Hord, 1987; Martin and Mazmanian, 1991; Ottoson, 1993). Some of these changes may be easy and even fun, like learning how to be a better gardener or skier. Other changes may be difficult and painful, such as learning to cope with a major illness or learning how to lay off large numbers of staff due to funding cutbacks or economic conditions.

Although most educational programs focus on the learning of individuals, often some of what has been learned cannot be applied unless changes are also made in current practices, organizations, and/or society. This is especially so when what is learned has to be applied primarily in a work or other organizational setting and/or depends on others having to agree to or also make those changes. For example, a teacher may want to try using some cooperative learning strategies and self-directed learning projects that he learned about at a summer institute but encounters a stumbling block in his department chair and principal, who voice strong opposition; they claim that these kinds of learning techniques, especially for science and math education, are just a waste of good teaching time. A more global example would be the current proliferation of educational programs on the importance of cultural diversity in major corporations and governmental bodies offered by and for organizations in which senior management, board members, and high-level governmental officials are still predominately Caucasian.

The Importance of Planning for Learning Transfer

There are a number of reasons why planning for the transfer of learning (also termed "transfer of training" and "follow-up to training") has become so important. First, as noted above, both sponsoring organizations and participants are asking for outcomes that are applicable, are practical, and can make a difference. For example, a variety of U.S. organizations, according to Broad and Newstrom (1992), are spending billions of dollars each year on employee training and development programs. Yet these authors believe that much of this training is wasted, "because most of the knowledge and skills gained by workers (well over 80% by some estimates) is not fully applied by those employees on the job" (p. ix). These same authors go on to assert that for organizations to remain competitive in the global marketplace and prepare highly skilled workers, improving the transfer of learning must be a high priority.

Second, there are many issues and concerns related to the lives of adults that can and should be at least partially addressed through educational programs—health-care reform, violence in our communities, restructuring of public education, world peace, and environmental concerns, just to name a few. What is critical about so many of these issues and concerns is that solutions were needed yesterday. Therefore, what has so often been left to chance by educators—whether people, as a result of attending a variety of educational programs, can apply what they have learned to solving these complex problems—is no longer either a viable or an ethical option.

And third, many people need assistance in reflecting on and planning for changes that must be made in themselves, other people, organizations, and/or society before what they have learned can be translated into concrete results. For example, Broad and Newstrom (1992) contend that only limited transfer of learning occurs in terms of job performance through voluntary transfer of knowledge and skills by individual learners. What is needed for any dramatic increase in learning transfer in the work world, from their perspective, is the full cooperation and specific assistance of supervisors and managers.

Factors Influencing the Transfer of Learning

Numerous reasons have been identified to explain why participants either do or do not apply what they have learned as a result of attending educational programs. Examples include the perceptions of program participants about the value and practicality of program content, the presence or absence of follow-up strategies as part of the program design, and supervisory and organizational attitudes toward changes required to apply what has been learned.

In thinking through the many ideas that have been discussed about why people do or do not apply what they have learned, it is useful to categorize these ideas into a clear and manageable number of key influencing factors, as displayed below (Fox, 1984; Hall and Hord, 1987; Laker, 1990a, 1990b; Perry, 1990; Kemerer, 1991; Broad and Newstrom, 1992):

- *Program participants.* Participants bring to educational programs a set of personal characteristics, experiences, and attitudes and values. These influence both what they learn and whether they can and want to apply what they have learned to their personal, work, and/or public lives.

- *Program design and execution.* Program planners can include as part of designing and conducting educational programs strategies for the transfer of learning. These strategies can be implemented before, during, and/or after the program has been completed.

- *Program content.* The knowledge, skills, and/or attitudes/values that are addressed through the program activities make up the program content. Program participants may or may not learn this material, either because they choose not to or because the program instructors did not teach what they said they would teach (or both).

- *Changes required to apply learning.* The nature of the changes required in people, professional practices, organizations, communities, and/or society to apply the learning describes the scope, depth, and enduring consequences of those changes. It also takes into account the complexity of the change process and who is responsible for making the changes.

- *Organizational context.* The organizational context consists of the people, structure, and cultural milieu of an organization, and it either supports or inhibits the transfer of learning. The context includes the value the organization places on continuous learning and development and the concrete support it gives to educational programs.

- *Community/societal forces.* The social, economic, and political conditions that exist in a specific community or society in general also play a role. This factor includes support by key leaders and groups in the community, region, and/or international arena.

These six key factors, depending on how they play out in the transfer-of-learning process, can be barriers or enhancers to that process (Martin and Mazmanian, 1991; Kemerer, 1991). Examples of specific barriers and enhancers linked to each factor are highlighted in Figure 8.1.

Figure 8.1. Examples of Barriers and Enhancers to the Transfer of Learning.

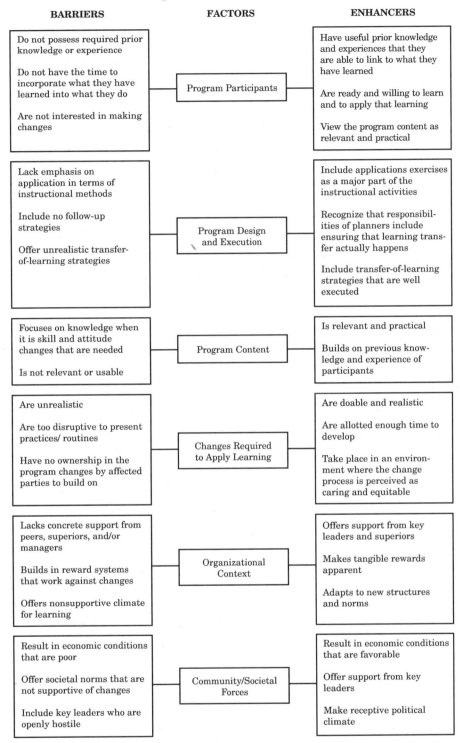

BARRIERS	FACTORS	ENHANCERS
Do not possess required prior knowledge or experience Do not have the time to incorporate what they have learned into what they do Are not interested in making changes	Program Participants	Have useful prior knowledge and experiences that they are able to link to what they have learned Are ready and willing to learn and to apply that learning View the program content as relevant and practical
Lack emphasis on application in terms of instructional methods Include no follow-up strategies Offer unrealistic transfer-of-learning strategies	Program Design and Execution	Include applications exercises as a major part of the instructional activities Recognize that responsibilities of planners include ensuring that learning transfer actually happens Include transfer-of-learning strategies that are well executed
Focuses on knowledge when it is skill and attitude changes that are needed Is not relevant or usable	Program Content	Is relevant and practical Builds on previous knowledge and experience of participants
Are unrealistic Are too disruptive to present practices/ routines Have no ownership in the program changes by affected parties to build on	Changes Required to Apply Learning	Are doable and realistic Are allotted enough time to develop Take place in an environment where the change process is perceived as caring and equitable
Lacks concrete support from peers, superiors, and/or managers Builds in reward systems that work against changes Offers nonsupportive climate for learning	Organizational Context	Offers support from key leaders and superiors Makes tangible rewards apparent Adapts to new structures and norms
Result in economic conditions that are poor Offer societal norms that are not supportive of changes Include key leaders who are openly hostile	Community/Societal Forces	Result in economic conditions that are favorable Offer support from key leaders Make receptive political climate

Not all of the major factors that influence the transfer of learning come into play for every educational program, of course. Rather, as illustrated in the following two examples, only a few of the factors may apply for some programs, whereas for others all may be applicable.

Scenario 1

An initial one-day training session is required for all new Reach for Recovery volunteers. All volunteers must have had breast cancer and be willing to make home or hospital visits to newly diagnosed breast cancer patients. The objectives of the training session are fourfold: (1) to help potential volunteers explore their motivations for being volunteers, (2) to share current information about breast cancer and the Reach for Recovery program, (3) to review what is expected of volunteers on patient visits, and (4) to provide opportunities to do "simulated" patient visits. In addition, volunteers are paired with experienced volunteers to assist them with their first few visits and are given material about where to seek additional support or information. *Applicable factors:* program participants, program design and execution, and program content.

Scenario 2

An organization-wide training program has been initiated on diversity in the work force. The major goals of the program are (1) to have all employees of the organization examine their own attitudes and values related to diversity issues in the workplace, (2) to provide opportunities for managers and supervisors to acquire additional knowledge and skills for working with employees who have diverse backgrounds, (3) to encourage the formulation of ad hoc teams to work on diversity issues within each division of the organization, and (4) to increase the number and percentage of employees in supervisory and managerial positions who are women, ethnic minorities, and/or disabled. The program is envisioned as a two-year intensive effort and is supported by both the top executive officer and the board. *Applicable factors:* program participants, program design and execution, program content, changes required to apply learning, organizational context, and community/societal forces.

As is readily apparent in the above examples, the more complex the program's scope and goals, the larger the number of people affected, the greater the magnitude of the changes, and the less control over organizational and societal forces, the more difficult the transfer-of-learning process becomes.

Program planners have varying levels of control over the decisions they can make related to the factors that influence the transfer of learning. For example, an in-house program planning team consisting of team members who have the authority to make organizational changes (such as purchasing new equipment, changing the reward system) has greater control over learning transfer than do program planners who design programs for audiences from diverse settings (for example, national conferences and workshops). This span of decision-making control over the transfer function may remain constant for some program planners but be continually changing for others (depending on the specific programs they are planning).

Generally, though, program planners have more control over some factors than they do others:

- *Level 1 (most control).* Program design and execution
- *Level 2.* Program participants, program content
- *Level 3.* Organizational context
- *Level 4.* Changes required to apply learning
- *Level 5 (least control).* Community/societal forces

Because the one factor that almost all program planners have the greatest decision-making power over is the design and execution of the program, it is important that planners consider planning for the transfer of learning an integral part of the planning process.

A Framework for Planning for the Transfer of Learning

To plan for the transfer of learning as part of the process of designing and conducting educational programs, three key elements need to be addressed: when the transfer strategies should be employed, the key players who need to be involved, and strategies that each of these players can use to help in applying what has been learned (Ford, 1990; Laker, 1990a; Silberman, 1990; Ottoson, 1994; Broad and Newstrom, 1992; Killion and Kaylor, 1991).

As for the timing, transfer strategies can be used before the program begins, while the program is in progress, and/or after the program is completed. Transfer strategies employed after the program is completed are usually the most difficult for program planners to influence, because of the cost and staff time that follow-up activities usually require (Wenz and Adams, 1991).

Key players—the second element to be addressed—are the people and/or groups who need to be involved to have the transfer of learning actually happen (Broad and Newstrom, 1992). Program planners must take into consideration the participants, others who have been involved in the planning process, and the program instructors in preparing transfer plans. In addition, there may be other key players who, though not involved in programs, need to be included in transfer plans. For example, in work situations, colleagues, supervisors, and/or senior managers may be critical players; in community action programs, city council members, area business people, and other community leaders may need to be included. To ascertain these other players, program planners contemplating transfer plans need to consider whether the changes related to the applications of learning are being newly initiated, are in progress, or simply need to be maintained (Rogers, 1983; Laker, 1990a). Where people and/or organizations are in the change process affects both who needs to be involved in the transfer-of-learning process and the strategies to be employed.

The final element that needs to be considered in planning for learning transfer is determining what strategies or methods are the most useful in assisting participants to apply what they have learned to their personal, work, and/or public lives. Examples of various strategies, along with an indication of when they are most useful in the planning process and who is most likely to use them, are displayed in Table 8.1 (Perry, 1990; Silberman, 1990; Wenz and Adams, 1991; Killion and Kaylor, 1991; Broad and Newstrom, 1992).

Table 8.1. Applying Various Transfer-of-Learning Strategies.

Strategies	When Strategies Are Most Useful			Who Could Use or Be Involved in Strategies			
	Before Program	During Program	After Program	Participants	Program Planners	Instructors	Other Key Players
Involve key people in the planning process.	x			x	x	x	x
Pretrain supervisors of participants.	x				x	x	x
Have participants select projects to complete prior to the start of a program.	x			x	x		x
Build into organizational policies, practices, and procedures (for example, personnel systems) recognition for meeting the goals of educational programs.	x				x		x
Develop individualized learning plans or contracts.	x	x	x	x	x	x	x
Use the formal supervisory process.	x	x	x	x			x
Provide mentors for participants.	x	x	x	x	x		x
Use organizational development interventions.	x	x	x		x		x
Involve people in conducting the program (for example, in on-site coordination and instruction).		x		x	x	x	x
Use applications exercises and simulations.		x		x		x	
Use participant self-assessments for what has been learned and what participants believe they can apply.		x		x		x	
Give assignments/activities that need to be completed after the program.		x		x		x	
Provide a session on reentry advice.		x		x	x	x	
Develop individual action plans.		x	x	x	x		x
Develop self-help groups.		x	x	x	x		x
Develop support groups.		x	x	x	x		x
Supply and use job aids and other resource materials.		x	x	x	x	x	x
Model skills or attitudes/values needed for learning transfer.		x	x	x		x	x
Provide and use peer coaches or teachers.			x	x	x		x
Develop self-monitoring instruments and techniques.			x	x	x		x
Involve key players in follow-up activities.			x	x	x		x
Schedule learner refresher sessions.			x	x	x	x	

Careful thought must be given to matching transfer strategies to the preferences and capabilities of specific individuals and/or groups of people. For example, peer coaching and support groups may be very effective for people who like to work collaboratively but may not work for people who need a supervisor to intervene before they will change the way they behave or practice.

Accounting for Other Factors in the Process

In planning for the transfer of learning as part of the design and execution of educational programs, program planners often must take into account the other five factors that influence the transfer of learning (program participants, program content, changes required to apply learning, organizational context, and community/societal forces). For example, program planners may need to use transfer strategies that are targeted primarily at the organizational context (such as formal supervisory processes or organizational development interventions) to ensure that the learning transfer can actually happen. This requires that planners be adept and have the authority to initiate such strategies (and/or have access to people who do).

What becomes readily apparent to many program planners as they plan for the transfer of learning is that they have little influence or control over some (or even most) of the key factors that must be addressed for the transfer of learning to happen. As noted earlier, this is especially true when the change is extensive and the organizational, community, and/or societal forces are complex and far-reaching. Does this mean program planners should ignore this part of the transfer-of-learning process or spend little time planning for it? Obviously, the answer is no; but it does mean that program planners must understand their span of decision-making control, recognize their own limits for action, and know when and how to call on people who can and will be helpful players in the transfer-of-learning process.

Chapter Highlights

Preparing transfer-of-learning plans—helping learners and program sponsors to systematically think through how program participants can apply what they have learned back at work, in their personal lives, and so forth—has been, until recently, a neglected part of the program planning process. It has been assumed that this application of what was learned at an educational program would somehow just happen and that the proposed changes as a result of this learning were the worry of someone other than those responsible for planning the program.

Program planners may or may not have control over the many factors that enhance or inhibit this transfer-of-learning process (for example, the background and experience of the participants, the program content, the organizational and community/societal contexts). The one factor over which most planners *can* exert a major influence is the design and execution of the program itself. Therefore, it is important that program planners consider planning for the transfer of learning an integral part of their responsibilities. In preparing transfer-of-learning plans, planners must address the following tasks:

- Decide when the transfer-of-learning strategies should be employed.
- Determine the key players who need to be part of the transfer-of-learning process (for example, participants, program planning staff, instructors, work supervisors, community leaders).
- Choose transfer strategies that will be the most useful in assisting participants to apply what they have learned (for example, developing individualized learning plans, providing mentors or peer coaches, starting self-help or support groups, offering organizational development interventions).

Developing transfer-of-learning plans is tied directly to the program evaluation component of the planning process, which is described in the next chapter. Without clear and doable plans for how participants can apply what they have learned, it is often difficult to trace how program activities are related to program outcomes and to provide justification for the judgments made on the worth and value of a program.

Applications Exercises

The two Applications Exercises presented here are designed to help you facilitate the transfer of learning. The first will assist you in identifying those factors that enhance or inhibit the transfer of learning (Exhibit 8.1); the second will help you incorporate the transfer of learning into your program's design and execution (Exhibit 8.2).

Exhibit 8.1. Identifying Elements That Enhance or Inhibit the Transfer of Learning.

1. Describe briefly a program for which you need to plan for the transfer of learning.

_____

_____

2. Using the following chart, first list specific things (related to one or more of the six factors) that could enhance or inhibit the learning transfer. Next, indicate what span of decision-making control you have for each enhancer or inhibitor you listed. Finally, for those items for which you have indicated only some or little or no influence, list who could assist you in the transfer process.

Factors That Influence Learning Transfer	Enhancers	Decision-Making Control (a lot, some, little, none)	Who Could and Would Help If Needed?	Inhibitors	Decision-Making Control (a lot, some, little, none)	Who Could and Would Help If Needed?
Program Participants						
Program Design and Execution						
Program Content						
Changes Required to Apply Learning						
Organizational Context						
Community/ Societal Forces						

Exhibit 8.2. Planning for the Transfer of Learning in the Design and Execution of Educational Programs.

1. Using a program you are now planning or conducting, develop a transfer-of-learning plan in the chart below. List each strategy according to when it would be used and who would use it.

When to Use Strategies	List People to Be Involved and Strategies They Should Employ			
	Participants	*Program Planners*	*Instructors*	*Other Key Players (Specify for Each Strategy)*
Before the Program				
During the Program				
After the Program				

2. Review this plan with key individuals and/or your planning group and revise based on the feedback you receive.

Nine

Formulating Evaluation Plans

John R. wants to demonstrate that he is doing a good job as the new training coordinator for the safety training program, but he is not sure how to proceed. His predecessor was on the job for years and ran a rather informal shop; other than a big chart displaying the number of accident-free days for the company, he kept no systematic records on the safety training. John has access to some figures on the number and types of programs offered, with the number of participants in each program, but the data are incomplete; the figures were not kept for all programs, and there is a great deal of inconsistency in how the figures were gathered and recorded. John asked his predecessor if there were any evaluation reports on the program, and his predecessor's response was, "You'll know if they're bad, because the trainees and/or supervisors will tell you." John wonders how he can demonstrate that the safety program is doing what it is supposed to be doing—lowering the rate and severity of accidents in the plant.

John is not alone in inheriting an educational program that has had, at best, haphazard evaluation. Although evaluation is an essential part of the program process, until fairly recently it has seldom received in practice the attention it deserves (Laird, 1985; Dixon, 1990; Rothwell and Kazanas, 1993). How program evaluation is defined is addressed first in the chapter, followed by a description of a twelve-step process for conducting a systematic program evaluation. Explored next is how unplanned or informal evaluation opportunities can be used. Sample approaches or models for program evaluation are then reviewed, and descriptions are given of ways to collect and analyze evaluation data and to make judgments about programs on the basis of the data presented. The chapter concludes with a discussion of the notion of examining program failures as well as program successes and suggestions for ways to formulate recommendations for current and future programs.

Program Evaluation Defined

Program evaluation is a process used to determine whether the design and delivery of a program were effective and whether the proposed outcomes were met. Evaluation is a continuous process that begins in the planning phase and concludes with follow-up studies (Nadler, 1982; Brinkerhoff, 1987; Bramlay, 1991; Tracey, 1992). Evaluation done to improve or change a program while it is in progress (even in the planning phases) is termed *formative* evaluation. When evaluation focuses on the results or outcomes of a program, it is called *summative* evaluation.

The heart of program evaluation is judging the value or worth of an educational program (Brookfield, 1986; Cervero, 1988; Sork and Caffarella, 1989; Rothwell and Kazanas, 1993). This is not an easy task for three major reasons. First, it may be difficult to demonstrate that program outcomes are really tied to what happened in the program. Factors other than what participants did as part of a planned program and transfer-of-learning activities, as outlined in the previous chapter, may account for the occurrence or nonoccurrence of changes. For example, budget cuts or a lack of backing by key leaders.

Second, developing clear criteria upon which judgments can be made may be hard to do, especially for program outcomes that are not quantifiable or that are unclear at the onset of the program. Even for those outcomes that are quantifiable, the time and effort it takes to formulate the types of measures needed and to collect and analyze the data may not be reasonable in terms of current program resources. (This does not mean, as is explored later in the chapter, that criteria for program success should not be developed; but program staff may have to think differently about the evaluation processes they use and about who is involved.)

Third, some people who plan programs may not want to make judgments about their programs or have others make those judgments. This is especially true in environments where evaluations of any kind are seen as punitive or are used primarily to advance political or personal agendas.

Despite all the difficulties of making judgments about programs, program evaluation serves several purposes. More specifically, the process (1) helps keep staff focused on the goals and objectives of the program, (2) provides information for decision making on all aspects of the program, (3) identifies improvements in the design and delivery of the learning events, (4) increases application of the learning by participants, (5) allows for program accountability, (6) provides data on the major accomplishments of the program, and (7) identifies ways of improving future programs (Steel, 1989; Dixon, 1990; Bramlay, 1991; Branham, 1992). In essence, good program evaluation provides useful feedback to program planners, participants, supervisors of participants, managers and administrators, community groups, and other interested parties.

Planning for Systematic Program Evaluation

There is no one acceptable systematic process for conducting a program evaluation. Rather, a number of descriptions of the process have been developed (for example, Nadler, 1982; Kirkpatrick, 1987; Harris, 1989; Branham, 1992; Rothwell and Kazanas, 1993). A composite description of how to design a systematic evaluation process consisting of twelve steps is outlined. For each step, operational guidelines and an example from practice are given.

Steps	Operational Guidelines	Examples
1. Secure support for the evaluation from those who have a stake in the results of the evaluation (for example, funding agencies, senior management, program staff, community groups).	Receiving written and/or verbal support from those who will be most affected by the evaluation is key. This support may take the form of memos, formal agreements, public announcements, and the like. What should be clear is the scope of the evaluation and the general time frame for completion.	The director of the Division of Education and Training has received two memos, one from the vice president and a second from the major funding agency that endorses the overall scope and timeline for the planned evaluation.
2. Identify the individuals to be involved in planning and overseeing the evaluation.	An individual or team of individuals should be designated to plan and oversee the program evaluation process. Some larger organizations have personnel designated for this function. Others choose to hire outside consultants.	Two staff members from the Division of Education and Training are responsible for the overall design and execution of the evaluation. They will consult with other groups (managers/administrators, participants, funding agency) as needed.
3. Define precisely the purpose of the evaluation and how the results will be used.	The purpose of the evaluation should be stated clearly and understood by all parties involved. It is especially important to meet the expectations of the major stakeholders in the program (for example, participants, supervisors of participants, funding agencies).	The major purpose of the evaluation is to determine whether a specific educational program has produced a major change in the knowledge, skill level, and/or attitudes of the participants. A secondary purpose includes the improvement of the educational unit itself.
4. Specify what will be judged and formulate the evaluation questions.	Major areas that can be judged: • Participant learning • The educational program itself (for example, format, content, staff) • Outcomes of the program (such as changes in people or organizations) • The policies, procedures and practices of the educational unit/function (for example, the program planning process) • The impact of a program on subunits or whole organizations • The impact of a program on communities/society	The major area to be judged is the participants' changes in knowledge and skills (with the educational unit itself secondary). The evaluation questions are these: • Was there a change in the knowledge, skills, and/or attitudes of the participants as a result of the program? • Was this change in knowledge, skills, and/or attitudes maintained over a twelve-month period? • How could the Division of Education and Training be changed to better meet the requirements of the major funding agency and the organization as a whole?
5. Determine who will supply the needed evidence. *(continued on next page)*	Evidence can be gathered from a number of people, such as participants, their supervisors, program staff members, instructors, administrative/ management personnel, customers, community members, and outside consultants.	Evidence will be gathered primarily from participants, their supervisors, and the funding agency. Education and training staff will also be asked to supply some of the data.

Steps	Operational Guidelines	Examples
6. Specify the evaluation approach to be used.	The chosen approach should match the purpose of the evaluation, the nature of the program, and the evaluation questions. The optimal choice of approach may not always be the most feasible or practical.	An objectives-based approach will be used. The objectives to be focused upon are those related to participant learning and the operation of the educational unit.
7. Determine the data collection techniques to be used and when the data will be collected.	The techniques and timing of data collection should be primarily determined by the purpose of the evaluation and the approach chosen. In addition, characteristics of the respondents, the expertise of the evaluators, and the time and cost requirements should be considered.	Three primary techniques will be used to conduct the evaluation: interviews, written questionnaires, and a review of performance records. Data will be collected prior to the program, at the end of the program, and nine months after the program has been completed.
8. Specify the analysis procedure to be used.	The analysis procedures should be related directly to the evaluation questions, the approach, and the kind of data collection techniques used. For quantitative data, they can range from simple numerical counting or computing of percentages to very sophisticated statistical analysis. Qualitative data are usually reported in prose form, though some simple numerical tables are also used.	As the quantitative data are at the nominal level, the analysis will consist of frequency counting and a chi-square statistical procedure. The qualitative data from the interviews will be analyzed for patterns and general themes.
9. Specify what criteria will be used to make judgments about the program or what process will be used to determine the criteria.	The criteria chosen should indicate the level of learning or change that will be considered acceptable. Criteria should be set for each major evaluation question. For programs where the criteria cannot be predetermined, a process for how criteria will eventually emerge should be outlined.	• Participants must be able to demonstrate at the end of the program that they have acquired at least 90 percent of the knowledge and skills presented. Eighty percent of the participants must demonstrate at least 75 percent mastery of the knowledge and skills nine months after completion of the program. • Participant attitude changes will be assessed through the patterns and themes revealed from the interview data. • The Division of Education and Training must demonstrate at least five major changes they have made in policies, procedures, and/or productivity that better meet the requirements of the funding agency and the organization.

(continued on next page)

Steps	Operational Guidelines	Examples
10. Determine the specific timeline and the budget needed to conduct the evaluation.	The timeline may be set and specific (such as before and after a specified program) or be continuous (as in the recording of change in the learning of participants for all programs). Program evaluations cost money, so a realistic budget should be negotiated prior to initiating the process.	The timeline for the quantitative evaluation is this: • Pretest 1: April • Pretest 2: June • Pretest 3: August • Treatment: September • Posttest 1: October • Posttest 2: March Qualitative data will be collected throughout the project. The budget for the evaluation has been set at $3,000 (excluding staff time).
11. Complete the evaluation, formulate recommendations, and prepare and present an evaluation report.	The evaluation report should be clearly and precisely written and should focus on the purpose(s) for the evaluation. Recommendations for changes and future actions should be realistic and should include action strategies for addressing those recommendations. This report should be presented in written form and/or orally to key stakeholders.	An evaluation report will be prepared highlighting participant learning and the changes in the Division of Education and Training. Also included will be recommendations related to future programs and the division itself. The report will be distributed to the vice president and her staff, the head of the funding agency, and the staff of the division. Oral presentations will be given by request.
12. Respond to the recommendations for changes in the overall program, specific learning activities, and/or the educational unit or function.	Recommendations should be acknowledged and, where appropriate, implemented in a timely fashion. Key stakeholders and those affected by the recommendations should be kept informed and, as needed, involved in the change process.	Although it was recommended that this program should be continued, changes were suggested by participants in the format and the instructional methods used. In addition, the funding agency suggested that some of the content be revised. These changes were made and reported back to the participants in an in-house newsletter and the funding agency through three planning sessions. No further recommendations were made concerning the operation of the Division of Education and Training.

Although systematic program evaluations are a desirable and necessary part of the programming process, Knowles (1980), Mayo and DuBois (1987), and Rothwell and Kazanas (1993) have cautioned program planners of four major pitfalls. First, as noted earlier, the outcomes of some educational programs may be too complicated, and the number of variables affecting those outcomes too numerous, to allow planners to demonstrate that a given program actually produced the desired changes. For example, it appeared that one three-week (two hours per day, twice a week) training program increased the proficiency of staff in the use of a new computer networking system. This conclusion was reached by comparing pretest and posttest scores of all workshop participants on the use of the system once the program was completed. Yet when the participants were asked what key element had helped them to increase their proficiency, 95 percent cited on-the-job trial and error. They said that the training program had, in fact, hindered their progress more than helped, because the instructor often gave poor and incomplete descriptions of how to use the new system.

A second pitfall is that current evaluation procedures, however scientifically rigorous, may not be able to provide hard evidence that the more subtle, and at times the most important, aspects of the educational program have been achieved. This is especially so for educational programs whose objectives are to foster major changes in personal, organizational, and/or societal values and beliefs. Third, conducting systematic program evaluations costs time and money, neither of which some organizations and groups are willing to provide if they see no immediate payoff or value for evaluating programs. And fourth, when staff know that no action will or can be taken on the basis of evaluation findings, it may be better not to collect the data at all, because the evaluation process raises expectations on the part of participants and/or sponsors that changes will be forthcoming.

Informal and Unplanned Evaluation Opportunities

Although most models of program planning advocate a formal or systematic process of evaluating programs, informal and often unplanned evaluation opportunities are also very useful; and in some cases, in fact, they are a critical part of a program planner's responsibilities. As with systematic evaluation, these informal evaluation strategies can be used prior to the start of the program, during the program, or after a program has been completed. Several informal and/or unplanned evaluation strategies are illustrated in the following scenarios:

Scenario 1: Prior to the Program

Joan B., the director of the Maternal and Child-Care Department at Hope Hospital, has been overseeing, with the help of an outside consultant, the planning of a three-session staff development program for all of the nurses on her service. She has a gut feeling that what has been proposed—even though it seems to address the problems that have been identified with the delivery of services by her unit—is not really what the nurses need to know to do their jobs more effectively. She decides to talk with three key staff members—people she knows will give her direct and honest feedback about both the format and content of the proposed program. If their reactions are similar to hers, she has enough time and the authority to either ask for changes in the program or, if needed, cancel the consultant's contract.

Scenario 2: During the Program

The atmosphere of the workshop has been tense. The instructors during the morning sessions did not deliver what they had promised, and the participants have been very verbal about how poor the program has been thus far. Sally R., the program coordinator, decides to ask the instructors to meet with her over lunch. Prior to the luncheon meeting, she spends a quick fifteen minutes with three of the participants, getting their reactions to the morning session. Armed with that information and her own perceptions, Sally decides to "lay the major problems on the table" and hopes that the instructors will be able to respond in a positive manner.

Scenario 3: During the Program

Christina A., the vice president for human resource development, decides to attend part of the new training program for nonexempt personnel. She is interested in finding out how receptive the employees are to the training events. Christina randomly chooses three sessions that fit into her schedule. She times her arrival and departure around the coffee break so that she can hear what the trainees are saying informally about the program.

Scenario 4: After the Program

Dave R., the principal of Shelly High School, has heard both directly and through the teacher grapevine that a recent two-day districtwide conference on how to initiate a standards-based curriculum (a new districtwide initiative) was perceived by his teachers as worse than even he thought it was. The content was a jumbled mess of unclear information and how-to tips that were unrealistic for a district of this size. The major outcome of this program appears to be that some teachers are even more opposed to this new initiative; and even those who supported it before are having major doubts. Dave knows that the superintendent and the board are committed to implementing a standards-based curriculum within the next year. He decides to check with three or four other principals to see if they and their teachers reacted the same way to the program. If these principals and their staff had the same reaction, he will ask one or two of those principals to join him at an informal breakfast meeting with the assistant superintendent and the superintendent, who happen to be golfing buddies of his. At the breakfast, he plans to provide them with his informal feedback about the program and offer to help in planning further informational and action agendas around this new initiative.

What is common among these scenarios is that people were willing to both listen to feedback about programs and take action on what they learned.

Whether program evaluations are systematic or informal, it is useful for staff involved with the program planning process to have a working knowledge of the following components of the evaluation process: evaluation approaches, data collection techniques, data analysis procedures, program judgments, and recommendations. These components, which are discussed in the remainder of this chapter, are the nuts and bolts of the evaluation process.

Approaches to Program Evaluation

There are numerous approaches to or models of educational program evaluation. These consist of a framework with relatively explicit perspectives and procedural methods for conducting evaluation. Because evaluation is often a multifaceted endeavor, more than one approach or model may be employed in combination in the evaluation process.

Salient examples of evaluation approaches, along with sample questions and data collection techniques appropriate for each approach, are given in Table 9.1 (Kirkpatrick, 1987; Worthen and Sanders, 1987; McMillan and Schumacher, 1989; Marshall, 1989; Bradley, Kallick, and Regan, 1991; Branham, 1992). As is evident from the description of each approach, there are overlaps and commonalities of focus and techniques between and among the approaches. The broadest overlaps are between the objectives-based approach and the "levels of evaluation" approach, because these two approaches focus on similar areas. In addition, some of the approaches—for example, the case study method—are sometimes used as part of the data collection and analysis process for other approaches.

Table 9.1. Various Approaches to Program Evaluation.

Approach	Description	Sample Questions	Sample Data Collection Techniques
Objectives-Based Review	Determines whether stated objectives of a program have been met. The focus of the objectives is on the participants' learning (with resulting changes in the individual, organizations, and/or society) and/or the program operations.	Have the individual participants learned what they were supposed to learn? Did the program contribute to changes in the organization? Did the program contribute to changes related to societal issues and concerns? Were specified changes made in the program operations?	Observations Interviews Written questionnaires Tests Performance reviews Product reviews Case studies
Systems Evaluation	Provides feedback on the effectiveness of the program planning and execution process, the structure of the educational unit/function, and the efficiency of the use of resources in relation to the outcomes of educational programs. One emphasis is cost-benefit analysis.	Has the process of planning and implementing the program been effective and efficient? Have resources been used wisely in relation to the benefits of the program?	Written questionnaires Interviews Cost-benefit analysis

(continued on next page)

Approach	Description	Sample Questions	Sample Data Collection Techniques
Case Study Method	Gives a "thick description" of what a program looks like from the viewpoint of participants, staff, sponsors, and/or other appropriate groups. It characterizes how a program has been implemented and received.	What are the prominent events/activities respondents would highlight? What value do participants, staff, and stakeholders place on the program? What are the program's strengths and weaknesses from the participants' perspective?	Observations Interviews Organizational/ community records and documents
Quasi-Legal Evaluation	Determines program quality through adversarial hearings. Panels hear a range of evidence (for example, opinions, data-based studies, belief statements) presented in a legalistic fashion. The judgments rest with a majority opinion of the panel members.	Which point of view represents the best judgment about the value or worth of a program? Should the program be continued, modified, or eliminated based on a specified body of evidence?	Interviews Organizational/ community records and documents Product reviews Tests Cost-benefit analysis
Professional or Expert Review	Relies on a panel of experts making judgments, usually based on a predetermined set of categories and standards, about a program (such as program accreditation, formal program reviews). It most often focuses on the resources, processes, and outcomes of large educational programs.	Does the program meet a predetermined set of standards related to the processes and outcomes of the program? Is the program doing what it claims it is doing?	Interviews Organizational records and documents Product reviews
"Levels of Evaluation" Review (Kirkpatrick, 1987)	Measures four different levels or areas: (1) participant reactions, (2) learning, (3) behavior change, and (4) results or outcomes. Focus is primarily on participant reactions and changes and on organizational changes. This approach is most often coupled with the objectives-based model.	Did participants like the program? What knowledge or skills were learned? What values or attitudes were changed? What changes in participant behavior have resulted that can be linked to the program? What overall impact has program had on the organization (for example, reduced cost, improved quality, etc.)?	Written questionnaires Tests Performance reviews Product reviews Cost-benefit analysis

The "levels of evaluation" approach—more specifically, the participant level of that approach—is still the most generally used form of evaluation (Robinson and Robinson, 1989; Munson, 1992). Participants are usually asked to complete some form of questionnaire indicating their opinion on such items as content, instructions, instructional techniques, facilities, and food service. They are also sometimes asked to more generally list the strengths and weaknesses of the program, what they perceive they have learned, and recommendations for future activities. Soliciting participant reactions is most often done at the end of the program. In addition, some program planners also like to request participant feedback for individual sessions within longer programs. For example, at workshops or conferences where there are numerous instructional events, from small-group sessions to large-group presentations, evaluation data are sometimes collected at the end of each session. When evaluation data are generated for individual sessions, these data are used in two ways. The first is to provide feedback to individual instructors and presenters. The second is to contribute to a larger data set focused on evaluating the program as a whole. Two examples of participant reaction forms—a brief form and a more comprehensive one—are given in Exhibits 9.1 and 9.2.

Exhibit 9.1. Sample Participant Questionnaire (Short Form).

Title of Program: _____ Date: _____

Please circle the ratings that best describe your reaction to this session:
1 = No   2 = Somewhat   3 = Yes, definitely

1. Were the session objectives clear?   1   2   3

2. Were the instructional techniques and materials helpful
in your learning of the material?   1   2   3

3. I would rate the instruction overall . . .   1   2   3

4. I would rate the program overall . . .   1   2   3

5. Some information and/or skills I can use from the program: _____

_____

_____

_____

6. Some suggested improvements for this program: _____

_____

_____

Exhibit 9.2. Sample Participant Questionnaire (Long Form).

Title of Program: _____ Date: _____

Please assist us in evaluating the quality of the program by completing this questionnaire. For each question, circle the number that best represents your view: *1 ("No"), 2 ("Somewhat"), and 3 ("Yes, definitely")*. Your specific comments and suggestions for improvement would be most appreciated, especially for those items you marked "No" or "Somewhat."

Have you had prior experience and/or training in this content area? If so, what?

_____

_____

Part 1: Session Content and Process

1. Were the program objectives clear and realistic?   1   2   3

   Comments/suggestions: _____

   _____

2. Did you learn what you expected to learn?   1   2   3

   Comments/suggestions: _____

   _____

3. Was the material presented relevant and valuable to you?   1   2   3

   Comments/suggestions: _____

   _____

4. Was the material presented at an appropriate rate?   1   2   3

   Comments/suggestions: _____

   _____

5. Was there an adequate amount of time allotted to each topic?   1   2   3

   Comments/suggestions: _____

   _____

6. Did the instructional and presentation techniques used adequately
   assist you in learning the material?   1   2   3

   Comments/suggestions: _____

   _____

7. If there were opportunities for you to actively participate
in the various sessions, was this participation beneficial to you?   1   2   3

Comments/suggestions: _____

_____

8. Could you relate the material to your particular life situation?   1   2   3

Comments/suggestions: _____

_____

9. Did the instructional materials and aids used (transparencies,
manuals, videotapes, and the like) enhance the learning process?   1   2   3

Comments/suggestions: _____

_____

10. Was the program well organized and effectively conducted?   1   2   3

Comments/suggestions: _____

_____

Part 2: Presenter Skills*

1. Were the presenters enthusiastic?   1   2   3

Comments/suggestions: _____

_____

2. Were the presenters well prepared?   1   2   3

Comments/suggestions: _____

_____

3. Did the presenters have expert knowledge of the content?   1   2   3

Comments/suggestions: _____

_____

4. Did the presenters make an effort to help you feel comfortable?   1   2   3

Comments/suggestions: _____

_____

5. Did the presenters provide you with adequate assistance in learning the material?   1   2   3

Comments/suggestions: _____

_____

6. Did the presenters communicate well with the participants (for example, use nonsexist language, attend to diversity of audience)?   1   2   3

Comments/suggestions: _____

_____

7. Did the presenters hold your interest?   1   2   3

Comments/suggestions: _____

_____

8. Did the presenters cover the content adequately in the allotted time?   1   2   3

Comments/suggestions: _____

_____

Part 3: Logistical Arrangements

1. Were the registration procedures "participant-friendly"?   1   2   3

Comments/suggestions: _____

_____

2. Was the program schedule well planned (allowing enough time between sessions and for lunch, for example)?   1   2   3

Comments/suggestions: _____

_____

3. Would you recommend that these facilities be used again?   1   2   3

Comments/suggestions: _____

_____

4. Would you want the same food menus again for breaks and meals?   1   2   3

Comments/suggestions: _____

_____

Part 4: Overall Program

1. Will you be able to apply what you have learned in your work, at home, and/or in your personal life? 1 2 3

Comments/suggestions: _____

_____

2. Were you challenged by the content and the way the material was taught?

1 2 3

Comments/suggestions: _____

3. How do you rate the program overall? 1 2 3

Comments/suggestions: _____

_____

4. Please comment on the major strengths of the program and changes you would recommend.

Major strengths: _____

_____

Suggestions for improvement: _____

_____

Any other observations:_____

_____

Thank You for Your Help!

*Part 2 could be modified to enable participants to give feedback on individual presenters/instructors; alternatively, separate evaluation forms could be used for each session.

A second approach that is also often used for program evaluation is the objectives-based approach. In this approach, the program objectives serve as the basis for program evaluation. The purpose, design, and criteria for the evaluation are all drawn from these objectives. This does not mean that other aspects of the program (such as facilities or on-site coordination) are excluded from the evaluation; rather, the program objectives serve as the primary guidepost for the evaluation process. Within this approach, the objectives may address changes in individual participants, in the procedures and practices of the educational unit or the program itself (for example, program formats, instructor competence, program coordination), in the organization, and/or in the community or society.

Collecting Evaluation Data

There are a number of techniques that can be used to collect evaluation data. Each technique can be used alone or in concert with one or more techniques, depending on the purpose, the evaluation approach, and the type of information needed. Other important variables to consider are the types of people administering and responding to the evaluation and the cost of using a given technique. Nine of the most widely used techniques for collecting evaluation data are described below, along with a list of operational guidelines:

Technique	Description	Operational Guidelines
Observations	Watching participants at actual or simulated tasks and recording the knowledge, skills, and/or values/attitudes participants display.	Determine whether these should be open-ended or formally structured (with specific variables to investigate). Observers must have a clear picture of who, how, and what they are observing.
Interviews	Conversations with people (for example, participants, program planners, supervisors, customers) individually or in groups, either in person or by phone.	Determine whether these should be open-ended or formally structured (with specific questions to ask). For formally structured interviews, the interview schedule should be pilot-tested. Interviewers must listen to responses without judging.
Written Questionnaires	Gathering of opinions, attitudes, perceptions, or facts by means of a written series of questions.	Choose from among a variety of question formats: open-ended, ranking, checklists, scales, or forced choices. These can be administered by mail or given to individuals or groups to complete.
Tests	Paper-and-pencil or computer-generated tests used to measure participants' knowledge, skills, or values/attitudes.	Know what the test measures (knowledge, skills, or attitudes/values) and use it as an evaluation tool for only those areas. In addition, make sure the test is both reliable and valid. Choose a test carefully. Check to see whether what it measures is important and relevant.
Product Reviews	Tangible items that participants produce as a result of the program (for example, written materials, portfolios, clay pots, rebuilt engines, flower arrangements, videotapes).	Clearly and precisely define the nature of the project and the criteria on which it will be judged. Participants, whenever possible, should be able to use the products.

Technique	Description	Operational Guidelines
Performance Reviews	Demonstration of a specific skill or procedure (for example, team building, responding to customer complaints, answering a health information line) in either a simulated or a real situation.	Identify specifically what the elements and criteria are for the performance to be evaluated. Determine what tool will be used in the process (such as checklist, rating scale, expert judgment) and ensure consistency.
Organizational/ Community Records and Documents	Written materials developed by organizations and communities. Examples include performance appraisals, production schedules, financial reports, records of absenteeism or attendance, job efficiency indexes, annual reports, committee and board minutes, and records showing hours of training time and numbers of participants involved.	Systematically collect and record data so that they are easy to retrieve and sort.
Portfolios	A purposeful collection of a learner's work assembled over time that documents events, activities, products, and/or achievements.	Include items produced by the learners and attestations from others (for example, honors, awards certificates). These should be used as a vehicle for engaging learners in active reflection.
Cost-Benefit Analysis	A method for assessing the relationship between the outcomes of an educational program and the costs required to produce them.	Develop the cost side of the equation. Include both direct and indirect costs. Calculate the benefit side by focusing on either increasing revenues or decreasing expenses. Evaluators must have quantitatively measurable outcomes to use this technique.

Helpful resources that include more detailed descriptions of specific evaluation techniques include Harris (1989), Robinson and Robinson (1989), Dixon (1990), Simerly (1990), Bradley, Kallick, and Regan (1991), and Tracey (1992).

Many of the same data collection techniques are used both for program evaluation and for generating ideas for educational programs (see Chapter Five). This overlap is not surprising, because pretest or preprogram data are often acquired through a formal needs assessment process. For example, information gathered by on-the-job observations as part of a needs analysis could be used as baseline data for an evaluation study. After an educational program was completed, the change in job performance would be measured against the original needs analysis data. (The type and form of the data would need to be equivalent in both phases, of course.) In addition, some of these techniques (for example, tests, product reviews, and interviews) are also used for instructional evaluation.

Evaluation data can be collected at three major points: prior to the program, during the program, and after the program is completed. The types of information collected at these three major points and examples of where and how this information is gathered are outlined as follows:

When and Where Data Are Collected	Type of Data Collected	How Data Might Be Collected
Prior to the start of the program; at the program site and/or in the environment of the participant	Baseline data on participants' present knowledge, skills, and/or values/attitudes; group, organizational, or community/societal information (for example, policies, operating procedures, specific behaviors, expressed values/attitudes)	Observations and interviews Review of group, organizational, and community records, reports, and so on Questionnaires Tests
During the program; at the program site	Data on participants' learning; participant and staff reactions to the program while it is still in progress	Questionnaires Interviews Tests
At the end of the program; at the program site	Data on participants' learning; participant and staff reactions to the program	Questionnaires Interviews Tests
Well after the program (follow-up studies); in the environment of the participant	Data on participants' knowledge level, performance, and/or values/attitudes; organizational information (for example, changes in policies, procedures, costs); community/societal information (for example, knowledge, actions, values/attitudes)	Observations Interviews Reviews of organizational records Cost-benefit analysis Written documents Questionnaires Product/performance reviews

Evaluation data that are collected before, during, and at the close of programs may include information that is tied directly into the instructional processes (see Chapter Twelve). One example of this type of data is information that instructors request either prior to or right at the start of a learning activity, such as the current knowledge and skill levels of participants in relation to the content being taught. A second example is the data collected either during or after the instructional portion to determine what participants have learned. For programs where only instructional data are collected, these data become the main criteria for making judgments about the value of the program. For example, if the major objective of a program is to teach individual participants specific skills (such as CPR or other emergency medical procedures), then the only data needed might be those that are collected during the instructional phase. For educational and training programs that have objectives beyond individual change, the evaluation data generated as a part of the instructional portion of the program are only one part of the data bank that is needed.

Likewise, evaluation data collected as part of follow-up studies may be gathered during the transfer-of-learning activities (see Chapter Eight). For example, evaluation data could be collected as part of support-group activities through group interviews or observations. Again, as stressed throughout the book, the various components of the program planning and implementation process often overlap and therefore are not necessarily done as separate tasks.

Data Analysis

At whatever point the evaluation data are collected, it is important to have set procedures for analyzing the data, because one of the most frequent flaws in the evaluation process is the inadequate planning of data analysis procedures (Knox, 1986). The following scenario illustrates this problem:

Scenario

Karen W., the director of judicial education for the state and municipal court system, has been asked to prepare an evaluation report covering the last two years of the program. She believes that this should be a fairly easy process, because she has required the collection of evaluation information on all programs. Due to the time constraints of her staff, very little actual analysis of the data has been completed, however (especially in the last year), except on the new educational activities. Karen decides to do a cursory review of the data prior to turning the information over to the two new members of her staff who will actually complete the analysis and do a draft of the report. To her dismay, what she finds in the computer reports is a bunch of figures that do not make sense. Not only have the data been entered differently across programs, but the data recorded are not consistent from program to program. She also finds five file boxes full of written questionnaires that have never been entered into the system and a large stack of handwritten notes from evaluation interviews with key judges and administrative staff. Karen wonders how she and her staff are going to make sense out of all these different sets of data.

Two major kinds of data are generated from program evaluations: quantitative and qualitative (Marshall, 1989; Patton, 1990; Bogdan and Biklen, 1992; Borg, Gall, and Gall, 1993). Quantitative data give precise numerical measures, while qualitative data provide rich descriptive materials. What some program planners do not realize is that these two major types of data are very different and therefore require vastly different competencies of the staff in the analysis phase.

Let us look at how the quantitative and qualitative approaches differ in evaluations focusing on various issues:

Evaluations Focusing on Participants' Learning

Quantitative. Participants take tests that measure changes in their knowledge, skill levels, and/or values/beliefs. The test scores are recorded in the training records and compared to the pretest scores.

Qualitative. Observations are made by the instructors on the extent of change in participants' knowledge, skill levels, and/or attitudes. These observations result in twenty-five pages of acceptable data.

Evaluations Focusing on Program Operations

Quantitative. Using a five-point Likert Scale, department heads and selected participants rate specific procedures and practices of the educational unit (for example, ways program ideas are generated, program formats, how participants for programs are chosen, funding for programs). These ratings are then compiled and analyzed, and a two-page numerical summary is given to all education staff.

Qualitative. Department heads and staff are interviewed, using open-ended questions about their perceptions of the effectiveness of the educational unit. About 100 pages of transcripts, transcribed from ten audiotapes, need to be analyzed.

Evaluations Focusing on Organizational Issues

Quantitative. After a revised training program for new agency volunteers, the percentage of new volunteers who remain with the program will be assessed. The director of volunteers will do a percentage count after one month, and then again after three months, by checking the computer records kept on all volunteer activities.

Qualitative. The director of volunteers and the staff who work directly with the volunteers will be asked if the new training program made a difference in the way they provided services to the clients of the agency. Notes will be taken at each of the interviews and transcribed so that training staff can review them.

Evaluations Focusing on Societal Issues

Quantitative. A random sample of community members is surveyed via a structured telephone interview to determine whether a recent series of newspaper articles on violent acts in the community has led to more people becoming involved in neighborhood programs for safer communities. Whenever respondents indicate that they have become more active, the type of activity and the setting are recorded.

Qualitative. Staff and members of five neighborhood groups for safer communities are asked in group meetings if they perceive the newspaper articles as having been useful in generating community support for their programs. Extensive notes are taken by two recorders and then transcribed and reviewed.

For some evaluations, only quantitative data or qualitative data are needed; for others, both types of data are required. In addition, some program evaluations rely on single data sources (such as questionnaires or performance demonstrations), whereas others require multiple data sources before complete responses to evaluation questions can be provided. This notion of single and multiple data sources linked to specific evaluation questions, data collection techniques, and resulting types of data is illustrated in Table 9.2.

Table 9.2. Interrelated Issues of Data Collection in Evaluation.

Type of Data Source Needed	Sample Evaluation Questions	Sample Data Collection Techniques	Kinds of Data
Single data source	What new skills were learned by participants as a result of the train-the-trainer program?	Observations of participants before and after training	Qualitative Quantitative
	Did participants feel that the instructors were effective and the content was useful in the program on communication skills?	Questionnaires administered right after the program	Quantitative
	Did the parents believe that the information and skills taught them through a series of seminars on "Coping with Your Teenager" were useful?	Telephone interviews a month after the seminar series was completed	Quantitative Qualitative
	Was there a reduction in the rate of turnover for new employees that could be attributed to the orientation program?	Review of company turnover rates for new employees three months after the program	Quantitative
Multiple data sources	What changes in the participants' job performances were an outcome of the leadership development program?	On-the-job observations, interviews, and performance appraisals three and then six months after the programs	Qualitative Quantitative
	As a result of the training program, are the volunteers effective instructors and/or coordinators of educational programs?	Questionnaires, observations, and interviews three months after the program	Qualitative Quantitative
	Did the training of staff in total quality management (TQM) result in a cost savings to the organization?	Review of company records and a cost-benefit analysis on a quarterly basis for two years	Quantitative
	Are more and different groups of people participating in community performing arts events as a result of educational programs on the arts for children and parents in area schools?	Review of ticket sales over a six-month period and questionnaires sent to parents	Quantitative

When different kinds of data and multiple data sources are used, a failure to outline the data analysis procedures clearly beforehand can be especially problematic. (This was illustrated earlier in the scenario about Karen W.)

In choosing data analysis procedures, the evaluation questions, approaches, data collection techniques, and kinds of data collected must be considered. For evaluations that produce quantitative data, as noted earlier, some sort of numerical values are assigned, from simple counting to complex statistical analysis (Shavelson, 1988; McMillan and Schumacher, 1989; Krathwohl, 1993). Qualitative analysis provides in-depth descriptions, usually in the form of words or visuals rather than numbers (Patton, 1990; Glesne and Peshkin, 1992). Content and thematic analysis is one of the most often used methods for reviewing qualitative data. More detailed descriptions of specific analysis procedures can be found in Patton (1990), Bogdan and Biklen (1992), and Krathwohl (1993).

If the program planning staff are unfamiliar with how to do data analysis, especially when complex procedures are needed, an outside consultant is usually a good investment. "People with such expertise may be higher education specialists or may be engaged in evaluation or market research in a business or community agency" (Knox, 1986, p. 168).

Making Judgments About the Program

Program planners make judgments on the worth of the program as they interpret the data compiled during the analysis phase. This judgment process involves bringing together various pieces of the information gathered and supplying answers to the evaluation questions (Chalofsky, 1985; Tracey, 1992). Was what the participants learned in a program worthwhile? Were the objectives of the program addressed in an effective and efficient manner? Do management and administrative personnel believe the educational program gives vital assistance in fulfilling the mission and goals of the organization? Does the program address compelling community and societal concerns? These judgments provide the basis for making final conclusions and recommendations concerning the content and the operation of the educational program.

Judgments about programs should be based primarily on criteria related to the program processes and/or outcomes and should be reached by comparing results of the data analysis with the criteria that were set (or emerged) for each evaluation question or objective. For those criteria that were predetermined and are measurable, the judgments are quite simple: the changes produced by the program either meet the criteria as stated or they do not. Examples of this are given below.

Evaluation Question	Criterion	Findings Based on Analysis Process	Interpretation and Conclusions
Focusing on participants' learning. Did the participants in the program on supervisory skills gain sufficient knowledge in this content area?	Participants will score 85 or better on a knowledge test of supervisory skills.	Thirty-eight of the forty participants scored 85 or better on a knowledge test of supervisory skills.	The majority of participants mastered the material; thus the program was termed highly successful.

(continued on next page)

Evaluation Question	Criterion	Findings Based on Analysis Process	Interpretation and Conclusions
Focusing on program operations. Are the program staff effective instructors and facilitators for in-house educational programs?	The staff will achieve a four-point rating or better on a five-point scale on their skills as instructors and facilitators. The data will be drawn from twenty-five randomly selected programs over a six-month period.	All but one of the staff were given an overall four-point rating based on the data drawn from twenty-five program evaluations of randomly selected educational programs.	The staff as a whole were seen as very effective instructors and facilitators for in-house educational programs.
Focusing on organizational issues. Was there a reduction in the turnover rate for new employees that could be attributed to the orientation program?	There will be a reduction of 20 percent in the turnover rate of new employees over a six-month period.	The turnover rate was reduced by 10 percent during a specified six-month period.	The orientation program did not produce the desired effect. Therefore, the problem of high turnover needs to be examined for alternative interventions (for example, changes in supervisory behavior or working conditions).
Focusing on societal issues. Was there an increase in the number of people who became volunteers for their local neighborhood action programs for safer communities as a result of a series of newspaper articles, neighborhood informational meetings, and flyers sent to all community households?	There will be a 5 percent increase in the number of people who volunteer to work with their neighborhood action programs for safer communities.	The percentage of volunteers increased an average of 8 percent.	Since the increase in the percentage of new volunteers exceeded program goals, the educational efforts via newspaper articles, neighborhood meetings, and flyers were judged to be highly successful.

A word of caution must be included even for programs for which the criteria are predetermined and measurable: unless the evaluation design is sophisticated enough to control for all the variables that could affect the outcomes, program planners must be careful not to attribute success or lack of success to their educational program without considering other contextual variables.

It is much more difficult to make judgments about programs for which the criteria are less clear and/or cannot or should not be stated in advance. The following scenario illustrates a program for which criteria are difficult to develop. The planners for this program might not be able to describe up front exactly what the tangible outcomes might be.

Scenario

The major staff development goal for administrators and instructors of Mountain Plains Community College is to have all staff use open and honest communication styles and to work on rebuilding trust between and among staff members. Those who have been working at the college for the last two years know that communication has been a problem; little trust exists between the instructors and administrators and between and among some of the instructional staff. It is a tough agenda, but one that most staff are committed to—even those who have been the most angry and disillusioned. The catalyst for this commitment has been twofold: the hiring of a new president and public statements by respected instructors that students are being negatively affected by the actions of both instructors and administrators. A one-day retreat will be held at a rustic mountain resort as the initial activity for addressing this problem.

Educational programs that focus on the kinds of changes that are difficult, if not impossible, to quantify (such as the program described in the above scenario) challenge program planners to think differently about who should define criteria (and when and how) and the judgment process itself. The use of qualitative evaluation approaches such as in-depth case studies has recently become an accepted alternative to developing up-front criteria. In this sort of qualitative approach, the criteria for judging the worth and value of the program are grounded in the major themes that emerge during the evaluation process and are highly contextualized to that particular setting. Unfortunately, qualitative evaluations are usually costly and call for evaluators with high levels of expertise. So how else could this be done?

A second strategy in the case of hard-to-quantify outcomes is to ask program participants to serve as the primary judges of whether the program has worked. This means that the criteria for program success start with individual perceptions of worth and value rather than preset standards. For most programs, these criteria will continue to change as the program unfolds. For some programs, such as the program described in the scenario above, it is important to make the emerging individual criteria public, with the explicit goal of working toward criteria that are mutually agreed upon. For other programs, such as support- or self-help groups, the criteria could remain highly personalized for each program participant. Allowing participants the freedom to form their own criteria for judging program quality and success, whether these criteria remain personalized or become a collective statement, means acceptance by program planners of multiple ways of saying programs are worthwhile. For example, returning to the scenario of Mountain Plains Community College, criteria could range from explicit statements such as, "Trust means that when I ask people to do something they will do it, and do it well," to very open-ended observations such as, "I feel better, and therefore the program was great," or "The new communication system just *feels* right, even though I can't put my finger on exactly why it's working." Sample ways in which these kinds of judgments can be made include self-reflection, reflective group procedures, and reviews of participants' written logs. In some cases, an outside consultant may be needed to assist in making this kind of judgment process work.

Examining Program Failures

In interpreting the evaluation data on an educational program, both the successes and the failures should be examined in terms of the realities of the situation (Sork, 1991a). Too often only the successes are highlighted; the process of trying to understand the failures is neglected. Sork (1991b), based on his earlier work (1987) and that of Sork, Kalef, and Worsfold (1987), developed the following typology of four types of program failures.

In Type 1 problems, planning for the program is partially completed but is terminated before implementation. Likely causes of failure include the following:
- Unclear organizational goals or mandates
- Ill-defined client/customer systems
- Incomplete knowledge of resource constraints
- Excessively costly or complex tentative design
- Lack of follow-through

In Type 2 problems, planning for the program is completed, but because the program does not attract sufficient enrollment, it is canceled. These problems are often due to one of these causes:
- Inappropriate pricing, scheduling, and/or location
- Lack of interest by potential participants, organizations, and/or the community
- Poorly focused or timed marketing
- More attractive competition
- Market saturation
- Inadequate support services

In Type 3 problems, planning for the program is completed and the program is offered, but the program does not provide the participants what they expected. The participants then either fail to complete the program or react very negatively to it. The fault may lie with:
- Poor instructors
- Poor coordinator
- Unclear objectives
- Mismatch between content and the participants' needs
- Poor quality of non-instructional resources

In Type 4 problems, the program is offered and the participants express satisfaction, but there is clear evidence that the program failed to achieve the goals and objectives for which it was designed. Among the likely causes of failure are these:
- Ineffective instruction
- Unclear objectives

- Miscommunication of objectives
- Unrealistic expectations
- Mismatch between objectives and program format and instructional techniques
- Inadequate provision for transfer of learning

Source: Adapted from Sork, 1991b, pp. 90–92.

Sork (1991b) goes on to discuss how to use these program failures to develop sound principles and practices of program development. For example, a Type 3 failure—a program that does not provide participants what they expected—might be avoided by planners who pay careful attention up front to ensuring that the program objectives match the participants' needs, who select instructors who are competent, are knowledgeable, and have a reputation for delivering what they say they will deliver, and who are willing to make changes in the program while it is being conducted if it is not meeting the participants' needs and/or is not being delivered as promised.

In addition, Sork (1981, 1991a, 1991b) has outlined ideas for specific procedures for analyzing and responding to program mistakes and failures. One systematic process for doing this is a postmortem program audit (Sork, 1981; Sork, Kalef, and Worsfold, 1987). Samples of important questions used for such an audit are these:

- What was the dollar value of personnel time devoted to this activity?
- How much money (other than for personnel) was expended on this activity?
- What event or evidence led to this activity being judged a failure?
- What are the consequences associated with this failure?
- What could have been done to avoid this failure?

More specific procedures and worksheets for doing this kind of audit are contained in a manual by Sork, Kalef, and Worsfold (1987). These authors stress that postmortem program audits should be timely and include as many staff who were involved with the program activity as possible. In addition, they caution that these procedures can be very difficult to do, because not all the facts may be known and what *is* known may be the product of people's imagination.

Formulating Recommendations

One of the final steps in the evaluation process is formulating recommendations concerning the educational program (Chalofsky, 1985; Tracey, 1992). The recommendations should focus on both reviewing the current program and planning future programs. Recommendations can be made regarding program planning and delivery, program content, program outcomes and impact, ideas for new programs, and how the educational function could more effectively and efficiently serve the organization/community. For example, it might be recommended that administrators and managers become more active in planning programs for their staff.

The program recommendations should be grouped by major issues or topics, address the original evaluation questions, and include any new observations that might have emerged. Each recommendation should also include clearly described strategies for addressing the recommendations and a list of the resources that would be needed to respond. One useful format for recommendations is shown in Exhibit 9.3.

Exhibit 9.3. Sample Format for Program Recommendations.

Recommended Actions	Alternative Strategies for Addressing the Recommended Actions	Resources Needed to Respond

Recommendations regarding further evaluation efforts may also be helpful. These recommendations could address such issues as the usefulness of the evaluation questions, the appropriateness of the evaluation approach and data collection techniques, and the clarity of the analysis and reporting procedures. For example, specific recommendations could be made concerning the format and questions on an instrument used to gather evaluation information. (A questionnaire might have been perceived as too long, too technically worded, and thus too cumbersome for many of the respondents to complete, for example.)

Chapter Highlights

Program evaluation is a process used to determine whether the design and delivery of a program was effective and whether program outcomes were achieved—those outcomes that emerged as the program progressed as well as those that were anticipated. The heart of program evaluation lies in judging the value and worth of a program, which is not an easy assignment. The program design and delivery are usually easier to evaluate than program outcomes; because outcome measures are often elusive, their use in judgments as to whether a specific program was worthwhile or not is problematic.

Program planners should take advantage of informal and unplanned evaluation opportunities that take place throughout program development and implementation as well as systematically designed program evaluation procedures. In formulating evaluation plans, program planners should thus consider both formal and informal evaluation processes as valid sources of evaluation data. In preparing evaluation plans, program planners should concentrate on five major tasks:

- Specify the evaluation approach or approaches that will be used (for example, objectives-based, quasi-legal), including informal or unplanned evaluation opportunities.
- Determine how the evaluation data will be collected (for example, observations, questionnaires, product reviews).
- Think through how the data will be analyzed, including data that were collected through any informal evaluation processes.
- Describe how judgments will be made about the program, using predetermined and/or emergent evaluation criteria for program success.
- Develop recommendations for current and/or future programming based on the judgments that were made and suggest ideas for how to address these recommendations, including what resources would be needed.

In using the evaluation process as a tool for revising current programs and planning future programs, it is important to examine programs that were judged to be failures as well as those that were seen as successes. Often the success or failure of a program is tied to "behind the scenes" aspects of the planning process—those critical components and tasks that program participants are not usually aware of until they arrive on the scene (and perhaps not even then), such as choosing appropriate program formats, scheduling, budgeting, and marketing. These important components of the planning process are addressed in the next two chapters of the book.

Applications Exercises

These Applications Exercises will assist you in planning a systematic program evaluation (Exhibit 9.4), weighing evaluation alternatives (Exhibit 9.5), examining program failures (Exhibit 9.6), and formulating program recommendations (Exhibit 9.7).

Exhibit 9.4. Planning a Systematic Program Evaluation.

1. Briefly describe an educational program for which you need to do a systematic evaluation.

_____

_____

2. Using the following twelve-step process, develop a plan for evaluating the program you described in the previous question.

Steps	Your Evaluation Plan
1. Secure support for the evaluation effort from those who have a stake in the results of the evaluation.	
2. Identify the individuals to be involved in planning and overseeing the evaluation process.	
3. Define precisely the purpose of the evaluation and how the results will be used.	
4. Specify what will be judged and formulate the evaluation questions.	
5. Determine who will supply the needed evidence.	
6. Specify the evaluation approach to be used.	
7. Determine the data collection techniques to be used and when the data will be collected.	
8. Specify the analysis procedures to be used.	
9. Specify what criteria will be used to make judgments about the program or what process will be used to determine the criteria.	
10. Determine the specific timeline and the budget needed to conduct the evaluation.	
11. Complete the evaluation, formulate recommendations, and prepare and present an evaluation report.	
12. Respond to the recommendations for changes.	

3. Ask a colleague and/or your planning group to review what you have proposed, and revise your plan based on the feedback you receive.

Exhibit 9.5. Weighing Alternative Ways to Evaluate Educational Programs.

List at least three ways, other than a systematic evaluation process, that you have used in evaluating educational programs. Indicate next to each alternative whether what you did was helpful and describe briefly why or why not.

Alternative Ways to Evaluate Educational Programs	Helpful? (Why or Why Not)
1.	
2.	
3.	

Exhibit 9.6. Examining Program Failures.

1. Briefly describe an educational program you helped plan that, in your opinion, was a failure.

_____

_____

_____

2. Using the Sork typology as a guide, determine the type of program failure suffered by the program you named in the previous question. Then list the probable causes of the failure and outline what you could do differently next time to develop a better program.

Type of failure: _____

_____

_____

Probable causes of failure:_____

_____

_____

What you could do to develop a better program:_____

_____

_____

_____

Exhibit 9.7. Formulating Program Conclusions and Recommendations.

1. Using information from a program evaluation you have been involved with, fill in the following chart.

Evaluation Question or Area Judged	Way Data Were Collected and Analyzed	Criteria Used	Judgments Made	Recommendations Suggested

2. Were any of the processes or procedures used unclear? Are there blank spaces on your chart? If the answer to either question is yes, how might you have made this evaluation a more complete process? More specifically, what might you have done differently?

_____

_____

_____

_____

_____

Determining Formats, Schedules, and Staff Needs

As part of her work with the planning team responsible for putting together a three-year training grant for teachers working in literacy programs in both the public and private sectors, Rebecca M. has been asked to provide the group some alternative ideas for how the program could be structured. In the past, the training program has consisted primarily of a week-long summer workshop, a statewide resource center, and individual consultation services. This move to restructure the training program and provide some different formats for learning has come from two sources. The first is the funding guidelines, which specifically state that grants that incorporate a technological component as part of the training program will have a higher priority for funding. The second is that the background and needs of many of the teachers have changed. The teachers now tend to be older, have more experience with adult learners, and express more frustration with fitting the week-long training session in with their other professional and personal obligations. Rebecca wonders which of the many training formats might work best for what has become a very diverse group of learners. She is intrigued by new technology but unsure that present staff members have the expertise to implement the technological component without a lot of up-front training themselves. With these two parameters in mind, she decides the best strategy in suggesting how to restructure the training program is to link her suggestions to (1) completing a formal needs assessment of present teachers, which focuses on their preferences for learning formats, and (2) assessing what the different learning formats would mean in terms of current staff expertise and roles.

With the alternatives widening for how educational programs can be structured and delivered, dilemmas around the "right" choice or choices for learning formats (and what these formats mean for program scheduling and staffing) are not uncommon for program planners. In order to make good decisions, people who plan programs must first be aware of their choices of format and then understand how these choices affect how programs can be both scheduled and staffed. This chapter first describes five major formats for learning, with specific examples given for each. Outlined next are samples of program schedules, which demonstrate both single and combined uses of program formats. The chapter concludes with a discussion of staffing issues, including the different roles staff need to play, the use of external consultants, and the importance of obtaining effective instructors/facilitators.

Determining the Program Format(s)

Program format refers to how educational activities are structured and organized. Five kinds of formats are used in educational and training programs: formats for individual learning, formats for small-group (face-to-face) learning, formats for large-group (face-to-face) learning, formats for distance learning, and formats for community learning (Knowles, 1980; Levine and Broude, 1989; Seaman and Fellenz, 1989; Duning, Van Kekerix, and Zaborowski, 1993). These are not discrete categories; indeed, some formats can easily fit into more than one category. For example, although a workshop is usually viewed as a small-group activity, it can also be used for a large group of people (with the large group divided into smaller workgroups so that the flavor of the intensive interaction and product orientation is not lost). In addition, program formats are often used in combination. A video conference, for example, might be integrated into a locally sponsored program at which participants also become involved in face-to-face small- or large-group interactions and/or individualized learning formats.

In the past, educational programs for adults have been equated primarily with face-to-face learning in groups. With the advent of expanding technological options and the recognition that learning via individual modes is a key way through which adults learn, program planners are incorporating more such formats into their programs. Brief descriptions of a variety of options within each of the five categories of learning formats are given here:

Individual Formats

- *Apprenticeship.* Formal relationship between an employer and employee by which the employee is trained for a craft or skill through practical experience under the supervision of experienced workers.

- *Coaching.* One-on-one learning by demonstration and practice, with immediate feedback, conducted by peers, supervisors, and/or experts in the field.

- *Programmed instruction.* Use of programmed texts and booklets. Material is presented in a planned sequence of steps, with immediate feedback given on the extent of a person's learning.

- *Self-directed learning.* A form of study in which learners have the primary responsibility for planning, carrying out, and evaluating their own learning experiences. Adults use people (such as friends, family, content experts) and other types of resources in this process. A personalized learning plan or contract is often used to document this type of format.

- *Mentoring.* An intense, caring relationship in which someone with experience works with a less experienced person to promote both professional and personal growth. Mentors model expected behavior and values and provide support and a sounding board for the protégé.

- *Clinical supervision.* A collegial practice designed to support and provide feedback to experienced staff who generally are good at what they do. The process, consisting of five steps (preobservation conference, observation and data collection, analysis and strategy session, follow-up conference, and postconference analysis), is used to refine practice.

- *On-the-job training.* Instruction provided by a master or expert worker to a novice while both are on the job and engaged in productive work. This format is often used when the work is complex and the worker or craftsperson is the best person to pass on the knowledge and skills to other workers.

- *Computer-based instruction (CBI).* Delivery of instruction by a computer. This instruction may take the form of drill and practice, tutorials, simulations, modeling, and problem solving. CBI can also be used as a part of distance-learning programs.

- *Electronic mail.* The exchange of correspondence by way of computer. Although the correspondence can be much like traditional mail, it moves virtually instantaneously from sender to receiver. The receiver's computer has an electronic "mailbox" that holds the mail until it is read.

- *Writing.* Writing of all kinds (for example, reflective journals, articles, poetry, books). Although writing provides a powerful individual format for learning, it can also be used as a small-group format (if, for example, writers work together to share and critique their work).

Small-Group (Face-to-Face) Formats

- *Courses/classes.* Groups with a definite enrollment that meet at predetermined times for the purpose of studying a specified subject matter under the direction of an instructor. These classes may be part of a distance-learning program or be held at only one site.

- *Seminars.* A focus on learning from discussions of knowledge, experiences, and projects of group members. Participants in these groups must have knowledge and skills in the content of the seminar. Instructors act primarily as resource persons and facilitators.

- *Workshops.* Intensive group activities that emphasize the development of individual skills and competencies in a defined content area. The emphasis in this format is on group participation and products.

- *Collaborative research projects.* Groups of people working together to respond to research questions related to practice. The final product would include both research findings and conclusions and an action plan related to this material.

- *Clinics.* Sessions that focus on a single problem or skill as participants present case illustrations of practice problems to an expert or panel of experts. The experts serve in consultant roles.

- *Trips/tours.* A group field visit for on-site observation and learning. Trips provide the opportunity for further experiences with people, places, and situations that cannot be found in a formal classroom setting.
- *Support groups.* Groups in which people work together on shared problems or practices. Usually participation is voluntary, and sharing and equal status among group members are the norm. In some cases, a trained facilitator may work with this type of learning group.
- *Decision support labs.* Groups of learners, using an interactive computer network, can make group decisions and learn a variety of decision-making and problem-solving techniques.

Large-Group (Face-to-Face) Formats
- *Conferences/conventions.* One or more days of meetings, one of the primary purposes of which is education—to present information, exchange experiences, improve skills, learn new skills, and/or engage in problem-solving activities. Sessions include large- and small-group meetings, and a variety of instructional strategies are used.
- *Clubs and other types of organized groups.* Groups that frequently engage in activities that foster learning as part of their agenda (for example, hobby clubs, physical fitness groups, computer users groups), although hosting educational programs may not be their primary purpose. This can also be a small-group format, depending on the size of the club or group.
- *Networks.* Loosely configured groups of people with similar experiences, interests, problems, or ideas who come together to give and receive information and to provide mutual support and assistance.
- *Institutes.* Intensive sessions, usually over several days, emphasizing the acquisition of knowledge and skill in a specialized area of practice.
- *Lecture series.* A series of presentations by one or more speakers who offer material on a given topic over a specified period of time.
- *Exhibits.* A stationary display of ideas, products, and/or processes. Resource people may be available to respond to questions about the content of the exhibit.

Distance-Learning Formats
- *Correspondence study.* Prepared printed instructional materials (for example, course syllabi, manuals, texts, worksheets) that are delivered to the home or office. Participants engage in reading and/or other learning activities and send assignments to instructors to evaluate.
- *Audio-conferencing.* The linking of one or more sites by telephone to provide for live, interactive verbal exchanges of information between and among program participants and instructors. Conference phones and networks are used to enhance group interaction.

- *Video-conferencing.* Delivery of educational programs via one-way video or two-way video to one or more locations. With two-way video, distinct sites can send and receive both motion video and audio.

- *Broadcast/cable television.* Educational programs transmitted by private and public broadcasting stations as well as cable television companies. The television production may stand alone or be part of a larger program effort (for example, college courses that are offered via television).

- *Satellite communication.* Delivery of video and audio educational programs that can be picked up by satellite reception dishes in homes, hotels, businesses, and other sites. This does not generally provide for interaction between and among learners and instructors, however (as does video-conferencing).

Community-Learning Formats

- *Community resource centers.* Centers that offer learning opportunities to individuals and groups within the community. Examples of community resource centers include museums, libraries, community schools, and learning exchanges.

- *Community development.* Centered on educators who serve as resource people or consultants to action-oriented groups focusing on community change. The community serves as the laboratory for learning.

- *Community action groups.* Groups that are formed for the primary purpose of social action (for example, churches, human rights groups, civic organizations). Although their primary purpose may not be learning, many of these groups organize activities that foster learning and development.

More detailed information about these formats can be found in Levine (1989), Heinich, Molenda, and Russell (1989), Galbraith (1990a, 1990b), Ostendorf (1993), and Piskurich (1993). Again, as stressed earlier and noted in some of the format descriptions, this categorization of format examples is only *one* of the illustrative categorizations that could be used. What is key is that program planners think in terms of alternative formats for learning, recognizing that there is no one right (and sometimes no one *best*) way to structure a specific program.

In choosing a format or formats for learning, six factors should be considered: the background and experience of the participants, availability and expertise of staff, cost, types of facilities and equipment, program content, and program outcomes. Especially for more comprehensive programs, planners are advised to include more than one format so that a wide range of styles and conditions for learning can be accommodated. "Besides, a variety of formats adds to the aesthetic quality of a program by giving it a sense of liveliness and rhythm, and a richer texture" (Knowles, 1980, p. 130).

Scheduling the Program

Once the format is chosen, program planners can identify the appropriate length and breakdown of the program and set specific dates and program schedules. Three examples of program schedules are given in Exhibit 10.1.

Exhibit 10.1. Sample Program Schedules.

Example 1: Single-Format Three-Day Conference

Day 1	Registration	10:00 A.M.–Noon
	Opening luncheon with speaker	Noon–1:45 P.M.
	Session 1	2:00–3:30 P.M.
	Break	3:30–4:00 P.M.
	Session 2	4:00–5:30 P.M.
	Reception	6:00–7:00 P.M.
	Dinner with entertainment	7:00–9:00 P.M.
Day 2	General session	8:30–10:00 A.M.
	Break	10:00–10:30 A.M.
	Session 2	10:30–Noon
	Luncheon	Noon–1:30 P.M.
	Session 3	2:00–4:30 P.M.
	Tea time	4:30–7:00 P.M.
	Awards banquet	7:00–9:00 P.M.
	Reception	9:00–11:00 P.M.
Day 3	Session 1	9:00–10:30 A.M.
	Break	10:30–11:00 A.M.
	Closing session (2) and brunch	11:00 A.M.–1:00 P.M.

Example 2: Multiple-Format Field Trip

8:00 A.M.	Departure from home organizations
10:00 A.M.	Arrival at destination for site visit
10:00–11:00 A.M.	Refreshments and overall introduction to organization and program
11:00 A.M.–12:30 P.M.	Tour of facilities
12:30–1:30 P.M.	Lunch in organization's cafeteria
1:30–3:30 P.M.	Choice of one of three in-depth seminars related to different operating divisions of the organization
3:30–4:30 P.M.	Small-group sessions of electronic mail interest groups (with participants assigned according to job responsibilities)

4:30–5:00 P.M.	Wrap-up session
5:15 P.M.	Departure (trip includes dinner stop)
9:00 P.M.	Arrival at home organizations

Example 3: Multiple-Format One-Day Conference

8:00 A.M.	Registration and coffee
8:30–9:30 A.M.	Introductory session
9:30–10:00 A.M.	Small-workgroup sessions
10:00–10-30 A.M.	Break
10:30 A.M.–Noon	Video-conferencing with panel of national experts
Noon–1:30 P.M.	Lunch
1:30–3:30 P.M.	Small-workgroup sessions
3:30–3:45 P.M.	Break
3:45–4:30 P.M.	Development of individual action plans

In finalizing the dates for the program, planners must take care that the times chosen fit into the participants' personal and/or job schedules. Few, if any, educational programs should be scheduled around times when the target audience may have other pressing commitments, such as a seasonally heavy load at work, family responsibilities, and religious celebrations. For example, to hold educational programs for managers or their secretaries during budget preparation time is not advisable. Likewise, programs should not be planned on or near major holidays or vacation times, unless a vacation package option (including, for example, sightseeing tours and special hotel rates) is seen as part of the marketing strategy.

Identifying Program Staff

Staff are needed to design, coordinate, conduct, and evaluate educational programs. One person may take on all these tasks or the tasks may be divided among a number of people, depending on the size and complexity of the educational function and the program being planned. However the tasks are divided, program planners must take on these four major roles (Nadler, 1982; Harris, 1989; Birnbrauer, 1993; Rothwell and Kazanas, 1993):

- *Program designer.* Individual(s) responsible for designing the program. This entails such tasks as gathering ideas for programs, setting program priorities, developing objectives, planning transfer-of-learning activities, and preparing budgets and marketing plans.

- *Program coordinator.* Individual(s) responsible for coordinating the program and ensuring that all housekeeping tasks related to planning, conducting, and evaluating the program are completed in a timely manner. Such tasks include arranging facilities, registering participants, and doing the onsite monitoring of programs. In carrying out this role, individuals may act as information givers, brokers, counselors, resource specialists, and/or administrators.

- *Instructor/facilitator.* Individual(s) responsible for designing and/or delivering the instruction and directly assisting participants to achieve their learning objectives using a variety of learning techniques and devices. The development of more complex instructional packages (for example, mediated learning modules) requires staff with specialized expertise, from instructional designers to production teams.
- *Program evaluator.* Individual(s) responsible for making judgments about the value and results of the program (after specifying what will be judged, by whom, how, and on what criteria).

Some of the program designer's specific tasks (such as compiling lists of ideas and needs for programs, determining program objectives, and planning transfer-of-learning activities) are discussed in Chapters Five, Six, Seven, Eight, and Eleven and earlier in this chapter. A more detailed description of the evaluator role is given in Chapter Nine, while the roles of instructor and coordinator are discussed in Chapters Twelve and Thirteen, respectively. The various tasks of the four roles are not necessarily discrete. For example, although the program coordinator usually arranges the facilities and equipment, the program designer may choose to do this task because of specific design requirements that a coordinator may not understand. And for smaller programs, the roles of program designer, coordinator, instructor, and evaluator may all be handled by one person or shared by a team of people.

Deciding to Use External Staff

Program staff, whether they be paid or volunteer, may be internal to the organization or they may be hired from the outside. Sometimes a mix of organizational personnel and external consultants are used. For example, while an internal staff person may coordinate and evaluate an educational program, outside consultants may be responsible for the design and delivery of that program.

Munson (1992) has outlined five factors to consider in selecting external consultants:

- *Caliber of the people.* Are the individuals both competent and capable? Will they be credible to your organization and the participants?
- *Quality of their materials.* Are the materials the outside consultants will use or develop (for example, manuals, transparencies, videos) of good educational quality? Will these materials be useful to the participants?
- *Adaptability.* Are the outside consultants willing to adapt their materials and/or their presentations to fit the specific needs of the buying organization?
- *Scope and depth of available resources.* Do the outside consultants add to the scope and depth of the present educa-

tional resources of the organization?

- *Cost.* Will the outside consultants cost more than internal staff for the same activity? If so, is this additional cost justifiable?

There are two primary sources for locating outside staff: other organizations and private consulting firms. It is critical that program planners check out consultants carefully prior to signing a formal contract. This process should involve face-to-face discussions, a review of materials, and, when possible, sitting in on a session the person or consulting group is conducting. In addition, information about prospective consultants can be gathered by talking with knowledgeable colleagues and the consultants' former clients. In considering using university faculty as consultants, planners may find it helpful to also ask the opinion of current or former students of the faculty members.

Outside staff are usually paid in one of three different ways: by the hour, by the program, or by a percentage of income for a specific program (Nilson, 1989). No matter how they are paid, however, it is important that the hiring organization negotiate a written contract for services. The following checklist, based on the work of Nilson (1989), Munson (1992), and Tracey (1992), indicates what the negotiation process and the contract or letter of agreement should address:

- A brief description of the program, project, or service
- What the consultant's responsibilities will be (for example, developing instructional modules, serving as the instructor, developing and conducting the program evaluation)
- Time requirements and schedule for which the consultant will provide services (for example, two days of preparation work off-site and two days of program delivery time)
- Estimated costs for the consultant's professional fees and per diem expenses
- Estimated costs for program materials and aids (for example, media equipment, transparencies, slides, shipping charges, books, handouts, participant evaluations, and certificates)
- Expectations for on-site support services (such as secretarial help, copying, office space)
- Project or service start and completion dates
- Contract extension or termination conditions
- Internal staff contact (for example, project manager, principal, director of training, manager of human resource division, executive director, division director)
- How fees for services/expenses should be billed and any forms that need to be completed
- Rights to use any copyrighted material to be distributed and/or use such material after the contract is completed
- Protection of the employing organization's intellectual property (for example, a statement promising nondisclosure of proprietary information)

Negotiating a written contract or letter of agreement will help promote a more harmonious relationship between an outside consultant and internal staff and help to ensure the desired results.

Obtaining Effective Instructors/ Facilitators

Instructors/facilitators play a key role in making an educational event a success, because they are responsible for assisting participants to achieve what they want to learn. Therefore, it is very important to obtain effective personnel for this role. But how does one determine who will be good? Eight selection criteria that have proven helpful are outlined below (Munson, 1992; Powers, 1992; Tracey, 1992; Birnbrauer, 1993):

- *Knowledge of subject matter.* Instructors must be knowledgeable about their subject matter and, where applicable, be successful practitioners of their subject and/or skills.
- *Competence in the processes of instruction.* Instructors should be competent in a number of instructional techniques and skilled in matching those techniques to their subject matter and the audience. They should also know how to provide helpful feedback and evaluate what the participants have learned.
- *Ability to respond effectively to the background and experience of the participants.* Instructors should be able to work well with a specific group of participants (for example, an ethnically diverse group) and demonstrate that they know how to tap into their audience's experiences and background.
- *Credibility.* Instructors should demonstrate credibility based on their position, background, experiences, and/or personal impact. High credibility predisposes participants to accept more readily the material presented.
- *Enthusiasm and commitment.* Instructors should be enthusiastic about their subject and committed to teaching it to others.
- *Personal effectiveness.* Instructors should be organized and prepared. They should be able to use humor effectively and have a genuine interest in whether or not the participants learn. They should also be able to adjust their presentation to the needs of the audience and model the behaviors and/or attitudes they are teaching.
- *Enterprise knowledge.* Instructors need to have at least basic information about the organizations or groups from which the participants will come (for example, products, services, culture).
- *Educational level.* Instructors have to have a level of formal education appropriate to the content, the participants, and the organization or group sponsoring the event.

Instructors may come from a variety of sources, again both internal and external to the sponsoring organization(s). Although adult educators, trainers, and staff developers are a main source, there are many people without this specialized background who, through experience and/or training, are competent instructors

(Ginocchio, 1990; Tracey, 1992). For example, technical employees often provide instruction for other technical staff, and volunteers serve as peer coaches and instructors for other volunteers.

Geigold and Grindle (1983) have cautioned program planners to be on the lookout for "Dr. Fox" in choosing instructors. Dr. Fox is an instructor "who has a wealth of personal charm, podium presence, and funny stories, but who conveys little else to the group" (p. 63). Although Dr. Fox may demonstrate competence in the processes of instruction and personal effectiveness, he falls short in other criteria areas noted earlier: knowledge of subject matter, credibility, and commitment to teaching his subject matter to others. Although audiences may react positively to this instructor, they learn little, if anything.

Chapter Highlights

Making decisions about how programs should be organized, scheduled, and staffed is an important part of the program planning process. This component of the planning process has become more complex as format choices (and the expertise needed by staff designing and conducting these various formats) have expanded through the use of technology. More specifically, tasks that need to be addressed during this phase of the planning process are as follows:

- Choose the most appropriate format or combination of formats for the learning activity (for example, individual, small-group [face-to-face], large-group [face-to-face], distance-learning, or community-learning formats).
- Devise a program schedule that fits the format(s) chosen and the participants' personal and/or job commitments.
- Identify staff needs (that is, program designers, program coordinators, instructors/facilitators, and program evaluators).
- Determine whether internal staff (paid or volunteer) can plan and conduct the program and/or whether external consultants need to be hired.

Formats, schedules, and staff needs are often connected to the financial resources that are available. How to link these financial resources to the planning process is discussed in the next chapter, along with how to prepare marketing plans for educational programs.

Applications Exercise

This chapter's Applications Exercise is intended to assist you in determining program format and staffing (Exhibit 10.2).

Exhibit 10.2. Determining the Program Format and Staff.

1. Identify an educational or training program that you are in the process of developing and give a short description of that program.

   _____

   _____

2. Identify at least *two* alternative formats (or combinations of formats) that would be appropriate for the above program and outline the reasons you chose them.

   Alternative 1: _____

   _____

   Alternative 2: _____

   _____

   Which of these formats would you use, and why?_____

   _____

   _____

3. Using the following chart, identify the specific staff who will plan and carry out the program.

Staff Role	Specific Person or Persons Who Could Carry Out Each Role	Internal or External to the Organization?	Paid or Voluntary?
Program Designer(s)			
Program Coordinator(s)			
Instructor/ Facilitator(s)			
Program Evaluator(s)			

——— ∞ ———

Eleven

Preparing Budgets and Marketing Plans

Terri R., the director of continuing education at a small private college, has proposed her division increase its revenues by 10 percent for each calendar year for the next three years. She would like to use this additional money for two primary purposes: to provide faculty incentive funds for developing new programs for adults and to develop a distance-learning program for the nursing department that could be used as a model for other programs on campus.

Prior to making this proposal, Terri first discussed with her staff whether this program objective would be doable and, if so, what strategies they might use to accomplish it. Her staff were very positive—they saw the idea as a proactive way to respond to the needs of adult students and the faculty simultaneously. They were able to come up with at least three strategies for making this objective a reality. These strategies included marketing their student portfolio guide nationally to other small colleges, increasing the offerings for five current high-demand, high-revenue-generating programs, and charging fees for certain services that were formerly offered without charge.

Terri also conferred with a number of faculty leaders over lunch to see whether they believed faculty would be responsive to such an incentive plan for program development, and she had two preliminary planning sessions with the nursing chair and faculty. Again, Terri received positive feedback on her proposal. The faculty members were especially responsive to the idea of their being able to apply for incentive funds for planning. This would break with the current campus norm, whereby faculty were paid only for what they actually *delivered*, not for the time and effort of *developing* an innovative program.

As illustrated by the above scenario, planning programs requires a whole range of activities that go beyond thinking through the educational components of the plan. People who are responsible for program planning need to recognize that budget management and other such behind-the-scenes tasks are integral components of the planning process and may even serve as the driving force behind program development efforts. Two of these key tasks are discussed in this chapter: preparing program budgets and developing marketing plans. Outlined in the section on budgeting are critical details of the budgeting process, along with worksheets for program planners to use in estimating the cost and income for specific programs. This is followed by a description of what marketing educational programs is all about, including specific ways this task is accomplished.

Preparing Program Budgets

Preparing a program budget is essentially translating intended program activities into monetary terms. Some educational units are funded as a budget center and therefore have organizational funds in addition to whatever income they may generate; others operate on a cost basis and need to break even; while the remainder are required to be profit centers and make money (Simerly, 1990; Tracey, 1992).

Understanding the Terminology

In working with budgets, some key words and phrases are used (Matkin, 1985; Ericksen, 1994). A brief review of those here will help prepare us for the subsequent discussion.

- *Income and expense budget.* The income side of an income and expense budget includes whatever monies are generated to support educational activities, while the expense side includes the actual cost of developing and delivering those activities.

- *Direct and indirect costs.* Direct program costs are "out-of-pocket" expenses, such as instructors' salaries, travel costs, and money spent on instructional materials. Indirect program costs are those expenses that do not cost actual dollars, such as costs for space, utilities, administrative salaries, and equipment. "Indirect costs are often called overhead costs (or simply 'overhead')" (Matkin, 1985, p. 39). What are usually considered indirect costs may become direct costs (and vice versa), depending on the program and the organization. For example, if a staff development program is held at the host organization's facilities, the space and equipment items are usually considered indirect costs; if the program is housed at a motel or conference center, these same expenses are considered direct costs.

- *Fixed and variable expenses.* Fixed expenses are those items that usually remain stable no matter what the number of participants is (for example, publicity and staff costs). In contrast, variable expenses are costs that typically change depending on how many participants sign up for a program (for example, meal and break costs, participant materials). Again, as with the terms *direct* and *indirect costs,* what is a fixed expense for one program may be seen as a variable expense for another. For example, instructor fees, which are most often thought of as fixed expenses, are sometimes negotiated based on the number of participants who actually complete a program: the more participants who complete the program, the more the instructors will cost. In that case, instructor fees would be part of the variable costs.

- *Profit.* Profit refers to making money, whether it is the educational unit that makes money or the organization as a whole. As stated earlier, some organizations expect the educational function to turn a profit. Other organizations simply expect the outcomes of the educational program to have a positive effect on the overall profitability of that organization.

- *Return on investments.* The term *return on investment* (ROI) refers to how the costs of planning and conducting educational programs (the organization's "investment") relate to the benefits they produce. The central question underlying the ROI issue is this: Which educational activities work, and at what cost? The need to demonstrate a positive economic return has become more pressing in recent years; as organizations invest an increasing amount of money in educational programs, they question whether this investment is worth it, especially when financial resources are scarce. Yet despite this need for more explicit financial accounting, few cost-benefit studies on educational and training programs are actually done (Carnevale and Schulz, 1990; Mosier, 1990). Major reasons given by organizations for not doing cost-benefit analyses are time, cost, difficulty in producing the necessary quantifiable data, and lack of know-how by educators and trainers. Two ways program staff can address these concerns are to take time to become knowledgeable about how to do cost-benefit studies and to ask for assistance from others in the organization who are experts in financial analysis. Examples of helpful resources on how to do cost-benefit analysis for educational and training programs include Swanson and Gradous (1988), Blomberg (1989), Carnevale and Schulz (1990), Mosier (1990), and Tracey (1992).

Determining the Cost of Educational Programs

There are three basic kinds of costs associated with each program offered: development costs, delivery costs, and evaluation costs (Laird, 1985; Nilson, 1989; Tracey, 1992). Expense items in these categories usually include staff salaries and benefits, instructional materials, facilities, equipment, travel, food, promotional materials, and general overhead (for example, administrative costs and utilities). In developing budgets for specific programs, program planners must know ahead of time whether they need to account for both direct and indirect costs (rather than just direct costs) and which items are considered fixed versus variable expenses. A sample worksheet for estimating program expenses is outlined in Exhibit 11.1.

Tracey (1992) offers further guidance for estimating program development expenses. For example, he provides worksheets for computing costs for specific types of educational materials. As a sampling, the costs for audiovisual materials would include some combination of the following: purchase costs, rental costs, development costs (including materials, labor, and processing), and distribution costs. In addition, Tracey outlines detailed ways to figure other development costs, explaining how to do calculations for different types of indirect costs and unit costs (such as costs per square foot, costs per hour, and equipment costs per hour), for example.

Exhibit 11.1. Worksheet for Estimating Program Expenses.

Budget Items	Development Costs	Delivery Costs	Evaluation Costs	Subtotal
Staff Salaries				
Secretaries				
Program planners				
Instructors				
Staff Benefits				
Secretaries				
Program planners				
Instructors				
External Consultants				
Instructional Materials				
Videotapes				
Videodiscs				
Audiotapes				
35mm slides				
Overhead transparencies				
Manuals				
Handouts				
Computer programs				
Books and articles				
Other				
Facilities				
Meeting rooms				
Staff work rooms				
Hospitality areas				
Sleeping accommodations				
Staff				
Participants				
Food				
Meals				
Staff				
Participants				
Coffee breaks				
Other (such as cocktail hour)				
Travel				
Staff				
In-house				
External consultants				
Participants				
Equipment				
Promotional Materials				
General Overhead				
Administrative costs				
Utilities				
Maintenance				
Other				
Other				
Subtotal for each type of cost				
			Total Costs =	

Some organizations, especially for-profit companies, require that participant costs also be computed, either as a separate expense budget or as part of the total program budget. Although some of those items, such as costs for participant travel and accommodations, were included in Exhibit 11.1, others were not. Laird (1985) and Nilson (1989) offer these useful ideas for computing participant costs:

- Number of participants (by pay group) × median salary × hours/days of educational programming
- Number of participants × hourly fringe benefit charges × hours/days
- *Travel costs.* Total from expense reports (or median costs × number of participants)
- *Per diem.* Total from expense reports (or median allowance × number of participants × number of days)
- *Participant materials.* Material costs × number of participants
- *Participant replacement costs.* Number of hours × median salary
- *Lost productivity of participants.* Value per unit × number of lost units (or value per unit × the reduced production)

In calculating participant costs, you might use only some of the line items or all of them, depending on the situation.

As budgets take shape, sometimes the costs are higher than the actual dollars program planners have to spend. In that case, program costs have to come down. The following list of strategies for reducing program costs is based on Davis and McCallon (1974), Nilson (1989), and Bellman (1993):

Substitute less expensive instructional materials or eliminate certain materials altogether.

Reduce the number of staff needed to plan, conduct, and/or evaluate the program. Be especially cognizant of the cost of outside consultants.

Reduce the number of participants.

Employ less expensive learning format(s) and/or techniques so that the same number of participants (or more) can be involved.

Use either a less expensive facility or one that will not cost you any direct dollars.

Have the program at a facility to which participants can commute so they do not have to pay for overnight accommodations.

Have participants pay for their own meals rather than including meals as part of the program package.

Require that participants find the cheapest mode of travel to and from the program (for example, car pool, train, plane).

Change the program to a date when the prices for the facilities, meals, and so forth would be lower (for example, a weekend, a weekday, off-season for a resort area).

Make promotional material for the program less elaborate.

Shorten the program and tighten the design.

Use a lending library of materials rather than producing all the materials for the participants.

Take the program to the participants rather than gathering the participants at a different site if it would cost less to "deliver" the program.

Consider subcontracting some of the programs if the cost would thereby be lower.

Take a hard look at the program and cut out activities, services, and the like that do not need to be provided.

Determining How the Program Will Be Financed

The income sources for educational and training programs vary depending on the type of institution (that is, for-profit, nonprofit); the purpose, content, and format of the program; and whether or not fees are charged for the program. The primary income sources for educational programs are organizational subsidy, participant fees, auxiliary enterprises and sales, grants and contracts, government funds, and profits from the educational unit itself (Knowles, 1980; Bennett and LeGrand, 1990). Brief descriptions of these income sources are listed below, with examples of each. It is important that program planners have a good understanding of their funding sources and the policies and regulations that govern each revenue source.

Organizational subsidy. The educational function receives operating funds from the parent organization.

The Office of Staff Development receives an expense budget of $150,000 annually for salaries, materials and equipment, travel, general office supplies, and printing.

Participant fees. Participants are charged a fee for attending a program.

Eighty percent of all adult education programs sponsored by the local school district must break even. Thus the participants' fees must cover all expenses of those programs.

Auxiliary enterprises and sales. Revenue is earned from the sale of materials, publications, and services provided by the educational unit to other organizations and individuals.

A nationally prominent accounting firm has developed an excellent computer-based training program and is now selling it to other organizations for profit.

Grants and contracts from foundations and other private organizations. Private foundations and other private organizations award funds to an educational unit to develop a specific program. Usually these awards go to nonprofit organizations.

An award is given to a nonprofit hospital to develop a specific program on the prevention of AIDS.

Government funding (federal, state, and local). Government funds are awarded or given to an educational unit to develop a specific program. These funds may be given to for-profit or nonprofit agencies (depending on the regulations governing the funds).

A local community college, in partnership with a private business, is awarded a grant to initiate a job training program for unemployed workers.

Profit from the educational unit. The educational unit produces an overall profit from the operation, which in turn can be used for future programs.

The College of Continuing Education at XYZ University on average nets a 10 percent profit from the Conferences and Institutes Division, which is used to sponsor new program ventures.

Just as it is necessary to estimate the expense side of the budget, it is also necessary to account for the income side. This is especially true if a program is expected to break even or make a profit. A worksheet for estimating program income is displayed in Exhibit 11.2.

Exhibit 11.2. Worksheet for Estimating Income Sources.

Income Source	Amount of Income/Subsidy
Organizational subsidy	
Participant fees (fee × number of estimated participants)	
Auxiliary enterprises and sales (item or service to be sold × number of estimated customers)	
Grants and contracts (list each source of funding with amount):	
1.	
2.	
3.	
Government funds (list each source of funding with amount):	
1.	
2.	
3.	
Profit from the educational unit	
TOTAL INCOME =	

Keeping Accurate Budget Records

It is important to keep accurate financial records that are clear, simple, and practical. The type of formal record keeping that is readily available depends on the accounting system of the organization in which the program is housed. Most large organizations will have computerized systems, whereas some smaller organizations and groups still require manual entries. The specific system within an organization may not allow for program-by-program record keeping; if records of income and expenses for individual programs are desired despite that, program planning staff may need to develop their own set of record-keeping books.

Marketing the Program

For some programs, marketing is an essential element of the program planning process (Nadler and Nadler, 1987; Simerly and Associates, 1989; Simerly, 1990). This is especially true of educational programs where participation is voluntary and potential participants are not affiliated with the sponsoring organization. Successful marketing is defined by Simerly (1989a) as "a process for ensuring that an organization reaches its goals and objectives by exchanging its products, services and knowledge for program registrations" (p. 445). Marketing is done primarily for two reasons: to ensure adequate participation for a program and to communicate what the program is all about.

The Potential Audience

Knowing the sometimes diverse background and experiences of the potential audience for a program is one of the first steps in developing a marketing plan. Completing a target population analysis is one way to determine these characteristics. This process assumes that staff know which individual(s) or groups of people will or might be interested in attending the program to be offered. The target population analysis involves answering some or all of the following questions, depending on the potential participants (Hentges, Yaney, and Shields, 1990; Richey, 1992; Rothwell and Kazanas, 1992; Stuart, 1992):

How many people might be involved?

At what times might the potential participants be able to attend sessions?

Where are the potential participants located (for example, where geographically, all from one organization)?

What are the ages of the potential participants?

What are the educational levels of the potential participants?

What are the gender, ethnicity, and social-class backgrounds of the potential participants?

What is the primary language of the potential participants?

Do the potential participants have any disabilities (such as learning disabilities or loss of hearing) that might call for specific program formats, instructional strategies, and/or special services?

What can be assumed about the present and past knowledge, skills, and experiences of the potential participants in relation to the content being offered?

What are the learning-style preferences of the potential participants?

What are the potential participants' attitudes about educational and training programs? About the organizations or groups that are sponsoring these programs?

Are the potential participants in any identifiable career stages (such as the entry level or retirement) or life roles (for example, parent, spouse, partner, volunteer) that would influence the content or process of the program to be offered?

Why do the potential participants want to enroll or be involved in the program?

What are the costs (for example, for fees, loss of job time, travel, child care) to the potential participants for attending the program?

The target population analysis can be done in a number of ways. For example, program planners can use existing data bases that contain the needed information, conduct interviews, do observations, and conduct surveys (Smith and Ragan, 1993). The information obtained from this analysis can also be useful in choosing program formats and staff (see Chapter Ten). For those programs that have participant eligibility requirements (requirements about specific types of jobs or educational background, for example), the data from the target population analysis can also be used both in determining whether an audience for this program exists in the designated market area and as a screening device for potential participants (Tracey, 1992).

One note of caution in using a target population analysis to assess the characteristics and needs of the potential audience for the program: the potential program participants and the program audience may or may not be one and the same. For example, in planning an educational program for entry-level managers, program planners might assume that those entry-level managers are their prime audience; and this may in fact be so. But other scenarios could also be built, depending on the situation. The impetus for that particular program may have come from the supervisors of these managers, and thus a dual audience may exist: the entry-level managers and their immediate supervisors. In this latter instance, the supervisors may in fact be the primary audience, with the entry-level managers secondary. Therefore, program planners may need to go beyond a target population analysis (perhaps conducting interviews with the participants' supervisors) in order to get a complete picture of their audience.

The Product, Price, Place, and Promotion

In addition to a good picture of the potential audience, four key aspects of marketing should be addressed by program planners: product, price, place, and promotion (Farlow, 1979; Riggs, 1989; Simerly and Associates, 1989).

Obviously, program planners need to know their "product"; that is, they must be able to provide a comprehensive and understandable description of the programs for which they are responsible. They also need to be able to choose the right product (that is, the right program) to fit the needs and desires of their audience.

If there is to be a cost charged to participants for a program, the right price must be determined. How much are the potential customers—whether they be individuals, groups, or organizations—willing to pay? In thinking through costs, program planners must consider both the cost to participants for the program itself and the participants' travel expenses. In addition, some organizations compute costs in terms of participants' time away from the job. In setting prices, the actual cost of planning and implementing the program, the demand for the program, and the competition should be taken into consideration (Simerly, 1989a). Sometimes, for example, lowering the price to increase the demand for a program is a good decision, especially if the market is a highly competitive one. On the other hand, when the competition is marginal and the demand high, increasing the price may be appropriate.

Choosing where to offer an educational program is also important. The location should be consistent with the program design, audience, and budget (Carson, 1989). For example, hosting a three-day national conference in a place relatively inaccessible by air (which usually means higher airfares) is generally not a good decision, especially if the participants need to be able to obtain low airfares to attend the conference. Common mistakes made in marketing the location of the program include overemphasizing the place rather than the program and being too "glowing" about the features and attractions of the location.

The fourth key aspect of marketing—that is, promotion—will be discussed at some length in the next section.

Promotion of Educational Programs

Not all educational activities need to be promoted. Some are mandatory—the participants are told they *must* go. Others are in such high demand that the job of the program planners is to select participants from a large potential pool. For the most part, though, program planners must promote or sell their programs to the potential audience. Many programs fail because of poor promotion. "People just never heard about them [the programs] or did not realize how good they were" (Knowles, 1980, p. 176).

Promotion involves developing strategies and materials aimed at generating or increasing enrollments for educational programs. Examples of promotional materials and strategies used to foster interest in educational programs are given in the following list (Coats, 1989; Holland, 1989; Nilson, 1989; Simerly and Associates, 1989):

Brochures. A written document describing a specific program or series of programs. A three-fold piece measuring 4 x 9 inches (which can fit into a business-size envelope) is used most often.

Direct mail

Placement in appropriate offices and public places (such as coffee rooms, cafeterias)

Participant packets (for brochures promoting future programs)

By hand at appropriate meetings

Flyers/announcements. A single sheet, 8½ x 11 inches, promoting an activity or a group of related activities to people with specialized interests.	Direct mail Bulletin boards Participant packets (for brochures promoting future programs)
Form letters. A letter that can be used in two ways: (1) as a cover letter mailed with a brochure or other promotional material (with the letter focusing the reader's attention on certain activities described in the promotional piece); (2) as a separate mailing to make a personalized appeal to a specific group of people.	Direct mail
Catalogues. A description of the programs and services of an organization's educational activities, with course descriptions usually included.	Direct mail Placement in offices and public display areas In-person distribution through various departments or units of an organization
Posters. A sign used to attract attention about a specific program or event. It should be attractive and eye-catching.	Bulletin boards and other appropriate places (such as office doors, cafeteria, coffee room)
Newsletter, newspaper, and magazine ads. An ad placed in appropriate publications announcing the program. There is usually a cost associated, except for local newsletters.	Distribution by the organization that owns or is responsible for the publication
Newspaper or newsletter publicity. An information piece describing a specific program or series of activities.	Distribution by the organization that owns or is responsible for the publication
Personal contacts. Program planning staff, other organizational personnel, and/or past participants who tell others about the program. This dissemination can be planned or done on an informal basis.	Individual in-person conversations, telephone conversations, and announcements in group meetings
Electronic mail and electronic bulletin boards. Electronic media used to describe an upcoming program or event. These should be used only if you know potential participants are networked into the system and use this form of communication on a regular basis.	Internal organizational electronic mail More widely used communication networks external to the organization

Audio/visual media. Program information provided via radio, television, videotape, or other forms of media. Production of these are often costly, but free air time may be given to nonprofit organizations.	Local radio and television stations Direct mail (for example, videotapes)
Telemarketing. Use of the telephone to promote programs to past and possible participants. The timing of calls is important, as is the script used by callers.	Calls over telephone lines (with written material often sent as a follow-up)
Exhibits at conferences, conventions, trade shows, and other public places. Displays that clearly portray the goals and objectives of the program. The size of the exhibit is determined by space allocations, cost, expected attendance, storage, and available staff.	Conferences, trade shows, conventions, libraries, museums, and shopping malls (with information given by staff or, if exhibit is not staffed, picked up by interested parties)

More complete descriptions of how to develop these types of materials and strategies are given in Nilson (1989) and Simerly and Associates (1989).

The Marketing Campaign

Having a clear picture of the audience to be reached, as noted earlier, is the essential first step to any marketing campaign. For example, a promotional piece targeted at older adults may be poorly received if in fact many of the people who receive the material do not consider themselves to be old. This audience targeting does not have to be done in an overt way but can come through in a more subtle manner—for example, in the illustrations, pictures, or language used in a brochure.

It is also essential that the marketing campaign be well planned. The planning phase includes building a promotional budget and determining how that budget will be spent. Two examples illustrating this planning process are outlined in Exhibit 11.3.

The third marketing step is preparing and distributing the promotional material. The most popular promotional materials are brochures, announcements, and newsletter articles. The writing of copy that is readable and attractive is key to this third step. Shipp (1981) and Simerly (1989b) have outlined four classic elements of a good promotional piece. The copy should catch the reader's attention, create interest, engage the reader, and inspire action. More specifically, Shipp and Simerly give the following nine pointers for writing good promotional materials:

- Define clearly the target audience—demographic characteristics, location—and indicate what type of promotional material may be most effective.
- Keep it simple. Use short sentences and familiar words.

Exhibit 11.3. Sample Marketing Campaign Plans.

Name of Program	Target Audience	Type of Promotional Material to Use	Target Time for Distribution	Proposed Cost
Example 1				
Working with Diverse Student Populations	Teachers and principals	Flyers	November 1	$ 25.00
		Organizational newsletters	November newsletter	$150.00
		Word of mouth	Push two weeks prior to program	No cost
Example 2				
Conducting Cost-Benefit Analysis (ASTD Workshop for Area Chapter)	Entry- and midlevel managers	ASTD newsletter	January newsletter	$350.00
		Brochure mailed to all members	January 15	$200.00
		Word of mouth and telephone calls	Push three to four weeks before workshop	No cost

- Use as few words as possible. Say what you want to say, then quit.
- Use the present tense and action words to make the message have a sense of urgency.
- Use personal pronouns. Talk to the audience just as you would to a friend.
- Do not use jargon and do not overpunctuate. This kills the copy flow.
- Emphasize benefits. Clearly outline what participants will learn and be able to do.
- Write with enthusiasm. Convince the consumer to share your excitement.

Developing a fact sheet before writing the actual copy may be helpful. The questions on the fact sheet are the same ones that program planners need to answer when preparing the actual program: who, what, when, where, why, and how (Nilson, 1989).

Your Promotional Assets

Ascertaining and strengthening your promotional assets and capabilities is an important part of any marketing effort. Program planners can use the following checklist (Farlow, 1979; Nadler and Nadler, 1987; and Simerly and Associates, 1989) for doing this task, rating each asset and capability as present, readily obtainable, or hard to obtain:

- Personnel (paid staff and/or volunteers)
  Copy writers
  Photographers
  Graphic artists
  Design specialists
  Desk-top computer publishers
  Clerical help (for example, to stuff and stamp envelopes)
  Other staff
- Access to printers, duplicating equipment and/or print shops
- Access to copy machines for small jobs
- Up-to-date mailing lists
- Coding and tracking system for mailing lists
- Established relationships with media people (for example, those working with newsletters, newspapers, radio, TV)
- Access to electronic mail and bulletin boards
- Access to a good reference library
- Access to good demographic studies of potential audiences

Chapter Highlights

Preparing program budgets and preparing marketing plans are sometimes two of the most important components of the planning process, depending on the organizational setting in which the programs are being planned. If the programs are expected to be break-even or profit-making ventures, these aspects of the overall plan are critical to the very survival of the planning enterprise. In carrying through these important components, program planners should focus on five major tasks:

- Estimate the expenses for the program, including costs for the development, delivery, and evaluation of the program (for example, staff salaries, participant expenses, facilities costs, instructional materials expenses, transfer-of-learning costs).
- Determine how the program will be financed (for example, by participant fees, organizational subsidy, government funding).
- Conduct a target population analysis to help determine the background and experiences of the potential audience as one of the foundational pieces of the marketing plan.
- Select and prepare promotional materials for the program (such as brochures, electronic mail messages, flyers) that "tell the story well" of the who, what, where, why, and how of the program.
- Prepare a targeted and lively promotional campaign, paying careful attention to the target audience, the type of promotional materials you want to use, the time frame, and the cost.

These two behind-the-scenes tasks of preparing program budgets and preparing marketing plans can have disastrous effects on the learning portion of the program if they are not done well.

Now we again move to the more visible portions of the planning process—more visible to the participants, at least—in the next two chapters, which deal with the instructional plans and the logistical details (including on-site coordination of the program).

Applications Exercises

This chapter's Applications Exercises address the issues of budgeting for and marketing educational programs. The first is designed to help you create a budget for your program (Exhibit 11.4), the second is a tool for identifying potential participants (Exhibit 11.5), and the third deals with marketing a program (Exhibit 11.6).

Exhibit 11.4. Preparing Program Budgets.

1. Choose an educational program that you are presently planning and prepare an estimated expense budget for that program using the following chart. Put an X in the space provided if no costs are incurred for that item.

Title of Program: _____

<table>
<tr><th colspan="5">Program Expense Budget</th></tr>
<tr><th>Budget Items</th><th>Development Costs</th><th>Delivery Costs</th><th>Evaluation Costs</th><th>Subtotal</th></tr>
<tr><td>Staff salaries</td><td></td><td></td><td></td><td></td></tr>
<tr><td>Staff benefits</td><td></td><td></td><td></td><td></td></tr>
<tr><td>Instructional materials</td><td></td><td></td><td></td><td></td></tr>
<tr><td>Facilities</td><td></td><td></td><td></td><td></td></tr>
<tr><td>Food</td><td></td><td></td><td></td><td></td></tr>
<tr><td>Travel</td><td></td><td></td><td></td><td></td></tr>
<tr><td>Equipment</td><td></td><td></td><td></td><td></td></tr>
<tr><td>Promotional materials</td><td></td><td></td><td></td><td></td></tr>
<tr><td>General overhead</td><td></td><td></td><td></td><td></td></tr>
<tr><td>Other</td><td></td><td></td><td></td><td></td></tr>
<tr><td></td><td></td><td></td><td>Total =</td><td></td></tr>
</table>

2. If you need to cover all or part of these program costs, identify what sources of income you will use and estimate how much funding will come from each source.

Income Sources	Estimated Funding

3. If your expense and income sources are not in line, describe how would you adjust either one or the other in order to achieve your budget objective (for example, breaking even on expenses, earning 10 percent over cost).

_____

_____

_____

_____

4. Review your budget plans with other members of your planning team and/or with people from your organization or sponsoring group. Revise your expense and income estimates and your ideas on how to meet your budget objective as needed.

Exhibit 11.5. Identifying Potential Participants.

1. Identify an educational or training program that you are in the process of developing and give a short description of that program.

   _____

   _____

2. Complete a target population analysis for that program by responding to any of the following questions that are appropriate for your situation.

   a. How many people might be involved?

   _____

   b. At what times might the potential participants be able to attend programs?

   _____

   _____

   c. Where are the potential participants located? (For example, are they all from the same geographic region and/or the same organization?)

   _____

   _____

   d. What are the ages of the potential participants?

   _____

   _____

   e. What are the educational levels of the potential participants?

   _____

   _____

   f. What are the gender, ethnicity, and social-class backgrounds of the potential participants?

   _____

   _____

   g. What is the primary language of the potential participants?

   _____

   _____

h. Do the potential participants have any disabilities that might call for different program formats and/or learning strategies?

_____

_____

i. What can be assumed about the present knowledge, skills, and experiences of the potential participants in relation to the program content being offered?

_____

_____

j. What are the learning-style preferences of the potential participants?

_____

_____

k. What are the potential participants' attitudes about educational and training programs and about the organizations or groups that are sponsoring these programs?

_____

_____

l. Are the potential participants in any identifiable career stages or life roles that would influence the content or process of the program to be offered?

_____

_____

m. Why do the potential participants want to enroll or be involved in the program?

_____

_____

n. What are the costs (for example, for fees, loss of time on the job, travel, child care) to the potential participants for attending the program?

_____

_____

3. How can you use the information you have generated from the target population analysis in the planning process?

_____

_____

Exhibit 11.6. Marketing the Program.

1. Choose a program for which you need to do a marketing plan. Using the following chart, outline how you would go about preparing the plan.

Name of Program and Proposed Date	Target Audience	Type(s) of Promotional Material to Use	Target Time for Distribution	Proposed Cost

2. Ask at least two people who are either involved in the planning process with you or are knowledgeable about your organization and/or the program to review your plan. Based on their feedback, complete a revision of the marketing plan as needed.

Twelve

Designing Instructional Plans

Preparing instructional units involves planning the interaction between learners and instructors and/or learners and resource materials for each educational activity. Outlined in instructional plans are the learning objectives, content, instructional techniques, materials and equipment, and evaluation procedures. Instructional plans may be developed by instructors of educational activities, program planners, instructional designers, or a combination of these people. The staff responsible may be paid or volunteer, internal to an organization or external.

Most instructional plans are developed by those who will be delivering the instruction. These individuals may receive assistance in putting the plan together, but the responsibility for the final product is theirs. There are times, though, when designing instructional plans is a team effort, especially when the educational activities are very complex and comprehensive. The composition of these design teams will vary, depending on the purpose, format, and content of the educational activity; but usually three types of staff are involved: instructional designers, content specialists, and persons representing the overall planning team or educational unit (Nadler, 1982; Tracey, 1992). For example, the design team for a mediated learning module for experienced literacy volunteers would probably involve an instructional designer, an adult educator, and the director for literacy training.

This chapter addresses the various components of instructional plans, how they are put together, and helpful hints for instructors as they put their plans into operation. It first describes learning objectives and how they are constructed and then offers suggestions for selecting and sequencing the content to be taught. Selecting instructional techniques and materials and developing the evaluation component of the instructional plan are the subjects reviewed next, followed by a sample instructional plan. The chapter concludes with a discussion of ways instructors can make the instructional plans work for them and their learners.

Developing Learning Objectives

Learning objectives describe the outcome of a specific educational activity (Mager, 1984; Tracey, 1992). They should be set in the context of the program objectives (those focused on participant learning) so that there is a sense of continuity between the two sets of objectives. Learning objectives must be selected carefully, because they set the tone and direction for what participants will be expected to do and learn during the instructional activity. Therefore, in preparing learning objectives, the developer must have in mind a clear picture of the proposed learning outcomes for the instructional unit.

There are four major categories of learning outcomes: acquiring new knowledge; enhancing thinking skills, developing psychomotor skills, and changing attitudes, values, and/or feelings (Bloom, 1956; Dick and Carey, 1990; Rothwell and Kazanas, 1992). The following are examples of learning objectives illustrating each category of learning outcomes:

- *Acquisition of knowledge.* Participants will be able to describe what a Ropes Course is and identify the basic principles of team building.
- *Enhancement of thinking skills.* Participants will analyze each of the team-building exercises and translate what they have learned into one or two proposed changes in their professional practice and/or personal lives.
- *Development of psychomotor skills.* Participants will demonstrate that they can do at least two of the physically challenging exercises included in the Ropes Course.
- *Changes in attitudes/values and/or feelings.* Participants will be willing to share their feelings about the Ropes Course and discuss how taking part in course activities has affected them either personally or professionally.

Learning objectives are useful for four major reasons (Mager, 1984; Tracey, 1992). They provide consistency in the design of instruction, guidelines for choosing course content and instructional methods, a basis for evaluating what participants have learned, and guidelines for learners to help them organize their own learning.

As with program objectives, learning objectives should be "stated clearly enough to indicate to all rational minds exactly what is intended" (Houle, 1972, p. 149). Tracey (1992) has outlined five general rules for communicating objectives clearly and correctly: avoid unfamiliar words, do not confuse or misuse words, be concise, seek simplicity, and review what has been proposed to make sure the objectives say what you want them to say.

The focus of each learning objective should be the program participants. Therefore, objectives should be stated in terms of what learners will be able to know, do, or feel. They should consist of an opening statement ("The participant will be able to . . ."), an action verb, and a content reference (which describes the subject being taught). Four sample learning objectives are given below:

The Learner	Action Verb	Content
The participant will be able	To detect	When the new equipment is not operating at 80 percent efficiency
The trainee will be able	To demonstrate	Effective and efficient use of parts 1 and 2 of the newly installed word-processing program
The learner will be able	To describe	Five appropriate methods for teaching adult students with learning disabilities
The learner will be able	To express	Her attitudes and feelings about working with diverse populations

In developing learning objectives, people sometimes have difficulty coming up with a variety of action words that fit each category of learning outcomes. To assist staff in this task, a sampling of such words is given below (Rothwell and Kazanas, 1992; Tracey, 1992):

Acquisition of Knowledge	Enhancement of Thinking Skills	Development of Psychomotor Skills	Changes in Attitudes, Values, and/or Feelings
To identify	To reflect	To demonstrate	To challenge
To list	To compare	To produce	To defend
To define	To contrast	To assemble	To judge
To describe	To catalogue	To adjust	To question
To state	To classify	To install	To accept
To prepare	To evaluate	To operate	To adopt
To recall	To forecast	To detect	To advocate
To express	To formulate	To locate	To bargain
To categorize	To investigate	To isolate	To cooperate
To chart	To modify	To arrange	To endorse
To rank	To organize	To build	To justify
To distinguish	To plan	To conduct	To persuade
To explain	To research	To check	To resolve
To outline	To study	To manipulate	To select
To inform	To translate	To fix	To dispute
To label	To differentiate	To lay out	To approve
To specify	To analyze	To perform	To choose
To tell	To compute	To sort	To feel
	To devise	To construct	To care
	To review	To draw	To express
			To reflect

Although the three essential elements of all learning objectives are a statement of *who* (the learner), *how* (the action verb), and *what* (the content), other authors have suggested additional components that may be useful in clarifying further what learners are able to know, do, or feel. More specifically, Mager (1984) and

Dick and Carey (1990) have described two more elements of learning objectives: conditions under which the learning is to be demonstrated and the criteria for acceptable performance. Wording describing the given conditions might sound like this:

- Given a problem of the following type . . .
- Given a list of . . .
- When provided with a specific set of tools . . .
- Without the use of any reference materials . . .
- By checking a flowchart next to the property equipment . . .
- When a client is angry or upset . . .

Wording describing the criteria for acceptable performance might sound like this:

. . . with 98 percent accuracy

. . . getting sixteen out of twenty correct

. . . in a twenty-minute time period

. . . by brief responses (fewer than five sentences)

. . . with no mistakes

. . . with all irate clients

The latter two elements are appropriate only for learning objectives that are measurable through quantitative means. There are certain kinds of learning outcomes, as stressed in Chapters Seven and Nine, that do not lend themselves to precise behavioral or performance criteria. This is especially true whenever creativity, confidence, sensitivity, feelings, attitudes, and values are the focus of the learning activity (Knowles, 1980; Caffarella, 1992). For example, changes in deep-seated values and attitudes about race and gender are learning outcomes that are extremely difficult, if not impossible, to express in any meaningful way in behavioral terms. However the learning objectives are written, it is key that they have meaning for both the participants and the instructors, are understandable, and provide a clear direction for the educational activity.

Selecting and Sequencing Content

Selecting the content—that is, choosing what will be learned during a learning activity—is a challenge because instructors can rarely include all the material they would *like* to teach; they are limited by time constraints, format, background of the participants, and materials available.

The starting point for selecting the content is the learning objectives. Tracey (1992) recommends preparing a rough draft of proposed content by objective and then expanding that draft into a detailed statement of content. Especially when there are time constraints, it is useful to prioritize the content in terms of its importance and relevance (Nadler, 1982). Smith and Delahaye (1987) have provided a framework for doing this:

- *What participants must know.* Content that is essential to the objectives.
- *What participants should know.* Content that supplements the essential material and should be included if time allows.
- *What participants could know.* Content that is interesting and relevant but not essential for clear understanding.

As Tracey (1992) cautions, care must be taken to avoid leaving out important points and ideas, overemphasizing topics that do not merit extensive attention, and repeating the material presented.

The order (or sequence) in which the content is delivered is also important. There is no one way to order the content. For example, should the content flow from general to specific or vice versa? Should it flow from abstract to concrete or concrete to abstract? The ordering of the content depends on the participants' knowledge and experience, the nature of the content itself, and instructor preference (Houle, 1972; Smith and Delahaye, 1987).

Tracey (1992, p. 242) offers the following guidelines:

- Start the sequence with materials that are familiar to the participants and then proceed to new materials.
- [Give participants] a context or framework to use in organizing what they are to learn.
- Place easily learned tasks early in the sequence.
- Introduce broad concepts and technical terms that have application throughout the instructional process early in the sequence.
- Place practical application of concepts and principles close to the point of the initial discussion of the concepts and principles.
- Place prerequisite knowledge and skills in the sequence prior to the point where they must be combined with subsequent knowledge and skills.
- Provide for practice and review of skills and knowledge that are essential parts of tasks to be introduced later in the activity.
- Introduce a concept or skill in the task in which it is most frequently used.
- Structure objectives into closely related, self-contained groups.
- Do not overload any task with elements that are difficult to learn.
- Place complex or cumulative skills late in the sequence.
- Provide for practice of required skills and review of concepts and principles in areas where transfer of identical or related skills is not likely to occur unaided.

Source: Adapted, with permission of the publisher, from *Designing Training and Development Systems* (third ed.), by William R. Tracey, © 1992 AMACOM, a division of American Management Association. All rights reserved.

Selecting Instructional Techniques

How does an instructor decide which instructional technique might best fit a specific situation? Let's take a look.

Scenario

> Paul R., a department manager and training specialist for a large retail outlet, has set up a two-hour training session for all part-time sales personnel who have been hired to handle the Christmas rush. He knows he will have both experienced salespeople and people who have never sold before—about twenty-five in all. Paul has outlined what he believes to be a good set of learning objectives on areas such as customer relations, selling techniques, and general store operations. He is now trying to decide just how he should cover that broad array of content in a short period of time.
>
> Paul has outlined two possible alternatives. The first is to use a combination of lecturing and small- and large-group discussions. He would ask the more experienced people to serve as resource people and leaders in the small groups. His second idea is to use role playing, followed by small- and large-group discussions. He would then fill in with lecture material as needed. Paul decides to review his ideas with three of his experienced sales staff. He believes that an offer of a paid lunch would entice them to help him out.

Underlying Paul's quandary about instructional techniques is the assumption that there is no one best way of assisting people to learn. Rather, there are eight major factors that should be taken into consideration when choosing instructional techniques (Robinson, 1979; Apps, 1991; Rothwell and Kazanas, 1992; Tracey, 1992):

- *Learning objectives.* Is the focus of the objectives acquiring new knowledge, enhancing thinking skills, developing psychomotor skills, or changing attitudes, values, and/or feelings?
- *Instructors.* Are the instructors capable of using the techniques, and do they feel comfortable doing so?
- *Content.* Is the content abstract or concrete? What is the level of complexity and comprehensiveness of the material?
- *Participants.* How many participants will there be? What are the characteristics of these participants? What expectations do the participants have in terms of the techniques to be used (and are they capable of learning through those techniques)?
- *Characteristics of the teaching techniques themselves.* What can realistically be done with the techniques? How difficult are the techniques to use?
- *Time.* What time period is available?
- *Cost.* Are the costs, if any, associated with the techniques chosen realistic?
- *Space, equipment, and materials.* Are the space, equipment, and/or materials necessary to use the techniques readily available?

Of these eight factors, the first two—the focus of the learning objectives and the capability of the instructor to use the chosen technique—are key. To address the first factor, a variety of instructional techniques appropriate for each category of learning outcomes—acquiring knowledge, enhancing thinking skills, developing psychomotor skills, and changing attitudes, values, and/or feelings—are listed here:

Acquisition of Knowledge

Lecture. A one-way organized, formal talk is given by a resource person for the purpose of presenting a series of events, facts, concepts, or principles.

Panel. A group of three to eight people present their views on a particular topic or problem.

Group discussion. A group of five to twenty people have a relatively unstructured exchange of ideas about a specific problem or issue.

Buzz group. A large group is divided into small "huddle" groups for the purpose of discussing the problem or subject matter at hand.

Reaction panel. A panel of three or four participants react to a presentation of an individual or group of individuals.

Screened speech. Small groups of participants develop questions they wish resource persons to respond to extemporaneously.

Symposium. A series of related presentations (three to six) are offered by persons qualified to speak on different phases of a subject or problem.

Listening group. In groups, participants are asked to listen to or observe an assigned part of a speech, panel, or the like.

Enhancement of Thinking Skills

Case study. A small group analyzes and solves an event, incident, or situation presented orally or in writing.

Game. An individual or group performs an activity characterized by structured competition that provides the opportunity to practice specific thinking skills and actions (such as decision making).

In-basket exercise. In a form of simulation that focuses on the "paper symptoms" of a job, participants respond to material people might have in their in-baskets.

Critical incident. Participants are asked to describe an important incident related to a specific aspect of their lives. This is then used as a basis for analysis.

Debate. A presentation of conflicting views by two people or two groups of people helps to clarify the arguments between them.

Reflective practice. Thoughtfully reflecting on one's actions, including the assumptions and feelings associated with those actions, can be done individually or as a part of a small-group discussion.

Observation. After an individual or group systematically observes and records an event using a specific focus (for example, leadership style, group interactions, instructor behavior), the data are analyzed and discussed (either one on one or in a group format).

Quiet meeting. Participants who know each other well sit quietly and reflect on a topic or question, sharing from time to time an idea on the area presented. No reaction is given to these comments, although others are free to share their ideas also. The power of this technique is in the silence, not the talking or listening.

Development of Psychomotor Skills

Demonstration with return demonstration. A resource person performs a specified operation or a job, showing others how to do it. The participants then practice the same task.

Simulation. Participants practice skills in a learning environment that simulates the real setting in which those skills are required.

Trial and error. Participants are encouraged to figure out individually or in groups a way to do a hands-on job effectively.

Skill practice exercise. Participants repeat performance of a skill with or without the aid of an instructor.

Behavior modeling. A model or ideal enactment of a desired behavior presented via an instructor, videotape, or film, usually followed by a practice session on the behavior.

Changes in Attitudes, Values, and/or Feelings

Role playing. The spontaneous dramatization of a situation or problem is followed by a group discussion.

Simulation. This is a learning environment that simulates a real setting, with the focus on attitudes and feelings related to the situation presented.

Group discussion. A group of five to twelve people have a relatively unstructured exchange of ideas focused on the attitudes and values they hold about a specific issue or problem.

Storytelling. Participants "tell their stories" about an experience that all or most group members have in common.

Metaphor analysis. Participants construct metaphors—concrete images—that describe, in a parallel yet more meaningful way, a phenomenon being discussed.

Game. Participants take part in an activity characterized by structured competition to provide insight into their attitudes, values, and interests.

Exercise, structured experience. People participate in planned exercises or experiences, usually using some instrument or guide, and then discuss their feelings and reactions.

Reflective practice. Thoughtfully reflecting on one's actions, including the assumptions and feelings associated with those actions, can be done individually or as a part of a small-group discussion.

More in-depth descriptions of these and other instructional techniques can be found in Seaman and Fellenz (1989), Brookfield (1990), Galbraith (1990a), Silberman (1990), Mezirow and Associates (1990), Apps (1991), and Davis (1993).

Although this categorization of techniques offers a good representation of how each instructional technique fits with a type of learning outcome, in actual use the categories of techniques are not clear-cut. One technique may be appropriate for two or three categories of learning outcomes. For example, group discussion could be used in both the knowledge and attitude categories, while a simulation could be used to impart knowledge, teach psychomotor skills, and develop thinking skills.

The second key factor in choosing instructional techniques, as stated earlier, is the capability of the instructor. Does the instructor have the knowledge, skill, and confidence to handle a particular technique? Does he or she feel comfortable using it? If not, the instructor's discomfort may be distracting. For example, an instructor who employs a new technique that does not seem to work the way she thought it should may continually apologize to learners.

The principle of active learner participation has also been stressed by Knowles (1980), Silberman (1990), and Munson (1992). "Given the choice between two techniques, choose the one involving the learners in the most active participation" (Knowles, 1980, p. 240). A sample of techniques with high, medium, and low participant involvement is given below:

High Participant Involvement
Group discussion
Buzz group
Case study
Game
Simulation
In-basket exercise
Structured experience
Critical incident
Trial and error
Metaphor analysis

Medium Participant Involvement
Reaction panel
Screened speech
Listening group
Behavior modeling
Role playing
Storytelling
Quiet meeting
Observation
Reflective practice

Low Participant Involvement
Lecture
Panel
Symposium
Demonstration

Assembling Instructional Materials

Carol B., a new part-time instructor in the continuing education division, attends a half-day workshop on selecting and using different media in classroom instruction. She really gets turned on to the use of these materials and decides to incorporate them into her classes as often as she can. Carol's colleagues can always tell who the instructor is for a particular session by the amount of equipment and handouts in the room. To Carol's surprise, she finds that not all participants are receptive to her use of supplemental materials, and she wonders why. Carol sincerely thinks they make her presentations much more interesting and lively, but she wonders if she is doing the right thing.

According to Dick and Carey (1990) and Tracey (1992), there are seven selection guidelines for choosing instructional materials:

- Select materials that fit the maturity, interests, and abilities of the participants.
- Select materials that fit with a particular learning activity.
- Maintain a balance in the types of materials used.
- Avoid the overuse of materials.
- Select materials that complement rather than duplicate other learning resources available.
- Choose materials that fit what is being taught (for example, knowledge versus thinking skills).
- Select materials that are available now or can be designed in the needed time frame and can be delivered effectively in the environment where the learning activity is to be held.

Carol B. violated at least two, if not more, of these basic guidelines—avoiding the overuse of materials and selecting materials that fit with a particular learning activity.

Types of Materials and Aids Available

A wide variety of instructional materials and aids can be used. A listing of the most popular materials follows (Robinson and Robinson, 1989; Rothwell and Kazanas, 1992; Tracey, 1992):

Worksheets, content outlines, observation guides

Workbooks, manuals, programmed texts

Books, articles, pamphlets, newspapers

Flipcharts, chalkboards, whiteboards, easels

Models, real objects, mock-ups, specimens, storyboards

Photographs, maps, charts, diagrams, pictures, drawings

Transparencies, slides, filmstrips

Audiotapes, compact discs

Computer programs

Films, videotapes, videodiscs, television

Multimedia presentations (some combination of text, graphics, animation, motion video, and digitized audio controlled by a computer)

Again, materials and aids should be selected carefully to enhance the learning efforts of the participants.

Buying or Making Instructional Materials

Before developing or buying new instructional materials, program planners should explore what materials already exist in-house. Are suitable materials available that could be used as is or with some modification? If not, are organizational staff available and able to develop the needed materials, or would it in any case be more cost-effective to buy materials from an external vendor (Dick and Carey, 1990; Rothwell and Kazanas, 1992)?

If the decision is to make the materials in-house, this can be done in a number of ways. For fairly simple materials, such as worksheets and content outlines, the instructor or the coordinator of the program may develop the materials. The same is now true for transparencies, charts, and diagrams, for staff who have access to computer graphics and word-processing programs.

When preparing more elaborate materials, such as videotapes or the components of computer-based instruction, a more complex process is used, usually involving a team effort (Dick and Carey, 1990; Tracey, 1992; Smith and Ragan, 1993). A typical team is composed of an educational specialist, a content expert, and an instructional designer. The team's role is to plan and oversee the production of the needed materials. Individual members of the team, depending on their expertise, may also do the actual production activities. It is important to validate complex materials with actual participants prior to using them on a large-scale basis (Dick and Carey, 1990; Tracey, 1992; Smith and Ragan, 1993). The validation process may be done with individuals or with groups, depending on the nature of the materials developed and how they will be used.

Nadler (1982) notes that program planners who decide to buy all or part of the instructional materials for an educational program, should consider five questions that address possible restrictions on the use of those materials:

Can the program [or materials] *be bought outright? Are there any restrictions on the use of the materials? Must subsequent use be authorized by the vendor? What is the cost for subsequent use? Can the learning materials be reproduced by the designer, or must supplies continually be purchased from the vendor?* [p. 141]

Nadler (1982) also cautions that it is unusual for materials purchased from outside vendors to meet all the requirements of a particular program. Therefore, modifications may have to be made to the materials themselves or to the instructional activities. For example, the sequencing of content of a particular program may need to be changed to match more closely the sequence of the purchased materials.

Whether the decision is made to use or prepare in-house materials or obtain materials from an outside source, Tracey (1992) notes that "the major criterion of selection is simply this: Will it advance learning; is it needed? A training aid must actually aid learning and not be mere 'eye wash' " (p. 292).

Preparing for Instructional Evaluation

Instructional evaluation is done for four major reasons: to assess participants' background, experiences, and readiness for learning when they enter an activity or program; to improve the instructional process and materials; to ascertain whether the instructional event has actually produced the desired results; and to assist participants to be more effective learners (Dick and Carey, 1990; Brookfield, 1990, 1992; Bennett and Clasper, 1993). Each of these purposes is discussed in the following subsections.

Evaluation at Entry

Evaluation done either prior to or at the start of a learning activity allows the instructors to know what the participants know and can do and/or how they feel about the content to be presented. Evaluation methods at this stage can range from asking participants to complete simple questionnaires (on who they are, what background knowledge and experiences they have related to the content, and the like) to administering comprehensive tests on prerequisite knowledge or skills (Bennett and Clasper, 1993). The data obtained can also be used as baseline data for evaluations given after the activity has been completed (see Chapter Nine).

Evaluation of the Instructional Process and Materials

Using instructional evaluation to improve the instructional process and materials can be done during the instructional event (formative evaluation), afterwards (summative evaluation), or at both times. This type of evaluation is usually completed by the instructors themselves and/or by the participants (Brookfield, 1990; Apps, 1991; Munson, 1992; Powers, 1992). Instructors can benefit greatly by reflecting on the instructional process and the content both during the session and after it is over. One way for instructors to formalize this reflection is to keep a teaching journal or log in which, after each session, they jot down and reflect on what was done well, what could have been done better, and what could be done differently (Apps, 1991). Team teaching with a colleague also encourages instructors to reflect on instructional activities, as long as both instructors agree that debriefing sessions will be a regular part of their team-teaching process.

Participant evaluation of the materials and process can also be very useful (especially when the session is still in progress), but only if instructors are willing to make changes based on the feedback given to them. Again, this evaluation can be done in a variety of ways, from questionnaires to small-group feedback sessions to large-group discussions. Sample questions to guide participant reactions are as follows:

- Were the handouts and other materials understandable and useful to you?
- Which instructional techniques were the most helpful to you in the learning process? Which were the least helpful?
- What was especially good about the session, and what could have been improved?
- Were the physical facilities comfortable and appropriate for the learning activities?
- Was the instructional climate welcoming, or did it inhibit your learning? Please give specific examples of factors that enhanced and/or blocked your willingness and/or ability to learn.
- Was the participation level appropriate and helpful to you as a learner?
- Are there any points and/or specific skills covered that you do not understand or do not know how to do? What do you believe would help you in gaining a better grasp of the content?
- Did the instructor respect differing viewpoints?
- Did the instructor invite and encourage participation from the group and individuals?
- Were the instructional aids (for example, overheads, videotapes, charts, and graphs) helpful, or did they distract from the presentation?

With instructional segments that will be used on a large scale with a variety of groups, a more comprehensive process of formative evaluation is used to evaluate the instructional materials and process. Usually this evaluation is done with small test groups before the materials are used on a regular basis. For a more complete description of this type of formative evaluation for instructional units, see Dick and Carey (1990), Rothwell and Kazanas (1992), and Smith and Ragan (1993).

Evaluation of the Results

The starting point for evaluating the results of the instructional unit is the learning objectives. The evaluation techniques chosen need to match the focus of those objectives—knowledge acquisition, enhancement of thinking skills, development of psychomotor skills, and/or changes in attitudes, values, and/or feelings. (As noted in Chapter Nine, evaluation techniques used for this part of instructional evaluation are also used as part of the procedures for evaluating total programs.) Some of the most widely used techniques for evaluating what has been learned are listed below (Smith and Delahaye, 1987; Harris, 1989; Silberman, 1990; Tracey, 1992; Bennett and Clasper, 1993):

Acquisition of Knowledge
- *Paper-and-pencil tests.* Participants respond to a printed set of questions. The test may consist of multiple-choice, true-false, matching, and/or sentence-completion items.
- *Essays.* Participants respond in writing to one or more questions or problem situations. They may be asked to compare, discuss, analyze, criticize, evaluate, or the like.

- *Oral tests.* Participants respond to a set of questions orally, usually on an individual basis.
- *Oral presentations.* Participants give a formal oral presentation to a selected group on a specific topic area.

Enhancement of Thinking Skills
- *Case studies.* Participants analyze and give alternative solutions to an event, incident, or situation that is problematic. This may be done in written or oral form and be either a group or individual exercise.
- *Essays.* Participants respond in writing to one or more questions or problem situations. They may be asked to demonstrate their ability to analyze, compare and contrast, criticize, or evaluate.
- *Interviews.* Participants conduct individual and/or group interviews. The focus of the exercise is to demonstrate the ability to analyze, criticize, or evaluate a specific problem or situation.

Development of Psychomotor Skills
- *Performance tests.* Participants perform a skill, operation, or practical application. Specified equipment and/or materials are often used. A clear statement of the standards required must be developed, and all parties must understand those standards.
- *On-the-job observations.* Participants, under the eye of the evaluator, carry out a set of performance behaviors on the job. Again, clear standards for performance must be set.
- *Product reviews.* Participants produce a product for review by the instructor and/or an outside expert or panel of experts.

Changes in Attitudes, Values, and/or Feelings
- *Role playing.* Participants role-play a situation, focusing on attitudes and feelings.
- *Paper-and-pencil tests.* Participants answer a printed set of questions that focus on specific attitudes. Although these tests are difficult to construct, they can provide a very useful measure.
- *Exercises.* Participants take part in exercises that display their attitudes about a particular topic or situation.

Although categorizing evaluation techniques is helpful, program planners should note that, depending on how a technique is designed, it (like instructional techniques) may fit into more than one category of learning outcomes. For example, written tests, depending on the type of test items, can measure knowledge acquisition, enhancement of thinking skills, changes in attitudes, values, and/or feelings, or all of the above.

Smith and Delahaye (1987) have outlined four important points to consider when administering an instructional evaluation. First, many participants are very anxious about any type of evaluation related to what they have learned. Educators need to respond to this anxiety with both concern and respect for the participants' feelings. Second, clear and complete instructions about how the evaluation will be conducted should be provided. Specified should be the date, time, and place of the evaluation; the format and length of the evaluation; what the evaluation will require participants to do; and what participants can or cannot bring with them on the day of the evaluation (such as their own computers, resource materials). Third, a comfortable environment should be provided. Fourth, all materials (such as paper, pencils, equipment) needed to complete the evaluation should be available.

Evaluation to Assist Learning

The final reason to do instructional evaluations is to assist learning (Brookfield, 1990, 1992). As Brookfield (1992) notes,

> To be helpful an evaluation should be educative. . . . (1) It should help the recipient become more adept and critically reflective in regard to the specific learning activity involved, (2) it should assist learners to develop insight into their own habitual learning process and rhythms so that they can make some judgments about when these should be given free rein and when they should be held in check, and (3) it should assist adults to develop self-concepts of themselves as learners as a way of nurturing their self-confidence and encouraging their belief that areas of skill, knowledge, action, and insight that they had formerly considered as being closed to them are actually accessible. [p. 22]

Brookfield goes on to describe seven indicators that can help instructors judge whether their evaluation processes are useful and significant to learners as they engage in the learning process:

- *Clarity*. Describing clearly, precisely, and in language understandable to the learners the criteria that will be used to judge their learning.
- *Specificity*. Outlining precisely the criteria for what is expected of learners (for example, in terms of in-class participation, written assignments, other products) and specific actions they can make to enhance their learning efforts.
- *Immediacy*. Giving feedback as soon as possible after the activity has been completed.
- *Accessibility*. Providing opportunities for learners for additional discussions about their evaluation.
- *Affirmation*. Acknowledging participants' efforts and achievements, no matter how large or small.
- *Future-orientation*. Giving clear suggestions for future changes and actions.
- *Justifiability*. Making sure that learners understand how the evaluation will help them in their learning efforts.

Of these seven, the indicators of affirmation and future-orientation are the most challenging and helpful to both instructors and participants.

Sample Instructional Plan

When clearly and concisely developed, instructional plans provide roadmaps that help instructors get where they want to go and remind them of their intended route (Smith and Delahaye, 1987; Harris, 1989). Three major advantages of preparing these plans are these: instructional plans help instructors (1) stay within the time frame for various parts of the educational activity, (2) know whether they have wandered too far off the topic (and how they can regain their focus), and (3) complete the learning activity in the allotted time.

There is no set form for an instructional plan as long as these major components of the activity are outlined:

- Learning objectives
- Content areas and key points to emphasize
- Techniques and materials to be used
- Evaluation plan
- Estimated time for each major part of the learning activity or activities

A sample instructional plan is given in Exhibit 12.1.

The instructional plan should be used as a guide for how the instructor and the participants spend their time in the session, not as a document that dictates precisely what each person must do when. There must be room for flexibility and change in both the content and the learning process, depending on the learners and what happens in the learning situation (Brookfield, 1990; Apps, 1991).

Making the Instructional Plan Work

How instructors, whether they are leaders of individual sessions or keynote speakers, put their instructional plans into action can either foster or block a positive climate for learning. Instructors can enhance learning by sharing their content mastery, being helpful facilitators, using instructional techniques and evaluation strategies appropriately and well, and establishing good rapport with the participants (Knox, 1986; Brookfield, 1990; Apps, 1991; Sisco, 1991). All these actions assume that instructors have some level of knowledge about the participants and come to the learning event well prepared.

Motivating participants up front is a very important part of making the instructional plan work (Munson, 1992). One major way to capture participants' interest is to get them personally involved with the material. This could be done, in smaller groups, by starting with a question-and-answer period or breaking the group into dyads or small work teams, for example. In larger groups, presenters could use human interest stories or prepare participants by highlighting two or three new and exciting ideas at the outset. However participation and interest are fostered, the method should be well thought out and applicable to the

Exhibit 12.1. Sample Instructional Plan.

Title: A Program Planning Model—Checklist for Planning Successful Programs

Date and Time: Wednesday 9:30 A.M. to Noon

Learning Objectives	Content Heading	Key Points to Emphasize	Instructional Techniques	Estimated Time
The participants will be able to . . .				
Describe an eleven-component program planning model	Present program planning model	Point out that the model is a set of interacting and dynamic elements and that most program planners work concurrently on a number of the components. Describe the eleven components of the model. The key word in using the model is *flexibility*.	Lecture Question-and-answer period	30 minutes
Analyze a case study using the model presented	Analyze case study	In small groups of five people, have participants analyze a case study. Appoint a discussion leader and a recorder who will report back to the whole group the results of each small group's work.	Small-group discussion Report from small groups Large-group discussion	45 minutes
Critique the model in terms of its usefulness for on-the-job applications	Critique the model	Discuss the strengths and weaknesses of the model. How could the model be revised?	Buzz groups Large-group discussion	30 minutes
List two ways they can use one component of the model in their daily work activities	Apply the model	Point out how the model can be applied to what participants do in their jobs.	Dyads Round-robin listing of ideas in the larger group	30 minutes

Evaluation plan: Pretest and posttest on the program model. Review of case study analysis.

Instructional materials and equipment needed:

For Instructor	For Participants
Overhead projector	Handout on program planning model
Overheads	Case study
	Critique form
	Reference list on program planning

Room Arrangement Needed: Chairs arranged around tables, table up front for the instructor program content. There is nothing worse than starting a session in an unorganized and vague manner.

A second way to motivate the group is by having enthusiastic and energetic instructors. Instructors who are open to questions and comments, use humor, and interact in an active manner can spark the interest of even the more reluctant participants.

In assisting the participants to learn content, instructors need to present the material in an organized manner. A number of different instructional techniques, as described earlier in this chapter, can be used, with the emphasis placed on active learner participation whenever possible and appropriate.

Some helpful hints for instructors as they move through the instructional plan are listed here:

Remove or lessen anxieties of the participants.

Spell out clearly and up front the expectations for participants.

Set or develop group norms. (Let participants know, for example, that active participation is encouraged, divergent opinions are welcomed, and a question-and-answer period will be a part of the presentation.)

Share what you have in common with the participants.

Let learners know you are there to help them learn.

Use nondiscriminatory language that all participants can readily understand and treat participants in an unbiased way.

Give participants advanced "organizers" (such as five key points) to help them follow the ideas presented.

Use the resources and expertise of the participants.

Use an outline or notes rather than reading a formally prepared paper or script.

Restate important ideas.

Be generous with examples (both yours and the participants').

Listen carefully to all ideas presented by the participants and respond appropriately.

Keep a good pace and be aware of time.

Provide feedback and positive reinforcement to participants throughout the session.

Recognize that emotions play an important part in the learning process.

Be flexible with your presentation, instructional plans, and techniques (for example, build on the unexpected).

Be caring and openly committed to the participants' learning.

Use humor and laughter.

Have fun.

Be ethical in your practice.

Helpful resources that describe more fully what instructors can do to ensure a positive learning experience include Brookfield (1990), Silberman (1990), Apps (1991), Sisco (1991), and Powers (1992). Whenever possible, instructors should assist participants in examining how the new knowledge, skills, attitudes, values, and/or feelings they have learned can be applicable to their lives. (See Chapter Eight.) This can be done in numerous ways, as was illustrated in Table 8.1. Four key transfer-of-learning strategies are these: (1) using concrete application examples in formal presentations, (2) including applications exercises during the learning event (such as role playing, return demonstrations, simulations), (3) having participants develop individual action plans for how they will use their newly acquired knowledge, skills, attitudes, values, and/or feelings, and (4) modeling the skills, attitudes, and/or values needed for the learning transfer.

When participants develop individual action or learning plans, in most cases a draft should be prepared during the program (O'Donnell and Caffarella, 1990; Caffarella, 1993). In helping participants complete these plans, instructors should encourage participants to indicate specific individuals who could provide assistance and/or support, especially when they are committed to making major personal, work, or community changes. (This assistance and/or support could be given by a variety of people, such as fellow participants, work colleagues and supervisors, family and friends, and professional educators.) A sample form for an individual action plan is provided in this chapter's Applications Exercises (see Exhibit 12.6).

Chapter Highlights

Instructional plans provide the framework for the interactions between learners and instructors and/or learners and resource materials for each educational activity. They spell out the anticipated end product, the content, the instructional techniques, and the evaluation strategies that make up the instructional process. In designing instructional plans, the program planners need to complete the following tasks:

- Develop clear and understandable learning objectives for each instructional session.

- Select and sequence the content based on the participants' knowledge and experiences, the nature of the content itself, and instructor preference.

- Choose instructional techniques that match the focus of the proposed learning outcomes and that the instructor is capable of using. (These might include lectures, case studies, role playing, storytelling, games, and metaphor analysis.)

- Select and/or develop instructional materials that will enhance the learning effort.

- Choose an evaluation component for each instructional segment that will enhance participant learning and assist in ascertaining whether the instructional event actually produced the desired result.

Clear and concise instructional plans provide guideposts for instructors that can help them stay focused as they move through the instructional process. Making that process work is an extremely important component of program implementation.

In order for the instructional component to work well, the logistics of the program must be handled in a way that enhances the learning process. Managing these program logistics before, during, and after the program is the subject of the next chapter.

Applications Exercises

The Applications Exercises in this chapter will help you to develop learning objectives (Exhibit 12.2), select instructional techniques (Exhibit 12.3), develop an instructional evaluation process (Exhibit 12.4), complete an instructional plan (Exhibit 12.5), and prepare for the application of learning (Exhibit 12.6).

Exhibit 12.2. Developing Learning Objectives.

1. Describe briefly an educational program for which you will act as the instructor or be part of an instructional team.

_____

_____

_____

_____

2. Develop a set of learning objectives for your part of the program using the following format. Complete each part for each objective, as appropriate.

The Learner	Action Verb	Content	Conditions Under Which the Learning Is to Be Demonstrated*	Criteria for Acceptable Performance*
a.				
b.				
c.				
d.				

*These two elements of the learning objective are not applicable for learning objectives that cannot be stated in behavioral or performance terms._

Exhibit 12.3. Selecting Instructional Techniques.

For the same session you described in Exhibit 12.2, develop two alternative ways the material could be taught. In doing this task, keep in mind the focus of the learning outcomes and the type of participant involvement you want.

Alternative 1:

_____

_____

_____

_____

_____

_____

Alternative 2:

_____

_____

_____

_____

_____

_____

Exhibit 12.4. Developing an Instructional Evaluation Process.

1. For the same session you described in Exhibits 12.2 and 12.3, describe the major reason or reasons for completing an instructional evaluation.

   _____

   _____

   _____

2. Select and describe one or more techniques you will use to evaluate this instructional session.

   _____

   _____

   _____

3. Describe how you will ensure that the evaluation process exhibits the following qualities:

   Clarity: _____

   _____

   Specificity: _____

   _____

   Immediacy: _____

   _____

   Accessibility: _____

   _____

   Affirmation: _____

   _____

   Future-orientation: _____

   _____

   Justifiability: _____

   _____

Exhibit 12.5. Completing an Instructional Plan.

Using the material from Exhibits 12.2, 12.3, and 12.4, develop an instructional plan for a session for which you will be serving as the instructor.

Session Title: _____

Date and Time: _____

Learning Objectives	Content Heading	Key Points to Emphasize	Instructional Techniques	Estimated Time

Evaluation plan: _____

_____

_____

Instructional materials and equipment needed:

For Instructor   For Participants

Room arrangement needed: _____

_____

General notes/comments: _____

_____

Exhibit 12.6. Preparing for the Application of Learning.

1. Briefly describe an educational program you recently attended.

_____

_____

_____

2. Complete an individual plan, as outlined in the following chart, specifying how you will apply what you learned.

Individual Action Plan

List knowledge, skills, and/or attitudes/ values/ feelings learned.	Specify when, where, and how you want to apply what you have learned.	Name people who could offer assistance, support.	List other resources that might be helpful (such as books, training programs).	Specify how you will know you are successfully using the new knowledge, skills, and/or values/ attitudes.	Outline time frame.

3. Review this plan with at least one other person and make changes as appropriate.

Thirteen

Coordinating Facilities and On-Site Events

There is nothing more frustrating to program participants and presenters than discovering that the logistical end of the program has received little or no attention. This problem is illustrated in the following scenarios.

Scenario 1: Poor Choice of Conference Facilities

Sue P. is really not enjoying the conference, primarily because the facilities range from poor to mediocre. She has thought to herself a number of times that the meeting rooms must have been designed by people who never attend educational events. The chairs are extremely uncomfortable, the lighting is terrible, and the temperature fluctuates between too hot and too cold. The food service and quality have been poor both for the breaks and the meals, and the hotel rooms are noisy and quite small. In addition, because the hotel is located in a questionable part of the city, Sue does not really feel safe. She tells herself that this is the last time she will attend a conference sponsored by this group, even though the program itself has been good, especially since her complaints to the conference staff have been virtually ignored.

Scenario 2: Meeting-Room Problems

John B., a workshop presenter, arrives at the room in which he is to present and finds it in total disarray. The room has dirty glasses, napkins, and crumbs scattered all over the tables; and although he requested a specific seating arrangement, the chairs and tables are all over the place. In addition, the overhead projector and screen he ordered are not in place. He looks through his presenter packet to see if it has any instructions on how to get assistance. Finding none, John decides to remedy the situation as best he can by moving the chairs and tables and figuring out how to do his presentation without the overhead projector. This is a somewhat awkward endeavor, because the program participants have started to arrive. Then—when everything is as set as can be and John is about to start—who should arrive but the person who was supposed to make sure all the room arrangements were in order.

Scenario 3: Ignoring the Schedule of Events

The program participants are beginning to get restless. According to the schedule, this session should have been over fifteen minutes ago. A number of people have already walked out of the session, while new arrivals looking for their next session keep opening and closing the door. Still the presenter goes on and on, seemingly oblivious to the time. Finally someone who has just entered the room—the next presenter, as it happens—tries in a very diplomatic way to let the speaker know that her session is scheduled in this room next. His response to this interruption is to tell her to wait her turn because he still has some important material to cover.

Thinking through the many logistical details of educational programs is not always fun, but it is a task program planners must be willing to tackle (and *before* the last minute). One of the hallmarks of top-notch program planners, among those who have the responsibility for logistical pieces, is that they are detail-oriented and able to keep track of numerous tasks in a timely manner. The larger the program, the more important it is to spend the time and effort needed before, during, and after the program to make sure it runs as smoothly as possible.

This chapter first addresses the importance of obtaining suitable program facilities. Included in that discussion are both facility and meeting-room checklists for helping planners with this task. Explored next is the role of the on-site program coordinator, along with those logistical aspects of the program that program coordinators need to have in place prior to the opening of the program. This section is followed by a description of the coordinator's role in creating a positive climate for learning once the participants have arrived and ways coordinators can monitor the program once it is in progress. The chapter concludes with suggestions for tasks that program coordinators need to complete in closing programs and in tying up loose ends once the participants have left.

Obtaining Suitable Facilities

The environment in which educational activities take place affects participants' learning (Fulton, 1991; Hiemstra, 1991). A learning environment is defined by Finkel as "every space in a facility in which meeting activities occur and the degree to which each detail of those spaces can be designed to contribute to higher levels of learning" (1984, p. 32). The most important space for all educational programs is the meeting rooms, whether they are designed for group or individual learning. In addition, program planners must consider other space, such as places for meals and breaks, overnight accommodations, and opportunities for recreation and socializing.

Investigating Facilities

There are five types of facilities most often used for educational activities: in-house organizational facilities, hotel and motel facilities, conference and retreat centers, college and university facilities, and resort areas. Each type of facility has its advantages and disadvantages, depending on the objectives of the educational activity, the instructional techniques to be used, the participants, the leaders, the cost, the accessibility, and the type of services provided by the facility (Nadler and Nadler, 1987; Munson, 1992). For example, for an organization's three-hour workshop for in-house personnel, the seminar rooms of that organization would probably be the best choice of facilities. If that same workshop were offered to people from a wide geographic area, however, a central meeting place in a local hotel or community college would probably work better.

If facilities need to be rented, program planners should check them out thoroughly. The following checklist can help with this task (Nadler and Nadler, 1987; Vosko, 1991; Munson, 1992):

- Availability on program dates
- Costs
    Meeting rooms
    Food (meals and breaks)
    Lodging
    Recreation
    Equipment
- Location
    Safe and secure lighting
    Barrier-free access
    Parking
    Convenience
- Transportation convenience
    Public
        Convenience
        Frequency
        Cost
    Private
- Meeting rooms
    Size
    Appearance
    Lighting
    Decor
    Furnishings
    Ventilation, heating, and cooling
    Sound projection
- Supporting services
    Food
    Accommodations
    Recreation
    Fitness facilities
    Public telephone
    Quality of service
- General factors
    Attractions in the area
    Experience in housing educational programs
    Site personnel
    Safety issues

Simerly (1990) stresses that "there are many legal issues to be aware of and traps to avoid" (p. 103) for planners attempting to negotiate favorable contracts for rental space. (He goes on to outline seventeen helpful tips for securing favorable contracts for meeting space, lodging, and meals.)

Choosing Meeting Rooms

Different learning activities require different types of meeting rooms (from large auditoriums to small seminar rooms) and seating arrangements. For example, instructors who want to foster group interaction and team building should not choose a huge room and arrange chairs in rows (preventing participants from facing each other). Rather, they should place chairs around a table or in a circle in a small room; that arrangement provides a much better learning environment for these kinds of activities. In addition, some types of learning activities require special facilities, such as space for prototype machinery or equipment.

In choosing meeting rooms, the accent should be on detail. "Details that contribute to learning are kept or added; ones that hinder participant learning or leader effectiveness are changed or eliminated" (Finkel, 1986, p. 52). Important details that should be checked when arranging for meeting-room space are outlined in the following list, which includes recommendations for each factor (Finkel, 1986; Nadler and Nadler, 1987; Vosko, 1991; and Munson, 1992).

Access. Choose rooms that are barrier-free and accessible (that is, having ramps, elevator access, braille directions).

Room size. Avoid overcrowding and cavernous, oversized rooms.

Room structure. The ideal room structure is square. Watch out for narrow rooms and posts in the wrong places.

Windows. Choose rooms with no windows or rooms whose windows can be completely covered.

Furnishings. Make sure tables and chairs are movable. Chairs need to be padded and provide good back support.

Color. Look for pastel shades of green, blue, and yellow. Stay away from white and dark colors.

Adornments. Check to see whether pictures, sculptures, or other types of adornment can be taken down.

Floor coverings. Choose rooms carpeted in solid shades, not patterns.

Lighting. Look for indirect, warm fluorescent lighting and rheostatic controls. For notetaking, a minimum of thirty to fifty footcandles is recommended.

Glare. Eliminate all sources of glare.

Temperature. Make sure you are able to regulate the temperature. Keep the temperature between sixty-five and seventy degrees. If you err, err on the cool side.

Ventilation. Keep the air circulating in the room. Allow no smoking.

Noise. Check for noise from heating and air-conditioning units in adjoining rooms, corridors, and outside the building.

Acoustics. Check on the bounce and absorption of sound. Use different types of voices for this testing process.

Electrical outlets. Identify the location and type of outlets (for example, prong outlets).

Computer hookups. Check for telephone jacks that would allow for computer hookups.

Access to other areas. Check for easy access to restrooms, vending machines, eating facilities, and so on.

Reality often sets in with a bang for those selecting meeting rooms. Some program planners have no real choice. For example, they may have to use the space available in their organization even though it is not the best environment for learning. In situations like this, it is important to think how the available space can be used to its best advantage. If the lighting is poor, can extra lights be obtained for the session? If the placement of outlets is inconvenient, are extension cords available and can they be placed so that people are not constantly tripping over them? If the room is too warm, could quiet fans be used to cool it down? Could more comfortable chairs be borrowed from another room just for this session?

Arranging Meeting Rooms

This question is often asked of program staff: "How do you want the meeting rooms arranged?" Often the response is a quickly scribbled picture on a napkin or other scrap of paper. It would be more helpful to have a set of diagrams available to give to the persons responsible for arranging the room (such as custodial staff, convention center managers). Figure 13.1 presents diagrams of the most frequently used small-room arrangements, while Figure 13.2 shows options for larger rooms:

Figure 13.1. Arrangements for Small Meeting Rooms.

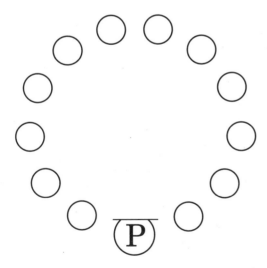

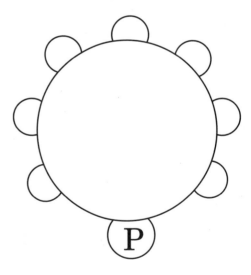

Chairs in a Circle

Round Table with Chairs

Figure 13.1. Arrangements for Small Meeting Rooms *(continued).*

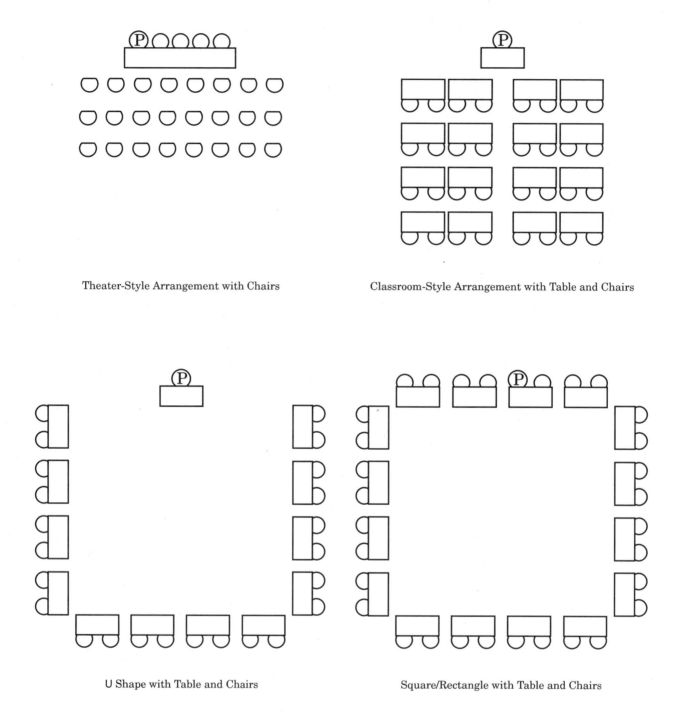

Theater-Style Arrangement with Chairs

Classroom-Style Arrangement with Table and Chairs

U Shape with Table and Chairs

Square/Rectangle with Table and Chairs

Figure 13.1. Arrangements for Small Meeting Rooms *(continued)*.

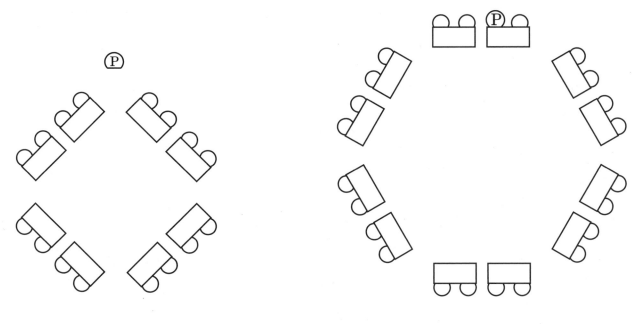

Diamond with Table and Chairs

Hexagon with Table and Chairs

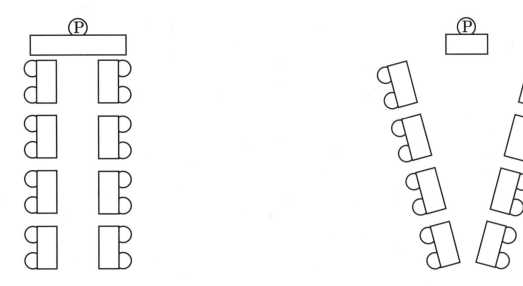

T Shape with Table and Chairs

Classroom-Style V Shape with Table and Chairs

Source: Nadler and Nadler, 1987, pp. 109–116. Reprinted by permission of Jossey-Bass Inc., Publishers.

Figure 13.2. Arrangements for Large Meeting Rooms.

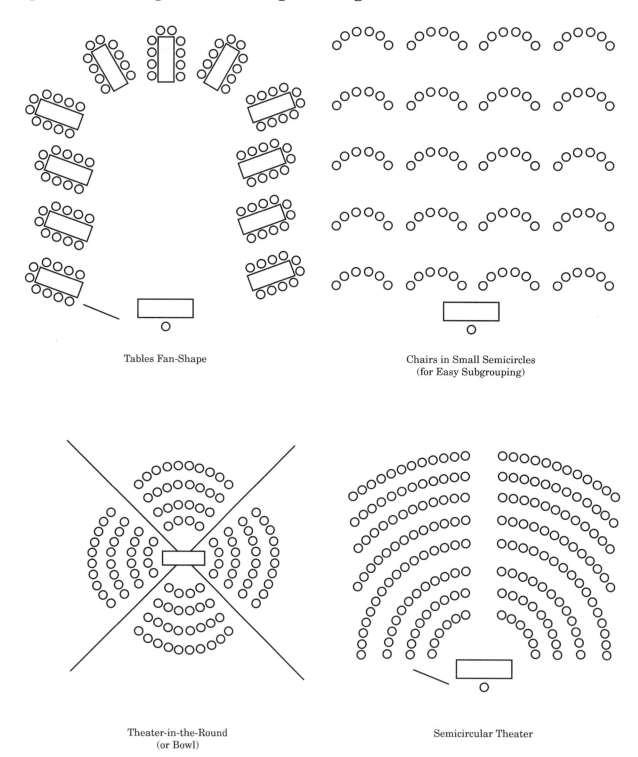

Tables Fan-Shape

Chairs in Small Semicircles
(for Easy Subgrouping)

Theater-in-the-Round
(or Bowl)

Semicircular Theater

Source: Malcolm S. Knowles, *The Modern Practice of Adult Education: From Pedagogy to Andragogy,* © 1980, p. 165. Reprinted by permission of Prentice-Hall, Englewood Cliffs, New Jersey.

Arranging for Instructional Equipment.

In arranging facilities, program planners need to know whether the necessary instructional equipment (for example, screens, overhead projectors, video players) is available at the site. For educational programs held at the host organization, this usually involves only scheduling the equipment, but equipment may also have to be borrowed or leased if the host organization does not own what is needed.

When facilities are rented, the arranging of instructional equipment may be more complicated. Equipment may be supplied by the host organization, presenters, the rental facility, or an outside rental agency. All of these arrangements have both advantages and disadvantages, as highlighted below:

Type of Arrangement	Advantages	Disadvantages
Supplied by host organization	The equipment usually will be in good working order. The program coordinator usually has control over scheduling and setting up the equipment.	Staff must be available to move and set up equipment in the rental facility. The program coordinator usually is responsible for making sure the equipment is set up properly and that it works.
Supplied by presenters	Presenters may feel more comfortable using their own equipment. Presenters may be able to supply highly specialized equipment that is not usually available (for example, CRT screens).	Many presenters do not have easy access to the equipment. Some presenters do not want or are not physically able to cart their own equipment.
Supplied by on-site rental facility	The equipment is available on-site, and therefore no arrangements need to be made to get the equipment to and from the host organization. Staff from the rental facility may handle all setting up and taking down of equipment.	The equipment may not be well maintained and thus may work poorly at best. Some control is lost by the program coordinator in regard to setting up the equipment.
Supplied by outside rental agency	The equipment is transported to and from the facility by the rental agency staff, who also usually handle all setting up and taking down of equipment.	The equipment may not be well maintained and thus may work poorly at best. Some control is lost by the program coordinator in regard to setting up the equipment. The program coordinator or presenter may not be familiar with how the rental equipment operates.

Whether planners are arranging for in-house or rental equipment, three considerations must be taken into account: Will the equipment be in good working order on the day of the program? Will the equipment definitely be available at the times requested? Who will be responsible for setting up and checking the equipment prior to presentation times? Previous experience can help in framing responses for the first two questions. If the organization responsible for the equipment has a good track record for supplying working equipment in a timely manner, then program staff can feel confident that this will be the case for their program. If, on the other hand, staff members have heard that this organization's equipment has not worked properly in the past and/or there have been scheduling difficulties, they may well decide that another company be brought in to manage the equipment for the program. The third task—setting up and checking the equipment—also needs to be assigned up front. Will staff from the host organization be responsible for this task, or will it be done by staff from the rental agency?

Doing On-Site Coordination

Bill Q. is busily checking all the last-minute program arrangements for a two-day conference that starts tomorrow. The conference is being held in one of the local hotels. This is the first time he has used these facilities, so he has been double-checking all the arrangements, such as accommodations, food, and equipment. Bill plans to go to the hotel later in the day to again meet with the hotel sales director to make sure all is in order. Bill's major worry at this point is the weather. Rain with heavy fog is forecast, and this could wreak havoc with the arrival of both conference participants and speakers. He has been thinking all day about possible contingency plans for use if one or more of the major speakers is not able to arrive on time. Bill has called an emergency meeting of the conference planning committee to help him work out the details of a possible reorganization for at least the first day of the conference. This committee will meet later over dinner.

Most personnel who coordinate educational programs agree that the actual carrying out of a program can be very hectic. All of the program arrangements must be checked, and thought must be given to how the program should be opened, monitored, and closed. One person may be responsible for all these tasks (as well as the instructional portion, perhaps) or a number of people may be involved, depending on the complexity of the event.

Smith and Delahaye (1987) have stressed how visible the coordination function is. Although most program participants are unaware of or indifferent to what went into *planning* a program, they are usually immediately cognizant of the details related to its on-site coordination; and they form opinions about the program based on those details (Smith and Delahaye, 1987). For example, were the registration procedures easy or difficult? Were all the meeting rooms clearly marked? Did the program start and end on time? Was there adequate parking? Because of this visibility, it is important that educational programs be well coordinated from start to finish, with special attention paid to those details that directly affect the participants.

Overseeing the Program Arrangements

One of the first tasks of program coordinators is to ensure that all program arrangements have been completed. This task should be done the day before, for the most part, although some things, such as checking on meeting-room arrangements and equipment, must be done on the day of the program. A program arrangements checklist follows, showing the items that need to be finalized prior to the start of the program (Nadler and Nadler, 1987; Smith and Delahaye, 1987; Silberman, 1990; Munson, 1992):

Items to Be Checked	Points to Be Considered for Each Item
Facilities to be used (such as rooms for large- and small-group sessions, meal and break areas, exhibit areas)	Lighting is adequate. Ventilation is good. Temperature is comfortable. Layout of room (for example, arrangement of table and chairs, placement of equipment) is what was requested.
Meals and breaks	Menus reflect what was requested. Final count of people for each meal and break is done. Exact times for meals and breaks are established.
Sleeping accommodations	Reservations are in order for both participants and staff. Rooms are clean and comfortable.
Instructors and program staff	All staff have a clear understanding of their roles. All presenters, leaders, and instructors are accounted for.
Equipment	The type and quantity of equipment requested is available. The right equipment is placed in the right rooms. All equipment is working properly. Backup parts and equipment are easily accessible.
Materials	All items are complete. The number of copies is correct. The materials are arranged in order of use.

Items to Be Checked	Points to Be Considered for Each Item
Travel	Transportation needs are provided for (for example, travel to the site, parking).
	Responsibility for assisting participants and/or program presenters with transportation is assigned.
	When transportation is needed, and for whom, is determined.
Program schedule	People have been assigned responsibilities for keeping the activities on time.
	Methods for keeping on schedule have been agreed upon.
On-site registration	Procedures are clear and customer-friendly.
	The physical setup is correct.
	The times when registration will be open are posted.
Message center	The form of the center has been decided.
	Who to staff the center has been determined.
	Ways to handle emergency messages are clear.

Not all items on this list need to be checked for every program, of course. What is important is that on-site coordinators know about and pay attention to those items that are essential for their specific programs. The key to finalizing the program arrangements is ensuring that everything that *can* be in place *is* in place *prior to the arrival of the participants* (Munson, 1992). There is nothing more frustrating to participants than having a learning event appear disorganized before it even begins.

Opening the Program

It is crucial to create a positive climate for learning at the opening of any educational event. Knowles has spoken often to this point: "I am convinced that what happens in the first hour or so of any learning activity (course, seminar, workshop, institute, tutorial, etc.) largely determines how productive the remaining hours will be" (1980, p. 224). Climate-setting starts as soon as the participants arrive. Are the participants greeted warmly and perhaps given a cup of hot coffee, or do they wander around trying to figure out where they should be? Is someone available to introduce the participants to one another and provide nametags? Are the people responsible for on-site registration friendly and helpful, or do they seem to be just doing a job? Do staff growl at participants who have problems with their registration materials, or do they really try to be of assistance? Do the coordinating staff seem harried, or do they appear calm and in control?

The way participants are oriented to the actual learning activities at the start is also very important (Smith and Delahaye, 1987; Silberman, 1990; Sisco, 1991). Items usually included in this orientation process are staff and participant introductions, an explanation of the objectives of the program, clarification of program requirements (such as attendance, outside assignments, instructor and participant expectations), and basic administrative information (for example, start and finish times, who should be contacted for assistance/problems). The orientation can be done formally (perhaps in a session whose sole purpose is orienting participants) or informally (at the opening of the program and/or in individual program sessions). The size of the group and the format for learning are two of the major factors that determine how the orientation process should be conducted.

For small and midsized groups (under 100), the orientation process is usually done with the whole group, whether as a separate session or as a part of opening the program. In most situations, the staff are introduced to the group first. If there are many staff members, only key personnel, such as the program coordinator and the primary instructors and resource people, should be introduced at this time. All these introductions should be brief and to the point.

If the group is small (fifteen or fewer), program participants should also be introduced to the whole group. If the number is greater than fifteen, the coordinator or instructor may choose to divide the group into smaller groups or into triads or dyads for the initial introductions. Although this grouping does not allow the learners to get a snapshot of all the other participants, it does give them the opportunity to become acquainted with at least one or more of the other participants. This type of activity is especially important when the learners do not know each other or have just a passing acquaintance.

How the actual participant introductions are done in small and midsized groups varies, depending on the objectives of the program and the time allotted for this part of the program. Participants may simply introduce themselves; they may, after an initial conversation with a second participant, introduce each other; and/or they may take part in more elaborate warm-up or icebreaker activities (Smith and Delahaye, 1987; Bianchi, Butler, and Richey, 1990; Corbett, 1992). What people say or do may be straightforward (such as the sharing of names, occupations, and reasons for attending the program); it may include other information about themselves (such as interests, hobbies, expertise they bring to the event); and/or it may take on different forms when icebreakers or warm-up activities are used. All but the straightforward introductions may also be used to address the program content in some way. For example, participants may be asked to share special problems, issues, or questions they hope to have addressed and/or to describe any prior knowledge and experience they have related to the program content.

For very large groups, orientation to the program is handled in a number of different ways: whole-group sessions set aside just for orientation, small-group sessions, written and/or computerized information, and individual assistance programs. For example, a major national conference may host small-group sessions for people attending for the first time, assign mentors or helpers to first-time attenders, and provide written and/or computerized information systems for all participants. In addition, individual volunteer or paid staff may be placed at key locations to offer help in answering questions and concerns. Two useful information sources for developing orientation activities and creating positive learning climates for programs that are very large are Nadler and Nadler (1987) and Simerly (1990).

The learning format also plays a part in determining what the orientation process should be like (and even what content should be addressed). For example, if the learning format calls for active involvement of the participants, then this should be modeled up front in the participant introductions. On the other hand, for learning situations that do not call for participant interaction, such as public lectures, participant introductions may not be needed or even appropriate.

Monitoring the Program

Experienced program planners know that things *do* go wrong while the program is in process (Bradley, Kallick, and Regan, 1991; Munson, 1992). Some of these things, such as a major speaker's illness, are out of the coordinator's control. Other problems are in the coordinator's control (and could have been avoided), such as having insufficient copies of handouts or non-functioning equipment. No matter what the source of the problems, the key is to find solutions that allow the program to keep functioning at an optimal level. This means program coordinators must continually monitor the program, remain flexible, and at times be highly creative. For example, if a major presenter becomes ill right before the start of a program, either another speaker has to be found or the order and timing of the program have to be rearranged. Either solution calls for fast action on the part of the coordinator and the ability to make sound, but quick, decisions.

Even if the program appears to be running smoothly, it is important that program coordinators continue to make sure this is so. This includes checking to see that all presenters and other staff are present and prepared, rooms continue to be arranged as requested as sessions change, participant concerns and problems are addressed in a timely and courteous manner, equipment is available and working, food and refreshments are well prepared and delivered on time, the correct handouts and other resources are available, evaluation data are being collected as planned, and the time schedule is being followed by the presenters (Smith and Delahaye, 1987; Munson, 1992).

An additional way to monitor the program is to have participants give evaluative feedback to program staff at designated times during the event. This type of feedback is especially useful for programs of more than one day, when changes in the program's format or content could realistically be made. There are a number of ways this kind of feedback can be obtained, including administering short written questionnaires and having the respondents critique the program in small groups.

In an intriguing variation on the small-group approach, program coordinators can conduct focus-group interviews with selected participants (Long and Marts, 1981; O'Donnell, 1988) using semistructured questions to find out what participants think of the program. The participants' perceptions are then given to program staff so that changes can be made in the program for the next day. This evaluation process should be integrated into the program, however—not just tacked on at the end of the day. Participants should be selected at random to participate and be given in advance an invitation requesting their involvement. Because the job of the focus-group leader is critical, he or she should be well versed in the process and be willing to record and share all comments, no matter how negative.

The most critical component of the monitoring process, no matter how it is done, is using feedback to make program adjustments, as needed, in anything from the time schedule to the content of the program. It is the responsibility of program coordinators to ensure that necessary changes are made.

Closing the Program

In closing the program, program coordinators need to accomplish three tasks. The first task is to ensure that all data needed for the evaluation have been collected. Depending on the evaluation design, the data collection may have been done throughout the program, at the end of the program, or both. Especially when participants are asked to give written evaluative comments, it is helpful to offer some kind of incentive for completion. Door prizes, for example, could be awarded to participants who complete session evaluations during individual program sessions. A candy bar or a piece of fruit to eat on the way home could be given to participants who complete participant reaction forms at the end of the program.

A second task is to give participants recognition for taking part in the program. For some programs, such as recertification programs for public school teachers and programs in continuing medical education, this recognition must be formal, whereas for other types of programs it can be more informal. One common practice for giving formal recognition is to award certificates (or other written documentation) to all participants who have successfully met certain preestablished minimum requirements. These requirements may range from simple attendance to participant demonstration that learning has occurred. A second practice is to give formal academic credit, often in the form of continuing education units, to participants who meet agreed-upon standards. The assignment of credit must be set up formally in advance, of course, with either an accredited postsecondary institution or a professional association. Other less formal but very effective ways to recognize successful program completion include giving mementos (such as mugs and T-shirts) to program participants, highlighting their involvement via in-house communications or the local press, and hosting informal celebrations.

The third task at the end of a program is to thank both participants and staff for being a part of the program. This can be done either at a group session and/or individually, depending on the learning format and what seems most appropriate. Where possible, these thank-yous should be personalized (for example, recognizing something unique a staff person has done) and expressed with sincerity.

Tying Up Loose Ends

The coordinator also has the responsibility for tying up all the loose ends, such as picking up extra handouts, returning equipment, and scrutinizing the bills, after the program is completed. If the coordinator makes a closing checklist prior to the *start* of the program, tiredness is less likely to overcome the need to pay attention to the wrap-up details. A sample checklist of tasks to complete after the program follows (Smith and Delahaye, 1987):

- Check facilities and, where necessary, put back in order.
- Pick up and store extra handout materials.
- Check out and store equipment.
- Complete all administrative forms.
- Scrutinize and pay all bills.
- Conduct a staff debriefing.
- Write thank-you notes to presenters and other resource people.
- Jot down suggestions for program improvements.

Chapter Highlights

Handling the logistical end of the program often seems like a thankless task, and yet if these chores are not done well, they can negatively affect all aspects of educational programs. One of the hallmarks of program planners who handle these types of arrangements in an effective and efficient manner is that they understand the importance of both keeping track of and keeping up with all of the detail work involved in this phase of the planning and implementation process. Seven specific tasks need to be addressed in this component:

- Obtain suitable facilities that will provide a good environment for learning and arrange for instructional equipment that works.
- Oversee all of the on-site program arrangements (those dealing, for example, with facilities, instructors and other staff, equipment, program schedules).
- Create a positive climate for learning from the moment the participants arrive, offering a user-friendly registration system, participant orientation, and introductions.
- Provide a system for monitoring the program and making sound, quick decisions when program changes are needed.

- Gather data for the program evaluation and provide incentives, when needed, for completing the on-site evaluation process.
- Give recognition to program participants (for example, certificates, mugs, celebrations) and thank both staff and participants for being a part of the program.
- Tie up all loose ends after the program is completed (such as storing equipment, completing administrative forms, conducting staff debriefings).

Once a program (or a series of programs) has been conducted, it is important to communicate the value of program activities to appropriate individuals and groups. This reporting function is discussed in the final chapter of the book.

Applications Exercises

This chapter's Applications Exercises focus on coordinating facilities and on-site events. The first is intended to assist you in choosing meeting rooms (Exhibit 13.1), the second will help you oversee the program arrangements (Exhibit 13.2), and the third addresses creating a positive climate for learning (Exhibit 13.3).

Exhibit 13.1. Choosing Meeting Rooms.

1. No meeting room is perfect. Knowing that, choose from the list below your top seven requirements for a room that is adequate for your educational program.
   - ❑ The room has barrier-free access.
   - ❑ The room is square.
   - ❑ The room has no windows.
   - ❑ The chairs are comfortable and movable, and there is adequate work space available for every participant.
   - ❑ The color of the room is cheerful.
   - ❑ The room is clean and well maintained.
   - ❑ The floors are tastefully carpeted.
   - ❑ The lighting is good.
   - ❑ There are no sources of glare in the room.
   - ❑ The temperature of the room can be controlled.
   - ❑ There is good air circulation.
   - ❑ There is no background noise that might distract participants.
   - ❑ The acoustics of the room are good.
   - ❑ There are plenty of electrical outlets spaced adequately around the room.
   - ❑ There are convenient computer hookups.
   - ❑ The room is a good size for the number of participants.
   - ❑ The room is close to restrooms, vending machines, and other needed conveniences.

2. Ask two or three other people to also do the above task. Were you all in agreement? If not, discuss your areas of differences and then come to a group consensus on the top requirements for choosing meeting rooms.

Exhibit 13.2. Overseeing the Program Arrangements.

Reflect on an educational program you recently attended or coordinated. Using the following chart, critique the program arrangements that were made. Write "NA" (not applicable) next to those items for which program arrangements were not needed.

Categories of Items	What Was Good About the Arrangements?	What Problems Were There with the Arrangements?	How Could the Arrangements Have Been Improved?
Facilities			
Meals and Breaks			
Sleep Accommodations			
Instructors and Program Staff			
Equipment			
Materials			
Travel			
Program Schedule			
On-Site Registration			
Message Center			
Other			

Exhibit 13.3. Creating a Positive Climate for Learning.

1. Outline, using the following chart, how you would create a positive climate for learning.

Part of the Program	How would you handle each item to help create a positive climate for learning?
Registration	
Introduction of Staff	
Introduction of Participants	
Introduction of the Program	
Other (Please Specify)	

2. Discuss your ideas with two or three other people. Do they view your ideas as helpful? What other suggestions do they have?

_____

_____

_____

_____

_____

—— ∞ ——

Fourteen

Communicating the Value of the Program

Tom G., the vice president for human resource development for a large power company, has just met with all the training directors from the various operational centers for the company, and the majority of them voiced concern over the training function's lack of visibility. Although these directors believed that they and their staff were doing a commendable job, their perception was that they received very little recognition for their work, especially from top management. They asked Tom for help "telling their story" better, so it would be heard by the right people. Tom wonders what kind of advice he should give to the directors and what his role should be in enhancing the image of the training operation.

Communicating the value of educational programs to the appropriate publics is a task that is often overlooked (Munson, 1992). Although program planners usually generate some type of reports on their programs, these reports tend to be uninteresting. Even when the reports are lively and interesting, often no real thought is given to getting key decision makers to review and then use the information.

This chapter outlines five important factors program planners should consider when preparing reports on educational programs. These are followed by a brief discussion of the audience for and timing of program reports. The chapter concludes by stressing the notion that follow-up with key individuals and/or groups may be needed to clarify questions about the program or to make sure the information has been heard by the right people.

Preparing Reports on Educational Programs

There are five important factors to consider when preparing reports on educational programs: function, scope, audience, content, and format (Knowles, 1980; Boyle, 1981; Knox, 1986; Brinkerhoff, 1987). Each of these factors is discussed in the following subsections.

Function

Reports on educational programs may fill one or more major functions. A report can be used to educate and gain support from key people and groups, to facilitate and inform decision making about current and future programs, to provide documentation for permanent records, to demonstrate program accountability, and/or to market the program (Brinkerhoff, 1987; Rothwell and Kazanas, 1992; Tracey, 1992). The people responsible for preparing the report must have a clear understanding of how the report will be used before they put it together.

Scope and Audience

Decisions must also be made about the scope and audience for the report. How comprehensive should the report be? Will it describe only a specific educational event, selected parts of a program, or the educational program as a whole? And who should receive the report? There may be one or multiple audiences, depending on the function and scope of the communication. Common audiences for reports on educational programs include the following (Brinkerhoff, 1987):

Past, current, and future participants

Instructors

Program planning staff

Supervisors of participants

Senior management/administrators

Members of advisory program committees or other ad hoc planning committees or teams

Clientele of the organization

Regulatory or licensing groups

Funding agencies

Professional groups and organizations

Community leaders

Community groups and organizations

Libraries and their clearinghouse units

The general public

Content

The content of a report should be tailored to the issues and concerns of its recipients (Knox, 1986). A typical content outline is shown in Exhibit 14.1

Exhibit 14.1. General Content Outline for Report on an Educational Program.

1. Introduction
   a. Purpose of the report
   b. How the information for the report was obtained
   c. What will be addressed in the report (an "advanced organizer")
2. Body of the Report
   a. Overview of the goals and/or objectives of the educational program or event
   b. Description of the program participants and activities
   c. Description of the results of the program or event
   d. Listing of conclusions and recommendations for future actions
3. Appendixes

Format

The format—the means by which the information is to be communicated to the appropriate audience(s)—can be handled in a number of ways, as outlined below (Brinkerhoff, 1987; Rothwell and Kazanas, 1993):

- *Formal written report.* A formal, detailed written description of program objectives, results, and recommendations. The depth and scope of the report depends on the purpose and audience for the document.
- *Executive summary of formal written report.* A one- or two-page summary of a formal written report highlighting the major components of that report. A summary may be found at the beginning of the complete report and/or be distributed separately.
- *Journalistic-style report.* A report written in newspaper style describing the program and highlighting a specific aspect of the program (for example, participants, activities, results).
- *Media presentation.* A formal presentation using some kind of media, such as presentation slides, videotapes, videodiscs, or transparencies. Often formal reports are enhanced by the use of media.
- *Case study report.* A report that describes a specific educational event or situation. The case is used to illustrate a major facet of the program.
- *Product display.* An exhibit of products produced as a result of an educational program. This is usually used in combination with a second format, such as a written report or an informational brochure.
- *Poster or display board.* A sign illustrating the results of an educational program. It can be used as part of an oral presentation or placed in a strategic place in the organization where key personnel will be able to see it.
- *Oral report.* A formal or informal oral presentation highlighting specific aspects of an educational program. Although this type of report can be planned, it is often given on a spontaneous basis at staff or committee meetings.
- *Informational brochure.* A written document describing the program or series of programs and highlighting the results. It can be mailed to people, placed in display racks, or handed out in organizational meetings or at future programs.
- *Electronic mail.* Text and/or graphics about a program entered into an electronic mail system. This is especially useful when key audiences are primary users of this form of communication.

Although a report may use a single format, a combination of formats may be more effective. For example, although a formal written report with an executive summary may be developed, in presenting the report program planners may wish to use slides and display boards to illustrate important content of the document. Whatever format or formats are chosen, the challenge is to find the best way to present the information so that the audience will be receptive and willing to "listen" to the materials (Rothwell and Kazanas, 1992).

Program reporters may find it helpful to map out each of the five factors prior to developing a report. One method for doing this, with specific examples given for each factor, is illustrated in Exhibit 14.2. Completing this sort of preliminary exercise should make it easier to develop a report that is well organized, clear, and concise.

Exhibit 14.2. Sample Applications of Factors to Consider When Reporting.

Primary Function	Scope	Audience	Content	Format
To educate and gain support from key people and groups	Selected parts of the program (for example, volunteer training and community action and information components)	Current and future participants Senior management Advisory board members Community leaders Community groups/organizations Public at large	Description of participants and program activities Results of the program Suggested recommendations for program changes and new programs	Journalistic-style report Media presentation Oral report
To influence and inform decision makers about current and future programs	Selected parts of the program (for example, new program initiatives)	Instructors Program planning staff Ad hoc advisory team Key supervisors Senior administrators	Short overview of previous programs Suggestions for new program initiatives	Written report Oral report Electronic mail
To provide documentation for permanent records	Educational program as a whole	Instructors Program planning staff	Numbers of participants who attended each event/program Types of activities Topic areas addressed Numbers of hours or days for each event/ program Program results	Written report Sample products

Primary Function	Scope	Audience	Content	Format
To demonstrate program accountability	Educational program as a whole	Senior managers/administrators Funding agencies Regulatory bodies	Brief description of program participants and activities Detailed description of program results in terms of on-the-job performance Recommended actions for organizational changes Cost-effectiveness of the program	Formal written report with executive summary Oral presentation using multimedia
To market the program	A specific educational event	Potential participants Supervisors Professional organizations and groups	Description of participants, topic areas, and program outcomes for similar audiences	Posters displayed in high-visibility areas Informational brochures

Communicating the Report to Key Individuals and Groups

"Reports should be made frequently to individuals and groups intimately involved in the program" (Knowles, 1980, p. 190) and at least annually, where applicable, to senior managers and administrators and to the public at large. As stressed earlier in this chapter, the audience for the report should be chosen carefully prior to the report preparation. The information has a much better chance of being "heard" if it is in the language and the "mindset" of the primary recipients. For example, program reporters addressing the general public as part of a marketing effort would in most cases do better to use a colorful poster highlighting the results of the program rather than a formally written report (even a short one). And if the primary language of that general audience is other than the official language of the area (for example, if a large percentage of the target group is Spanish speakers in an English-speaking area), whatever text is used in the poster should reflect both languages. This could be handled either through a dual printing (once in each language) or by incorporating both languages on a single poster. In contrast, a report prepared for organizational sponsors to demonstrate program accountability may stress program cost-effectiveness and, in addition to the more formal traditional text, include both elaborate graphs and tables demonstrating this fact. Again, the key is making the content and style of the report understandable to the primary audience.

The timing of the report may be critical in determining whether the information is actually used (Brinkerhoff, 1987). A report sent to work supervisors during their busiest production season will probably be put aside or given only a very cursory review, for example. On the other hand, a report sent to those same supervisors during budget preparation time and demonstrating that production costs were reduced by 5 percent as a result of the educational program will in all probability be given a very thorough review. Therefore, based on the situational realities, it is important to plan not only to whom and in what format the report should be released, but also when. The examples shown in Exhibit 14.3 offer guidelines for completing this task.

Exhibit 14.3. Sample Who/What/When Abstracts for Program Reporters.

Report Title (Content)	Who Should Receive Report	Format of Report	When Report Should Be Released
Technical Training: A Six-Month Review	Instructors Technical supervisors Training staff Technical training advisory committee Senior management	Journalistic-style report	Immediately after a successful changeover to new equipment requiring all technical staff to learn a series of new skills
The Leadership Development Program: Making Diversity Work	Participants Supervisors of participants Senior managers/ administrators Program planning staff Members of advisory committee	Formal report with an executive summary Oral presentation	Mid January, to coincide with Martin Luther King Day
The Wellness Program: A Year of Success	Program participants Program staff Community groups/organizations General public	Poster display Informational brochure	January 2 (right after the holiday season)
The Neighbor-to-Neighbor Program: Actions Speak Louder Than Words	Participants Community groups/organizations General public	Journalistic-style report Posters Community presentations Product display	After each successful project and/or when more community volunteers are needed

In summary, when communicating the value of educational programs, program planners should make sure the reports are clear and understandable. Careful thought should be given to the appropriate audience and timing of the reports.

Following Up

It may be important to initiate additional conversations with key individuals and groups after a report has been released, to clarify questions or concerns about the program or to make sure the information has been heard. This communication may be formal (such as further written documents or formal interviews) or informal (such as conversations over coffee or lunch), as the following scenario illustrates:

Scenario

Jean R., the director of human resources, believes it is important that all department heads of the organization thoroughly understand the implications and recommendations of her recent report highlighting the quality-of-service program spearheaded by her unit. Therefore, she and her associate director, Walter, will meet personally with each of the department heads to discuss the report and respond to any questions they may have. Jean decides to send each department head, prior to their meeting, a second copy of the executive summary of the report with an addendum outlining what actions have been taken thus far. In addition, Walter plans to buttonhole many of the first-line supervisors over coffee or lunch to gather their opinions on whether the program has made a difference in the day-to-day operations.

Chapter Highlights

Communicating the value of educational programs is often overlooked by program planners. Educators need to learn to tell their stories in such a way that the various publics hear their message and receive a clear picture of what educational programs for adults are all about—learning and change. In completing this component, program planners need to complete the following tasks:

- Prepare a program report (for example, journalistic-style report, media presentation, poster, product display) that addresses well the function, scope, and audience for the report.
- Ensure that the report is done in a format that portrays the message in such a way that the content is "seen and heard" by appropriate individuals, groups, organizations, and/or the general public.
- Be proactive in timing the release of the report.
- Follow up as needed with appropriate individuals and groups to clarify any questions or concerns about the program.

The benefits of this aspect of the program planning process are usually well worth the extra time and effort needed to put this type of communication together and disseminate it.

Applications Exercises

These Applications Exercises are designed to help you prepare reports on educational programs (Exhibit 14.4) and communicate program results to key individuals and groups (Exhibit 14.5).

Exhibit 14.4. Preparing Reports on Educational Programs.

1. Describe briefly a situation for which you need to prepare a report on a specific educational event or program.

_____

_____

_____

2. Using the following chart, outline the primary function(s), scope, audiences, content, and format(s) for that report.

Factors to Consider	Your Report
Primary Function(s) Educate and gain support Facilitate decision making Offer documentation Show accountability Assist marketing	
Scope Single educational event Series of educational events Whole educational program	
Possible Audience(s) Participants, instructors, program planning staff, supervisors of participants, senior managers/administrators, regulatory and licensing groups, funding agencies, professional groups and organizations, committee members, clientele of organizations, general public	
Content Information to be included	
Format(s) Written report, journalistic-style report, media presentation, case study report, product display, poster, oral report, informational brochure, electronic mail	

3. Review your plan for the report with a colleague and revise it as needed.

Exhibit 14.5. Communicating Program Results to Key Individuals and Groups.

1. Using the following chart, develop a one-year plan for communicating the results of your educational program to key individuals and groups, both internal and external to the organization.

Report Title (Content)	Who Should Receive Report	Format of Report	When Report Should Be Released

2. Review your plan with two or three colleagues and/or your planning team and then revise it as needed.

References

Apps, J. W. *Towards A Working Philosophy of Adult Education.* Occasional Paper no. 36. Syracuse, N.Y.: Syracuse University Publications in Continuing Education and ERIC Clearinghouse on Adult Education, 1973.

Apps, J. W. *Improving Practice in Continuing Education: Modern Approaches for Understanding the Field and Determining Priorities.* San Francisco: Jossey-Bass, 1985.

Apps, J. W. *Higher Education in a Learning Society: Meeting New Demands for Education and Training.* San Francisco: Jossey-Bass, 1988.

Apps, J. W. *Mastering the Teaching of Adults.* Malabar, Fla.: Krieger, 1991.

Belenky, M. F., Clinchy, B. M., Goldberger, N. R., and Tarule, J. M. *Women's Ways of Knowing: The Development of Self, Voice, and Mind.* New York: Basic Books, 1986.

Bellman, G. M. "Trimming Your Waste Line." *Training and Development Journal,* 1993, 47 (3), 28–31.

Belsheim, D. J. "Environmental Determinants for Organizing Continuing Professional Education." *Adult Education Quarterly,* 1988, 38(2), 63–74.

Bennett, G. J., and Clasper, T. D. "Training Evaluation." In G. M. Piskurich (ed.), Handbook of Instructional Technology. New York: McGraw-Hill, 1993.

Bennett, N. L., and LeGrand, B. F. "Developing Continuing Professional Education Programs." The Guide Series in Continuing Education. Urbana: Illinois University, Office of Continuing Education and Public Service, 1990. (ED 334 440).

Bianchi, S., Butler, J., and Richey, D. *Warmups for Meeting Leaders.* San Diego, Calif.: University Associates, 1990.

Birnbrauer, H. "Identifying, Selecting, and Training Instructors." In G. M. Piskurich (ed.), *Handbook of Instructional Technology.* New York: McGraw-Hill, 1993.

Blomberg, R. "Cost-Benefit Analysis of Employee Training: A Literature Review." *Adult Education Quarterly,* 1989, 39(2), 89–98.

Bloom, B. *Taxonomy of Educational Objectives: The Classification of Educational Goals.* New York: McKay, 1956.

Bogdan, R. C., and Biklen, S. K. *Qualitative Research for Education.* (2nd ed.) Needham Heights, Mass.: Allyn & Bacon, 1992.

Bolman, L. G., and Deal, T. E. *Reframing Organizations: Artistry, Choice, and Leadership.* San Francisco: Jossey-Bass, 1991.

Borg, W. R., Gall, J. P., and Gall, M. D. *Applying Educational Research.* (3rd ed.) White Plains, N.Y.: Longman, 1993.

Boyle, P. G. *Planning Better Programs.* New York: McGraw-Hill, 1981.

Bradley, M. K.; Kallick, B. O.; and Regan, H. B. *The Staff Development Manager.* Needham Heights, Mass.: Allyn & Bacon, 1991.

Bramlay, P. *Evaluating Training Effectiveness: Translating Theory Into Practice.* New York: McGraw-Hill, 1991.

Branham, L. A. "An Update on Staff Development Evaluation." *Journal of Staff Development,* 1992, 13(4), 24–28.

Brinkerhoff, R. O. *Achieving Results from Training: How to Evaluate Human Resource Development to Strengthen Programs and Increase Impact.* San Francisco: Jossey-Bass, 1987.

Broad, M. L., and Newstrom, J. M. *Transfer of Training.* Reading, Mass.: Addison-Wesley, 1992.

Brockett, R. G. (ed.). *Ethical Issues in Adult Education.* New York: Teachers College Press, 1988.

Brockett, R. G. (ed.). *Professional Development for Educators of Adults.* New Directions for Adult and Continuing Education, no. 51. San Francisco: Jossey-Bass, 1991.

Brookfield, S. D. *Understanding and Facilitating Adult Learning: A Comprehensive Analysis of Principles and Effective Practices.* San Francisco: Jossey Bass, 1986.

Brookfield, S. D. "Ethical Dilemmas in Evaluating Educational Programs." In R. G. Brockett (ed.), *Ethical Issues in Adult Education.* New York: Teachers College Press, 1988.

Brookfield, S. D. *The Skillful Teacher: On Technique, Trust, and Responsiveness in the Classroom.* San Francisco: Jossey-Bass, 1990.

Brookfield, S. D. "Giving Helpful Evaluations to Learners." *Adult Learning,* 1992, 3(8), 22–24.

Caffarella, R. S. "Identifying Client Needs." *Journal of Extension,* 1982, 20(7), 5–11.

Caffarella, R. S. "A Checklist for Planning Successful Training Programs." *Training and Development Journal,* 1985, 39(3), 81-83.

Caffarella, R. S. *Program Development and Evaluation Resource Book for Trainers.* New York: Wiley, 1988.

Caffarella, R. S. *Psychosocial Development of Women: Linkages to Teaching and Leadership in Adult Education.* Columbus, Ohio: ERIC Clearinghouse on Adult, Career, and Vocational Education, 1992.

Caffarella, R. S. "Facilitating Self-Directed Learning

as a Staff Development Option." *Journal of Staff Development*, 1993, *14*(2), 30–34.

Caffarella, R. S. "Characteristics of Adult Learners and Foundations of Experiential Learning." In L. Jackson and R. S. Caffarella (eds.), *Experiential Learning: A New Approach.* New Directions for Adult and Continuing Education, no. 62, San Francisco: Jossey-Bass, 1994.

Caffarella, R. S., O'Donnell, J. M. *Self-Directed Learning.* Nottingham, England; Department of Adult Education, University of Nottingham, 1989.

Caldwell, S. D. (ed.). *Staff Development: A Handbook of Effective Practice.* Oxford, Ohio: National Staff Development Council, 1989.

Carnevale, A. P., and Schulz, E. R. "Return on Investment: Accounting for Training." *Training and Development Journal*, 1990, *44*(7), S1–S32.

Carson, C. R. "Choosing the Best Locations for Continuing Education Programs." In R. G. Simerly and Associates, *Handbook of Marketing for Continuing Education.* San Francisco: Jossey-Bass, 1989.

Carter, M., and Powell, D. "Teacher Leaders and Staff Developers." *Journal of Staff Development*, 1992, *13*(1), 8–12.

Cervero, R. M. *Effective Continuing Education for Professionals.* San Francisco: Jossey-Bass, 1988.

Cervero, R. M., and Wilson, A. L. "Perspectives on Program Planning in Adult Education." Proceedings of the 32nd Annual Adult Education Research Conference, University of Oklahoma, Stillwater, Okla., 1991.

Cervero, R. M., and Wilson, A. L. "The Centrality of Negotiating Interests in Adult Education." Proceedings of the 33rd Annual Adult Education Research Conference, University of Saskatchewan, Saskatoon, Canada, 1992.

Cervero, R. M., and Wilson, A. L. *Planning Responsibility for Adult Education: A Guide to Negotiating Power and Interests.* San Francisco: Jossey-Bass, 1994.

Chalofsky, N. E. External Evaluation. In W. R. Tracey (ed.), *Human Resources Management and Development Handbook.* New York: AMACOM, 1985.

Coats, S. "Exhibiting at Conferences, Conventions, and Trade Shows." In R. G. Simerly and Associates, *Handbook of Marketing for Continuing Education.* San Francisco: Jossey-Bass, 1989.

Cohen, D. J. "The Pretraining Environment: A Conceptualization of How Contextual Factors Influence Participation Motivation." *Human Resource Development Quarterly*, 1990, *1*(4), 387–398.

Cohen, S. L. "The Art, Science, and Business of Program Development." *Training and Development Journal*, 1993, *47*(8), 49–56.

Corbett, A. H. "Give Participants Responsibility for Learning: Techniques for Opening a Workshop." *Journal of Staff Development*, 1992, *13*(1), 40–42.

Cross, K. P. "The State of the Art in Needs Assessments." Paper presented at the Conference on Lifelong Learning: Assessing the Needs of Adult Learners, Akron, Ohio, 1979.

Davis, B. G. *Tools for Teaching.* San Francisco: Jossey-Bass, 1993.

Davis, L. N., and McCallon, E. *Planning, Conducting, Evaluating Workshops.* Austin, Tex.: Learning Concepts, 1974.

Deal, T. E., and Kennedy, A. A. *Corporate Cultures.* Reading, Mass.: Addison-Wesley, 1982.

Dick, W., and Carey, L. *The Systematic Design of Instruction.* (3rd ed.) Glenview, Ill.: Scott, Foresman and Little, Brown Higher Education, 1990.

Diegmueller, K. "The Changing Role of Staff Developers." *Journal of Staff Development*, 1992, *13*(3), 8–10.

Dixon, N. M. *Evaluation: A Tool for Improving HRD Quality.* San Diego, Calif.: University Associates, 1990.

DuFour, R. P. *The Principal as Staff Developer.* Bloomington, Ind.: National Educational Service, 1991.

Duning, B. S., Van Kekerix, M. J., and Zaborowski, L. M. *Reaching Learners Through Telecommunications: Management and Leadership Strategies for Higher Education.* San Francisco: Jossey-Bass, 1993.

"Employee Training in America." *Training and Development Journal*, 1986, *40*(7), 34–37.

Ericksen, C. G. "Developing and Managing Adult Education Budgets." In P. Mulcrone (ed.), *Current Perspectives on Administration of Adult Education Programs.* New Directions for Adult and Continuing Education, no. 60. San Francisco: Jossey-Bass, 1994.

Farlow, H. *Publicizing and Promoting Programs.* New York: McGraw-Hill, 1979.

Federal Highway Administration, U.S. Department of Transportation. "Training Guide for Identifying, Meeting, and Evaluating Training Needs." Washington, D.C.: National Highway Institute, 1977. (ED 143 846)

Finkel, C. "Where Learning Happens." *Training and Development Journal*, 1984, *38*(4), 32–36.

Finkel, C. "Pick a Place, But Not Any Place." *Training and Development Journal*, 1986, *40* (2), 51–53.

Ford, J. K. "Understanding Training Transfer: The Water Remains Murky." *Human Resource Development Quarterly*, 1990, *1*(3), 225–229.

Forest, L., and Mulcahy, S. *First Things First: A Handbook of Priority Setting in Education.* Madison: Division of Program and Staff Development, University of Wisconsin Extension, 1976.

Forest, L., and Mulcahy, S. *First Things First Workbook,* Madison: Division of Program and Staff Development, University of Wisconsin Extension, 1979.

Foster, A. *Learning at a Distance.* Madison: Professional Development Program in Distance Education, Department of Continuing and Vocational Education, University of Wisconsin, 1993.

Fox, R. D. "Fostering Transfer of Learning to Work Environments." In T. J. Sork (ed.), *Designing and Implementing Effective Workshops,* New Directions for Adult and Continuing Education, no. 22. San Francisco: Jossey-Bass, 1984.

Fulton, R. D. "A Conceptual Model for Understanding the Physical Attributes of Learning Environments." In R. Hiemstra (ed.), *Creating Environments for Effective Adult Learning*. New Directions for Adult and Continuing Education, no. 50. San Francisco: Jossey-Bass, 1991.

Galbraith, M. W. (ed.). *Adult Learning Methods*. Malabar, Fla.: Krieger, 1990a.

Galbraith, M. W. (ed.). *Education Through Community Organizations*. New Directions for Adult and Continuing Education, no. 47. San Francisco: Jossey-Bass, 1990b.

Geigold, W. C., and Grindle, C. R. *In Training: A Practical Guide to Management Development*. Belmont, Calif.: Lifetime Learning, 1983.

Ginocchio, F. L. "Teacher-Clinicians Put Credibility into Staff Development." *Journal of Staff Development*, 1990, *11*(2),16–18.

Glesne, C., and Peshkin, A. *Becoming Qualitative Researchers*. White Plains, N.Y.: Longman, 1992.

Hall, G. E., and Hord, S. M. *Change in Schools: Facilitating the Process*. Albany: State University of New York Press, 1987.

Harris, B. M. *In-Service Education for Staff Development*. Needham Heights, Mass.: Allyn & Bacon, 1989.

Hart, M. U. *Working and Educating for Life*. London and New York: Routledge, 1992.

Heinich, R., Molenda, M., and Russell, J. D. *Instructional Media*. (3rd ed.) New York: Macmillan, 1989.

Hentges, K., Yaney, J., and Shields, C. "Training and Motivating the New Labor Force." *Performance Improvement Quarterly*, 1990, *3*(3), 36–44.

Hentschel, D. "Staff Development for Continuing Education Staff." *Adult Learning,* 1990, 1(7), 11–14.

Hiemstra, R. (ed.). *Creating Environments for Effective Adult Learning*. New Directions for Adult and Continuing Education, no. 50. San Francisco: Jossey-Bass, 1991.

Hiemstra, R., and Sisco, B. *Individualizing Instruction: Making Learning Personal, Empowering, and Successful*. San Francisco: Jossey-Bass, 1990.

Holland, B. R. "Successful Telemarketing Techniques for Continuing Education." In R. G. Simerly and Associates, *Handbook of Marketing for Continuing Education*. San Francisco: Jossey-Bass, 1989.

Hopfengardner, J. D., and Potter, A. R. "Staff Development: What We Are Doing—and What We Know We Should Be Doing." *American Secondary Education*, 1992, *20*(3), 2–7.

Houle, C. O. *The Design of Education*. San Francisco: Jossey-Bass, 1972.

Houle, C. O. *Governing Boards: Their Nature and Nurture*. San Francisco: Jossey-Bass, 1989.

Kaufman, R. "A Needs Assessment Primer." *Training and Development Journal*, 1987, *41(10), 78–83.*

Kaufman, R. "Needs Assessment: A Menu." *Educational Technology*, 1988, *28*(7), 21–23.

Kaufman, R., and Stone, B., *Planning for Organizational Success*. New York: Wiley, 1983.

Kemerer, R. W. "Understanding the Application of Learning." In T. J. Sork (ed.), *Mistakes Made and Lessons Learned: Overcoming Obstacles to Successful Program Planning*. New Directions for Adult and Continuing Education, no. 49. San Francisco: Jossey-Bass, 1991.

Killion, J. P., and Harrison, C. R. "An Organization Development Approach to Change." *The Journal of Staff Development*, 1990, *11*(1), 22–25.

Killion, J. P., and Kaylor, B. "Follow-Up: The Key to Training for Transfer." *Journal of Staff Development*, 1991, *12*(1), 64–67.

Kirkpatrick, D. L. "Evaluation." In R. L. Craig (ed.), *Training and Development Handbook*. (3rd ed.) New York: McGraw-Hill, 1987.

Knowles, M. S. *The Modern Practice of Adult Education*. New York: Cambridge University Press, 1980.

Knox, A. *Helping Adults Learn: A Guide to Planning, Implementing, and Conducting Programs*. San Francisco: Jossey-Bass, 1986.

Krathwohl, D. R. *Methods of Educational and Social Science Research*. White Plains, N.Y.: Longman, 1993.

Laird, D. *Approaches to Training and Development*, (2nd ed.) Reading, Mass.: Addison-Wesley, 1985.

Laker, D. R. "Dual Dimensionality of Training Transfer." *Human Resource Development Quarterly*, 1990a, *1*(3), 209–223.

Laker, D. R. "Final Word: Yes, the Water Remains Murky, But It Is Safe to Swim." *Human Resource Development Quarterly*, 1990b, *1*(3), 231–235.

Levine, S. L., *Promoting Adult Growth in Schools*. Needham Heights, Mass.: Allyn & Bacon, 1989.

Levine, S. L., and Broude, N. E. "Designs for Learning." In S. D. Caldwell (ed.), *Staff Development: A Handbook of Effective Practice*. Oxford, Ohio: National Staff Development Council, 1989.

Long, J. S., and Marts, J. A. "The Focused Group Interview—An Alternative Way to Collect Information to Evaluate Conferences." Pullman: Cooperative Extension Service, Washington State University, 1981.

Loucks-Horsley, S. "Managing Change: An Integral Part of Staff Development." In S. D. Caldwell (ed.), *Staff Development: A Handbook of Effective Practice*. Oxford, Ohio: National Staff Development Council, 1989.

McMillan, J. H., and Schumacher, S. *Research in Education*. (2nd ed.) Glenview, Ill.: Scott, Foresman, 1989.

Mager, R. F. *Preparing Instructional Objectives*, (2nd ed.) Belmont, Calif.: David S. Lake, 1984.

Marshall, J. C. "Assessing Program Effects." In S. D. Caldwell (ed.), *Staff Development: A Handbook of Effective Practice*. Oxford, Ohio: National Staff Development Council, 1989.

Martin, K. O., and Mazmanian, P. E. "Anticipated and Encountered Barriers to Change in CME: Tools for Planning and Evaluation." *The Journal of Continuing Education in the Health Professions*, 1991, *11*, 301–318.

Matkin, G. W. *Effective Budgeting in Continuing Education: A Comprehensive Guide to Improving Program Planning and Organizational Performance.* San Francisco: Jossey-Bass, 1985.

Mayo, G. D., and DuBois, P. H. *The Complete Book of Training: Theory, Principles, and Techniques.* San Diego, Calif.: University Associates, 1987.

Mehrens, W. A., and Lehmann, I. J. *Measurement and Evaluation,* (4th ed.) Troy, Mo.: Holt, Rinehart & Winston, 1991.

Merriam, S. B. *Case Study Research in Education: A Qualitative Approach.* San Francisco: Jossey-Bass, 1988.

Merriam, S. B. *An Update on Adult Learning Theory.* New Directions for Adult and Continuing Education, no. 57. San Francisco: Jossey-Bass, 1993.

Merriam, S. B., and Caffarella, R. S. *Learning in Adulthood: A Comprehensive Guide.* San Francisco: Jossey-Bass, 1991.

Merriam, S. B., and Cunningham, P. M. (eds.). *Handbook of Adult and Continuing Education.* San Francisco: Jossey-Bass, 1989.

Mezirow, J. *Transformative Dimensions of Adult Learning.* San Francisco: Jossey-Bass, 1991.

Mezirow, J., and Associates. *Fostering Critical Reflection in Adulthood: A Guide to Transformative and Emancipatory Learning.* San Francisco: Jossey-Bass, 1990.

Michalak, M. L., and Yager, E. G. *Making the Training Process Work.* New York: Harper Collins, 1979.

Mosier, N. R. "Financial Analysis: The Methods and Their Application to Employee Training." *Human Resource Development Quarterly,* 1990, *1*(1), 45–63.

Munson, L. S. *How to Conduct Training Seminars.* (2nd ed.) New York: McGraw-Hill, 1992.

Murk, P. J., and Wells, J. H. "A Practical Guide to Program Planning." *Training and Development Journal,* 1988, *42*(10), 45–47.

Nadler, L. L. *Designing Training Programs: The Critical Events Model.* Reading, Mass.: Addison-Wesley, 1982.

Nadler, L. L. *The Handbook of Human Resource Development.* New York: Wiley, 1985.

Nadler, L., and Nadler, Z. *The Comprehensive Guide to Successful Conferences and Institutes.* San Francisco: Jossey-Bass, 1987.

Newstrom, J. W., and Lilyquist, J. M. "Selecting Needs Analysis Methods." *Training and Development Journal,* 1979, *33*(10), 52–56.

Nilson, C. *Training Program Workbook and Kit.* Englewood Cliffs, N.J.: Prentice-Hall, 1989.

O'Donnell, J. M. "Focus Groups: A Habit-Forming Evaluation Technique." *Training and Development Journal,* 1988, *42,* 71–73.

O'Donnell, J. M., and Caffarella, R. S. "Learning Contracts." In M. W. Galbraith (ed.), *Adult Learning Methods.* Malabar, Fla.: Krieger, 1990.

"Organizational Development for Improving Schools." *Journal of Staff Development,* 1990, *11*(1), 2–42.

Ostendorf, V. A. *Distance Education Technology.* Madison: Professional Development Program in Distance Education, Department of Continuing and Vocational Education, University of Wisconsin, 1993.

Ottoson, J. M. "Implementation Research: Understanding the Application of Learning Following Continuing Professional Education." In D. Flannery (ed.), *Proceedings of the 34th Annual Adult Education Research Conference,* University Park, Penn.: Penn State University, 1993.

Ottoson, J. M. "Transfer of Learning: Not Just an Afterthought." *Adult Learning,* 1994, *5*(4), 21.

Patton, M. Q. *Qualitative Evaluation and Research Methods.* (2nd ed.) Newbury Park, Calif.: Sage, 1990.

Pennington, F., and Green, J. "Comparative Analysis of Program Development Processes in Six Professions." *Adult Education,* 1976, *27*(1), 13-23.

Perry, S. "Ideas for Improving Transfer of Training." *Adult Learning,* 1990, *1*(7), 19–23.

Piskurich, G. M. (ed.). *Handbook of Instructional Technology.* New York: McGraw-Hill, 1992.

Piskurich, G. M. *Self-Directed Learning: A Practical Guide to Design, Development, and Implementation.* San Francisco: Jossey-Bass, 1993.

Powers, B. *Instructor Excellence: Mastering the Delivery of Training.* San Francisco: Jossey-Bass, 1992.

Richey, R. *Designing Instruction for the Adult Learner.* London: Krogan Page, 1992.

Riggs, J. K. "Determining an Effective Market Mix." In R. G. Simerly and Associates, *Handbook of Marketing for Continuing Education.* San Francisco: Jossey-Bass, 1989.

Robinson, D. G., and Robinson, J. C. *Training for Impact: How to Link Training to Business Needs and Measure the Results.* San Francisco: Jossey-Bass, 1989.

Robinson, R. D. *An Introduction to Helping Adults Learn and Change.* Milwaukee, Wis.: Omnibooks, 1979.

Rogers, E. M. *Diffusion of Innovations.* (3rd ed.) New York: Free Press, 1983.

Rossett, A. *Training Needs Assessment.* Englewood Cliffs, N.J.: Educational Technology Publications, 1987.

Rossett, A., and Gautier-Downes, J. *A Handbook of Job Aids.* San Diego: Pfeiffer, 1991.

Rothwell, W. J., and Kazanas, H. C. *Mastering the Instructional Design Process: A Systematic Approach.* San Francisco: Jossey-Bass, 1992.

Rothwell, W. J., and Kazanas, H. C. *The Complete AMA Guide to Management Development.* New York: American Management Association, 1993.

Schlossberg, N. K., Lynch, A. Q., and Chickering, A. W. *Improving Higher Education Environments for Adults: Responsive Programs and Services from Entry to Departure.* San Francisco: Jossey-Bass, 1989.

Scott, J. *Social Network Analysis.* London: Sage, 1991.

Seaman, D. F., and Fellenz, R. A. *Effective Strategies for Teaching Adults.* Columbus, Ohio: Merrill, 1989.

Shavelson, R. *Statistical Reasoning for the Behavioral Sciences.* Needham Heights, Mass.: Allyn & Bacon, 1988.

Shipp, T. "Building a Better Mousetrap in Adult Education." *Lifelong Learning: The Adult Years*, 1981, *5*(1), 4–6.

Showers, B. H. "Synthesis of Research on Staff Development." *Educational Leadership*, 1987, *45*(3), 77–87.

Shroyer, M. G. "Effective Staff Development for Effective Organizational Development." *Journal of Staff Development*, 1990, *11*(1), 2–6.

Silberman, M. *Active Training.* San Diego, Calif.: University Associates; Lexington, Mass.: Lexington Books, 1990.

Simerly, R. G. "A Ten-Step Process to Ensure Success in Marketing." In R. G. Simerly and Associates, *Handbook of Marketing for Continuing Education.* San Francisco: Jossey-Bass, 1989a.

Simerly, R. G. "Writing Effective Advertising Copy: Eight Principles for Success." In R. G. Simerly and Associates, *Handbook of Marketing for Continuing Education.* San Francisco: Jossey-Bass, 1989b.

Simerly, R. G. *Planning and Marketing Conferences and Workshops: Tips, Tools, and Techniques.* San Francisco: Jossey-Bass, 1990.

Simerly, R. G., and Associates. *Handbook of Marketing for Continuing Education.* San Francisco: Jossey-Bass, 1989.

Sisco, B. R. "Setting the Climate for Effective Teaching and Learning." In R. Hiemstra (ed.), *Creating Environments for Effective Adult Learning.* New Directions for Adult and Continuing Education, no. 50. San Francisco: Jossey-Bass, 1991.

Sleezer, C. M. "Developing and Validating the Performance Analysis for Training Model." *Human Resource Development Quarterly*, 1991, *2*(4), 355–372.

Smith, B. J., and Delahaye, B. L. *How to Be an Effective Trainer.* (2nd ed.) New York: Wiley, 1987.

Smith, P. L., and Ragan, T. J. *Instructional Design.* Columbus, Ohio: Merrill, 1993.

Sork, T. J. *Development and Validation of a Normative Process Model for Determining Priority Needs in Community Adult Education.* Proceedings of the 20th Annual Adult Education Research Conference, Ann Arbor, Mich.: University of Michigan, 1979

Sork, T. J. "The Postmortem Audit: Improving Programs by Examining 'Failures.'" *Lifelong Learning: The Adult Years*, 1981, *5*(3), 6–7, 31.

Sork, T. J. *Determining Priorities.* Vancouver: British Columbia Ministry of Education, 1982.

Sork, T. J. "Toward a Causal Model of Program Failure in Adult Education." *Proceedings of the 28th Annual Adult Education Research Conference.* Laramie: University of Wyoming, 1987.

Sork, T. J. "Ethical Issues in Program Planning." In R. G. Brockett (ed.), *Ethical Issues in Adult Education.* New York: Teachers College Press, 1988.

Sork, T. J. "Theoretical Foundations of Educational Program Planning." *The Journal of Continuing Education in the Health Professions*, 1990, *10*, 73–83.

Sork, T. J. (ed.) *Mistakes Made and Lessons Learned: Overcoming Obstacles to Successful Program Planning.* New Directions for Adult and Continuing Education, no. 49. San Francisco: Jossey-Bass, 1991a.

Sork, T. J. "Tools for Planning Better Programs." In T. J. Sork (ed.), *Mistakes Made and Lessons Learned: Overcoming Obstacles to Successful Program Planning.* New Directions for Adult and Continuing Education, no. 49. San Francisco: Jossey-Bass, 1991b.

Sork, T. J., and Buskey, J. H. "A Description and Evaluation Analysis of Program Planning Literature, 1950-1983." *Adult Education Quarterly*, 1986, *36*(2), 86–96.

Sork, T. J., and Caffarella, R. S. "Planning Programs for Adults." In S. B. Merriam, and P. M. Cunningham, (eds.), *Handbook of Adult and Continuing Education.* San Francisco: Jossey-Bass, 1989.

Sork, T. J., Kalef, R., and Worsfold, N. E. *The Postmortem Audit: A Strategy for Improving Programs.* Vancouver, Canada: Intentional Learning Systems, 1987.

Sparks, D. "Becoming an Authentic Consultant: An Interview with Peter Block." *Journal of Staff Development*, 1992, *13*(3), 12–15.

Stark, A. T. "Conducting Training Programs." In W. R. Tracey (ed.), *Human Resources Management and Development.* New York: AMACOM, 1985.

Starratt, R. J. "Building an Ethical School: A Theory in Educational Leadership." *Educational Administration Quarterly*, 1991, *27*, 185–202.

Steele, S. M. "The Evolution of Adult and Continuing Education." In S. B. Merriam and P. M. Cunningham (eds.), *Handbook of Adult and Continuing Education.* San Francisco: Jossey-Bass, 1989.

Stuart, P. "New Directions in Training Individuals." *Personnel Journal*, 1992, *71*(9), 86–93.

Swanson, R. A., and Gradous, D. B. *Forecasting Financial Benefits of Human Resource Development.* San Francisco: Jossey-Bass, 1988.

Tracey, W. R. *Designing Training and Development Systems.* (3rd ed.) New York: AMACOM, 1992.

Tuck, J. W. "Professional Development Through Learning Centers." *Training and Development Journal*, 1988, *42*(9), 76–79.

Tyler, R. W. *Basic Principles of Curriculum and Instruction.* Chicago: University of Chicago Press, 1949.

Varney, G. H. "Organizational Development." In R. L. Craig (ed.), *Training and Development Handbook.* (3rd ed.) New York: McGraw-Hill, 1987.

Vosko, R. S. "Where We Learn Shapes Our Learning." In R. Hiemstra (ed.), *Creating Environments for Effective Adult Learning.* New Directions for Adult and Continuing Education, no. 50. San Francisco: Jossey-Bass, 1991.

Watkins, K. E., and Marsick, V. J. *Sculpting the Learning Organization: Lessons in the Art and Science of Systematic Change.* San Francisco: Jossey-Bass, 1993.

Welton, M. R. "The Contributions of Critical Theory to Our Understanding of Adult Learning." In S. B. Merriam (ed.), *An Update on Adult Learning Theory.* New Directions for Adult and Continuing Education, no. 57. San Francisco: Jossey-Bass, 1993.

Wenz, A., and Adams, C. D. "Life After Training: A Look at Follow-Up." *Journal of Staff Development,* 1991, *12*(1), 60–62.

Witkin, B. R. *Assessing Needs in Educational and Social Programs: Using Information to Make Decisions, Set Priorities, and Allocate Resources.* San Francisco: Jossey Bass, 1984.

Worthen, B. R., and Sanders, J. R. *Educational Evaluation.* White Plains, N.Y.: Longman, 1987.

Zemke, R., and Kramlinger, T. *Figuring Things Out.* Reading, Mass.: Addison-Wesley, 1982.

Zinn, L. M. "Appendix—Philosophy of Adult Education Inventory." In M. W. Galbraith (ed.), *Adult Learning Methods.* Malabar, Fla.: Krieger, 1990a.

Zinn, L. M. "Identifying Your Philosophical Orientation." In M. W. Galbraith (ed.), *Adult Learning Methods.* Malabar, Fla.: Krieger, 1990b.

Index

Ericksen, C. G., 164

Evaluation: approaches to, 125—127, 132—133; and causes of failures, 142—143; data analysis used for, 136—139; data collection for, 133—136; explanation of, 119—120; formulating recommendations regarding, 143—144; informal and unplanned opportunities for, 124—125; instructional, 194—197; making judgments during analysis phase of, 139—142; by participants, 128—133, 223; planning for systematic, 120—124; techniques for, 195—196

Exhibits, 154

Expense budget, 164, 167. *See also* Budgets

External contextual factors: explanation of, 47—48; information on, 48—49

F

Facilities: arrangement of, 213—217; choice of, 22, 212—213; instructional equipment and, 217, 218; obtaining suitable, 210—212; types of, 210

Farlow, H., 171, 175

Fellenz, R. A., 152, 191

Finkel, C., 212

Fixed expenses, 164

Ford, J. K., 113

Forest, L., 32

Formative evaluation, 119—120. *See also* Evaluation

Fox, R. D., 108, 110

Fulton, R. D., 210

G

Galbraith, M. W., 155, 191

Gall, J. P., 136

Gall, M. D., 136

Gautier-Downes, J. A., 92

Geigold, W. C., 161

Ginocchio, F. L., 161

Glasne, C., 139

Goldberger, N. R., 25

Gradous, D. B., 165

Green, J., 11, 26

Grindle, C. R., 161

H

Hall, G. E., 108, 110

Harris, B. M., 7, 17, 24, 120, 134, 157, 195, 198

Heinich, R., 155

Hentges, K., 170

Hentschel, D., 4

Hiemstra, R., 59, 210

Holland, B. R., 172

Hopfengardner, J. D., 56

Hord, S. M., 108, 110

Houle, C. O., 8, 17, 22, 24, 67, 102, 184, 187

I

Income, 164

Individual format, 152—153

Institutes, 154

Instructional equipment, arranging for, 217—218

Instructional materials: buying vs. making, 193—194; evaluation of, 194—195; selection of, 192; types of, 192—193

Instructional plans: application of, 198, 200—201; design of, 21—22; developing learning objectives for, 183—186; evaluation component of, 194—198; sample of, 198, 199; selecting and sequencing content for, 186—188; selecting instructional techniques for, 188—192

Instructors: capability of, 191; obtaining efficient, 160—161; responsibilities of, 158

Interactive program planning models: assumptions of, 22—24; components of, 17—18; determining which components to use of, 34—36; ethical approach to using, 37—39; personal beliefs and, 29—32, 41; sources for, 24—26; tasks within components of, 19—22; up-front assumptions and application of, 32—34. *See also* Program planning models

Internal contextual factors: explanation of, 46—47; information on, 48—49

K

Kalef, R., 142, 143

Kallick, B. O., 6, 24, 46, 67, 68, 77, 126, 134, 222

Kaufman, R., 68, 76, 87, 88

Kaylor, B., 108, 113

Kazanas, H. C., 3, 5, 24, 56, 57, 58, 59, 60, 68, 84, 86, 92, 119, 120, 123, 157, 170, 184, 185, 188, 192, 195, 229, 230, 231

Kemerer, R. W., 108, 110

Kennedy, A. A., 46

Killion, J. P., 108, 113

Kirkpatrick, D. L., 120, 126, 127

Knowles, M. S., 7, 17, 22, 24, 55, 56, 57, 70, 75, 101, 123, 152, 155, 168, 172, 186, 191, 216, 220, 229, 233

Knox, A., 136, 139, 198, 229, 230

Kramlinger, T., 75

Krathwohl, D. R., 139

L

Laird, D. R., 3, 17, 24, 84, 85, 92, 119, 165, 167

Laker, D. R., 110, 113

Large-group format, 154

Learning objectives: content selection and, 186—187; development of, 21—22; examples of, 184—186; explanation of, 183—184

Learning process, in adults, 30—32

Lecture series, 154

LeGrand, B. F., 67, 68, 168

Lehmann, I. J., 102

Levine, S. L., 25, 152, 155

Lilyquist, J. M., 75

Long, J. S., 223

Loucks-Horsley, S., 3

Lynch, A. Q., 59

M

Mager, R. F., 183, 184, 185—186

Management, building program support from, 54—55

Marketing: aspects of, 171—172; assets to use for, 175—176; campaigns for purpose of, 174—175; preparation of plans for, 21; and promotion methods, 172—174; target population analysis as task of, 170—171